OLD ROADS OF THE MIDWEST

OLD ROADS
OF THE MIDWEST

GEORGE CANTOR

ANN ARBOR
THE UNIVERSITY OF MICHIGAN PRESS

2000   1999   1998   1997   4   3   2   1

A CIP catalog record for this book is available from the British Library

Library of Congress Cataloging-in-Publication Data

Cantor, George, 1941–
      Old roads of the Midwest / George Cantor.
          p.   cm.
      ISBN 0-472-08288-4 (pbk. : alk. paper)
      1. Middle West—Description and travel.   2. Roads—Middle West.
   3. Middle West—History, Local.   I. Title.
   F355.C35   1997
   917.7—dc21   96-45829
                                                                CIP

Contents

U.S. 2

St. Ignace, Michigan, to Ironwood, Michigan

After taking a break of several hundred miles, U.S. 2, the most peculiar of old roads, resumes its westward journey at St. Ignace. No other federal highway has such a long interruption in its route, but the explanation is reasonable, if not simple.

U.S. 2 is the most northerly road in the old federal numbering system. It starts in Maine and runs across northern New England to Rouses Point, New York, near Lake Champlain. But then it has nowhere to go. To the west, Canada dips to its southernmost extremity, and the U.S. government couldn't very well run U.S. 2 through it. So to keep the numerical order consistent, U.S. 2 is simply discontinued until Canada is sufficiently out of the way to the north, at which point it starts up again.

The western part of the route is a scenic drive across the northern shore of Lake Michigan and then through the Upper Peninsula iron ranges. The highway eventually heads across the country and reaches Puget Sound at Everett, Washington.

Few old roads begin in as visually spectacular and historically significant a setting as does this one, which starts along the Straits of Mackinac. U.S. 2 officially resumes at the Interstate 75 interchange, just past the northern end of the Mackinac Bridge. But we will begin, instead, east of the interstate, in St. Ignace.

A Closer Look. When Europeans first came to the Straits of Mackinac in the late seventeenth century, they encountered a world in turmoil. Far to the east, the Iroquois Confederacy, sworn enemies of the French, had invaded the Huron homeland in 1649. The Iroquois felt threatened by the French presence on the eastern shore of Lake Huron and sent raiding parties to destroy their religious missions. The attacks

Mackinac Bridge. (Courtesy of Mackinac Bridge Authority, St. Ignace.)

uprooted the Huron Nation and sent it fleeing north and west, where the tribe intermingled with the Ottawa. This group was already in the process of moving into Michigan's Lower Peninsula and was, in turn, bumping into the Ojibwa, who were slowly migrating west to Wisconsin and Minnesota.

They all came together at St. Ignace. When the missionary-explorer Fr. Jacques Marquette arrived here in 1671, he found a large Huron village, as well as Ottawa and Ojibwa settlements, at the northern end of the Straits. Marquette had set up his first permanent mission at Sault Ste. Marie three years earlier, making St. Ignace the second oldest settlement in Michigan. The mission here was dedicated to St. Ignatius Loyola, founder of the Jesuits. It was one of Marquette's favorite spots. When he fell ill on a subsequent voyage, he asked to be returned to St.

Ignace for burial. He died in 1675 near the present site of Ludington, on Lake Michigan, and was interred there. When Native Americans from this mission learned the location of his grave, they retrieved the body the following year and reburied it in St. Ignace, according to the priest's wish.

Fort de Buade was established at St. Ignace in 1679 by the French and garrisoned for the next 22 years. Then the decision was made in Quebec to move its commander, Antoine de la Mothe Cadillac, and most of his troops to a more strategic outpost on the southern lakes. That settlement would grow into the city of Detroit. By 1706 there no longer seemed to be any valid reason for maintaining a mission at St. Ignace. To avoid it being desecrated, the church was burned. Over time, its location and the spot of Marquette's grave were forgotten.

For the next century, St. Ignace was home only to a few trappers and Native Americans. When the British took over the area, in 1763, they fortified Michilimackinac, at the southern end of the Straits, in Mackinaw City (see U.S. 23). The headquarters of the American Fur Co., the great economic force in this region in the early nineteenth century, was placed on Mackinac Island. Not until a rail ferry was completed across the Straits in 1881 did St. Ignace's years of isolation come to an end. The rail connection turned it into a major lumber port for the eastern U.P. In 1882, the county seat was moved here from Mackinac Island, and the town has maintained its primacy ever since. It is now the largest settlement on the Straits.

To walk St. Ignace's one main thoroughfare, State St., which parallels the waterfront, is to step back in time. The docks occupy one side of the street, the downtown area the other. It is a waterfront scene right out of another century, although the cargo is now tourists rather than timber. The car ferry, which once brought travelers from the Lower Peninsula into the heart of town, was replaced by the Mackinac Bridge in 1957. But three ferry companies still run boats to Mackinac Island, which lies about 15 minutes offshore. The street is always bustling with traffic.

The former site of Fort de Buade, on State St., is now a museum of the early French settlers. Two blocks farther north is the site of Marquette's mission. It was accidentally rediscovered in 1877 by construction workers, 201 years after the priest's burial there. A memorial has been placed on the spot, surrounded by a garden. This is one of Michigan's most important archaeological sites, with excavations yielding new information on Native American culture almost annually. The Huron village that stood here in Marquette's time has been reconstructed according to the outline that turned up in the dig. Adjacent to this village is the Museum of Ojibwa Culture, with displays relating to the history and family life of the most populous Native American group in the Great Lakes area.

A second memorial to Marquette, emphasizing his journeys through the upper Midwest, is located west of town on U.S. 2. It places the trips to the upper Mississippi Valley in a historical perspective and displays actual artifacts from these voyages of discovery.

The memorial grounds also command outstanding views of the Mackinac Bridge. The span is billed as the world's longest suspension bridge, and so it is if you measure the 8,614 feet between anchorages. The main span of 3,800 feet, however, comes in third, behind the Verranzano Narrows and the Golden Gate. The 5 miles it travels uninterrupted over open water is, indisputably, the longest in that category.

However the statistics come out, the "Big Mac" is a majestic sight. There had been sentiment for building a bridge across the Straits as far back as 1884. But each time it was brought up over the years it was dismissed as economically unfeasible and technologically impossible. An actual loan application was made to the Depression-era Works Progress Administration in 1935, but it, too, was turned down.

But the idea wouldn't die, and after World War II new studies were conducted to show how construction costs could be repaid by users. Its very existence, it was claimed, would generate the extra traffic required to raise the revenues. The forecasts turned out to be on the money. The Big Mac became a vital transportation link in the state as well as a visual delight, turning a crossing that once took hours during peak weekends into a matter of minutes. Only on Labor Day morning does it open for foot traffic, when a traditional walk across the span is always led by the governor of Michigan.

For the next 50 miles, U.S. 2 runs along the northern shore of Lake Michigan, at the edge of the Hiawatha National Forest. This is a spectacular drive, past miles of almost deserted public beaches (some with campgrounds) and expansive nautical views. The points of land still bear the names given to them by French sailors of the eighteenth century. Point La Barbe, the last cape before Mackinac, was given its name because of the custom of shaving off beards *(barbe)* before coming into port. Gros Cap was the biggest of the capes. The name Pointe aux Chenes referred to the oaks that grew there.

At Pointe aux Chenes, there is an information center for the national forest and a nature walk through an adjacent marsh. Hiawatha National Forest, established in 1931, covers the territory ravaged by overcutting of pine and hardwood during the lumbering era. It extends across the eastern third of the U.P., running its entire breadth from Lake Michigan to Lake Superior. The U.P. is referred to as the "Land of Hiawatha," because Henry Wadsworth Longfellow based his long narrative poem on lore from this area collected by Henry Schoolcraft, the Indian agent on Mackinac Island. The Hiawatha of history, however, was actually a Mohawk who lived in New York in the fifteenth century and was a leading force in unifying the Iroquois Confederacy.

Although not quite as spectacular as the Big Mac, the U.S. 2 bridge across the narrow Cut River, beyond Brevort, is a local landmark of sorts. The road used to dip into the valley, and when this imposing span was built, it was quickly nicknamed the "million-dollar bridge across a two-bit stream."

A few scattered buildings is all that remains of Epoufette. The old fishing and lumbering town was given its name, which means "place of rest," in a traditional belief that it was Fr. Marquette's first overnight stop on his final voyage from St. Ignace.

Naubinway marks the northernmost point on Lake Michigan. There is a roadside park along the highway at that spot.

Gould City, named in honor of a commercial fisherman, has one of the more remarkable roadside attractions in the area, Michihistrigan. It has a miniature golf course shaped like the map of Michigan. And that's not all. Its trout ponds are formed in the outline of the Great Lakes. It bills itself as unique, and that's no exaggeration.

From Gulliver, a county road leads to the lakeshore and the Seul Choix Point Lighthouse. Built in 1895, this is a national historic site, and its location at the head of a harbor is spectacular. The name means "only choice," because this was considered the only harbor of refuge between St. Ignace and Big Bay de Noc. The light is now run as a museum piece.

Manistique features another of the landmark bridges that seem to be a signature of this road. The Siphon Bridge, by which U.S. 2 crosses the Manistique River, has a road surface lower than the water level. Built by a local paper company in 1916, the bridge lies within a concrete tank. It dams the river and provides an artificial roadbed for the highway, situated below the impounded water. You really can't get the sensation when you drive it, but if you stand at the end of the bridge and look across it, you can see the waters above your vantage point. There are some good sand beaches in the area, making Manistique something of a summer resort.

The strangely shaped trout ponds back at Michihistrigan were impressive, but so is the real thing at Thompson. The State Fish Hatchery here is the largest of its kind in the world.

A short side trip, on Michigan 149, leads north to Palms Book State Park, on Indian Lake. This is where the Big Spring bubbles up through the limestone at the rate of 10,000 gallons a minute across a 200-foot-wide underwater fissure. You row a self-propelled raft from the shore to the spring to watch the phenomenon. To experience the full beauty of the setting, get there early in the morning, before the crowds arrive.

The road crosses the head of the Garden Peninsula, which extends south into Lake Michigan. It got the name Garden from its sheltered eastern shore, where the climate was so moderate that vegetables could be grown by the Native Americans.

The big trees of Hiawatha National Forest close in once more as the road skirts the northern edge of Big Bay de Noc. At Rapid River, named for the speed with which the stream empties into the lake, the road joins U.S. 41 (featured later in this book) and runs along the western shore of Little Bay de Noc. It passes through the towns of Kipling and Gladstone, two echoes of nineteenth-century Britain in the north country. British investors were important during the opening of these lands, and it was regarded as prudent to give new settlements names that would be familiar to these customers. In addition, the general manager of the Soo Railroad was a huge fan of the British writer Rudyard Kipling. He also named another town along its route Rudyard in his honor. Kipling was so tickled that he wrote a short poem to the man in 1896 in which he acknowledged "my sons in Michigan." Sad to say, both Rudyard and Kipling are now just wide spots in the road and don't even appear on some maps.

Gladstone, however, is a thriving resort town and in recent years has received attention for a local industry—the making of coffins for pets. The Hoegh Pet Casket Co. features a tour of the manufacturing process, and there is also a small but tasteful pet cemetery on the premises.

Escanaba grew up as a shipping port for lumber, and after the 1860s it became the only iron ore port on Lake Michigan. Much of the wood that built the cities of the prairie states sailed from the docks here. Even as late as 1936, maple used for paneling staterooms on the Cunard Line's Queen Mary was shipped from Escanaba. It continues to serve as an important lumber port, as the second growths of once-depleted forests are being harvested. Escanaba's escape on the lake is Ludington Park, a beautifully landscaped stretch of green on the waterfront. The park features a marina, tennis courts, picnic facilities, and the Delta County Historical Museum, which recounts the story of the great ships that sailed from this port and the cargoes they carried. A restored 1867 lighthouse is part of the museum.

Now U.S. 2 turns away from Lake Michigan and heads due west, following the old Chicago and Northwestern Railroad right-of-way through a succession of defunct former railroad stations. At Harris, the road enters Menominee County, where the clocks are turned back to Central Time. All the counties along the U.P.'s Wisconsin border are within the economic orbit of that state and run on its time.

The largest building in Hermansville was the office of the Wisconsin Land and Lumber Co., built in 1882. This was the home of IXL, once the largest wooden flooring plant in America. Displays of antique tools and examples of the hardwood floors that were made here are exhibited in the former factory. The town was named for Herman Meyer, son of a local lumberman, who grew up to become its first postmaster.

At Vulcan, the road enters the Menominee Iron Range, one of the U.P.'s three great iron mining areas. The Vulcan Mine, named for the Greek god of metals, opened here in 1877 on the range's vein of hematite. The ore was named for its reddish blue appearance, which resembles the color of blood. The primary vein ran between here and the town of Norway (named for the pines of that variety in the area), and this road was lined with mining camps through the late nineteenth century.

Vulcan is now home to the Iron Mountain Iron Mine, preserved as a living museum of the mining era. There are 2,600 feet of subterranean passageways, some of them extending 400 feet beneath the surface. Old mining machinery is demonstrated as visitors ride through the tunnels by train.

In the town of Iron Mountain, which grew up as the commercial center of the range, there are other reminders of the mining era. The Chapin Mine, discovered in 1879, was very rich and very wet. It was the second biggest iron mine in U.P. history in terms of production. But a special steam pump had to be designed to keep it dry. The Cornish engine, named for the nationality of most of the mine workers, was built in 1889 and stands 54 feet high. It was the largest steam-driven pump ever constructed in America, and at its peak capacity it could remove 3,000 gallons of water a minute from a depth of 1,500 feet. This tremendous machine is the focus of the Cornish Pumping Engine and Mining Museum, which also includes equipment used in the last underground mines in the area. The museum is run in conjunction with the Menominee Range Historical Museum, which deals with the entire sweep of history, from the Native Americans to today's dairy farmers, in the western U.P. It is housed in the former Carnegie Library, built in 1901.

Many of the old hills that were stripped to give up their ores have been converted into ski runs. Among them is Pine Mountain, which is just north of the town of Iron Mountain along U.S. 2. This is one of the top ski-jumping runs in the country and the site of many championship meets, with a 1,440-foot-long course.

Beyond Pine Mountain, U.S. 2 makes a short jog west into Wisconsin and then returns to Michigan near Crystal Falls. You may stay in Michigan by going north on Michigan 95, then west on Michigan 69, rejoining U.S. 2 at Crystal Falls.

Once the commercial center of the western section of the Menominee Iron Range, Crystal Falls is now primarily a resort town, with a historic courthouse dating from the 1880s. The falls for which the town was named were on the Paint River and are now dammed. Bewabic State Park, with its beautiful stand of trees on Fortune Lake, is just west of town.

Iron River was the last of the Menominee Range mining towns to develop. The Caspian Mine to the south, established in 1903, was its biggest moneymaker. During the earliest days of the camp, a young physician, Dr. Lewis Bond, set up practice in Iron River, moving from

Wisconsin with his wife, Carrie. In an autobiography written decades later, Carrie Jacobs Bond, who became a successful songwriter, said that the seven years spent here were the happiest of her life. But when the Depression of 1893 wiped out her husband's practice, the couple was forced to move. One year later, Dr. Bond died and his young widow had to take her children to Chicago, where she opened a small sewing shop and wrote songs in her spare time.

By 1900, she had written "I Love You, Truly," a composition probably played at more weddings during the first quarter of this century than any other. That made her reputation and her fortune. But her most enduring song was written 10 years later, after an automobile trip along the Mojave Desert at sunset. Returning to her hotel in Riverside, California, Mrs. Bond wrote the lyric to the song that would become "When You Come to the End of a Perfect Day." It enjoyed worldwide popularity and was a special favorite of American and British troops during World War I.

Mrs. Bond spent the remainder of her life in Los Angeles, with annual concerts held in her honor at the Hollywood Bowl. She died in 1946, but Iron River remembered her. When her former home here was threatened with demolition in 1978, a civic committee managed to raise the funds to move it to the Iron County Museum, in neighboring Caspian. It remains the most popular exhibit there. Other exhibits center around the history of the Caspian Mine and the early days of railroading and lumbering in the area.

The highway now enters the Ottawa National Forest, which covers much of the western U.P. U.S. 2 remains in this lake-studded semi-wilderness all the way to Wakefield, a distance of 60 miles. A visitors center near Watersmeet, at the junction with U.S. 45, has displays about the varieties of life found in this forest and maps of its facilities. Nearby is the J. W. Toumey Nursery, which provides seed stock to many of the state forests in the Great Lakes area. Watersmeet got its name because streams from three major watersheds—Lake Superior, Lake Michigan, and the Mississippi River—come together here.

West of Watersmeet the land steadily rises to the Gogebic Mountains, the last of Michigan's three iron ranges to be developed. Most of the Gogebic developed in the 1880s, a decade after the first Menominee mines. Wakefield was one of the mining camps that grew up then, although it is now better known to skiers as the home of Indianhead, regarded as a top downhill course in the upper Midwest.

The hematite ore found in the Gogebic Mountains was important in the Bessemer steel-making process, which was used to make rails. In fact, the name of one town a bit farther ahead is Bessemer. From Bessemer, U.S. 2 continues into Ironwood, the largest city of the Gogebic, on the Wisconsin border.

Instead of going to Ironwood, you might end this drive by heading north on County Road 513, the Black River Scenic Byway. This narrow, winding road through the Ottawa National Forest follows the Black River as it tumbles over a series of waterfalls and descends from the hills to the Lake Superior shore. This is a lovely drive, and turnoffs to five forest cascades are well marked. The end of the byway is Black River Harbor on Lake Superior, a fine spot for a picnic, for watching the lighthouse, or for simple contemplation of the road just traveled.

VISITING HOURS

St. Ignace

Fort de Buade Museum, at 334 N. State St. (906) 643–9494. Daily, 9–9, Memorial Day–mid-September. $2.

Marquette Mission and Museum of the Ojibwa Culture, at 500 N. State St. (906) 643–9161. Daily, 10–8, Memorial Day–Labor Day. Tuesday to Saturday, 1–5, rest of September. $2.

Father Jacques Marquette National Memorial and Museum, west of town. (906) 643–8620. Daily, 9–5, mid-June–September. $3.50 per vehicle.

Gould City

Michihistrigan, west of town. (906) 477–6983. Hours vary through the year. Fee for golf.

Gulliver

Seul Choix Point Lighthouse, east on a county road. (906) 283–3169. Monday to Saturday, 12–4, June–September. Donation.

Thompson

State Fish Hatchery, west of town. (906) 341–5587. Daily, dawn to dusk. Free.

Gladstone

Hoegh Pet Casket Co., at 317 Delta Ave. (906) 428–2151. Monday to Friday, 8–4. Free.

Escanaba

Delta County Historical Museum, on Ludington St., in Ludington Park. (906) 786–3428. Daily, 1–9, June–Labor Day. Free.

Hermansville

IXL Museum, south on Main St. and west on River St. (906) 498–2181. Daily, 1–4, Memorial Day–Labor Day. $1.

Vulcan

Iron Mountain Iron Mine, west of town. (906) 563–8077. Daily, 9–6, June–mid-October. $5.50.

Iron Mountain

Cornish Pumping Engine and Mining Museum, west on Kent St. (906) 774–1086. Monday to Saturday, 9–5, and Sunday, 12–4, May–October. $4.

Menominee Range Historical Museum, at 300 E. Ludington St. (906) 774–4276. Monday to Saturday, 10–4, April–November. $4.

Iron River

Iron County Museum, south on Michigan 189, in Caspian. (906) 265–2617. Monday to Saturday, 9–5, and Sunday, 1–5, June–August. Monday to Saturday, 10–4, and Sunday, 1–4, May and September. $2.50.

Watersmeet

Ottawa National Forest, Watersmeet Visitors Center, at U.S. 45. (906) 358–4724. Daily, 9–5, Memorial Day–September. Free.

Walker Tavern. (Courtesy Michigan Historical Center.)

U.S. 12

Ypsilanti, Michigan, to Beverly Shores, Indiana

U.S. 12 was once the Great Sauk Trail, the Native American road that connected the tribes on Lake Michigan to the Detroit River. It later became the Chicago Turnpike, the main stagecoach route between the two greatest cities on the Great Lakes, Detroit and Chicago.

Michigan's larger cities developed slightly to the north, along the route chosen by the Michigan Central Railroad. U.S. 12 leads to smaller, older communities, through surprisingly scenic country, and, finally, to the Indiana dune country at the threshold of Chicago. The highway eventually makes it all the way to the Pacific coast of Washington, reaching the ocean at the port of Aberdeen.

The Greek struggle for independence from Turkey in the 1820s captured the imagination of many Americans. They deeply identified with the country as the birthplace of the classical era, in whose writings and architecture all educated persons were steeped. It was also a Christian outpost trying to free itself from Muslim rule. So the valor of Demetrios Ypsilanti, a young general from the Greek family that led the insurrection, captured the hearts of admirers in Michigan. They decided to name a small settlement on the Huron River in his honor in 1832, and Ypsilanti has proudly borne the name of this Greek hero ever since. There is a memorial to him here, with a bust sculpted in Athens, next to the city's most identifiable landmark, the Old Water Tower. It is just west of the business district, on Cross St. The water tower itself dates from 1899 and is visible from all parts of town. Right across the road is Eastern Michigan University, with an enrollment of 23,000. Part of the state university system, the school is noted for its College of Education. A small collegiate shopping area is located opposite the entrance to the campus, on Cross St.

Most of historic Ypsilanti developed along U.S. 12. In town the highway is called Michigan Ave. and is the town's main business street. The highway carries that same name as it leaves downtown Detroit and also as it enters Chicago's Loop. East of Ypsilanti, it is a congested run through Detroit's western suburbs, so it is a better idea to pick the road up in Ypsilanti.

Much of the residential area north of Michigan Ave., just east of downtown, is a national historic district, with a wealth of fine nine-teenth-century homes. Many, appropriately, were built in Greek Revival style. One of them, at 220 N. Huron St., is now the Ypsilanti Histori-cal Museum, with exhibits on the history of the town during the Victo-rian period. Right around the corner, on E. Cross St., is Depot Town, another historic district, with a collection of nineteenth-century shops clustered around the town's old railroad station.

From Ypsilanti, the road crosses U.S. 23 (featured later in this book) and begins its journey, angling consistently southwest. Saline was named for the salt springs its settlers found useful when they arrived in 1824. Henry Ford took an interest in the area, establishing his first satellite parts plants here in the 1920s. It reminded him of the rural Michigan community in which he had grown up, and he contributed funds to the restoration of several local structures. The town has an attractive downtown section, with bricked sidewalks and old street-lamps.

Clinton was almost a mirror image of Saline through the nineteenth century, developing along the same lines and only 12 miles farther down the road. In the 1940 census, Clinton had exactly 17 more people than Saline. But Clinton remained outside the suburbanization process and now is only one-third the size of its neighbor. It also has a nicely pre-served business district, which features commercial structures dating back to the 1830s.

Past Clinton, the highway enters the hilliest portion of southern lower Michigan, an area known as the Irish Hills. An Episcopal priest from nearby Tecumseh, Rev. William N. Lyster, is credited with giving the area its name in the 1830s. He said the rolling, lake-dotted land-scape reminded him of his native land. The Irish Hills is a popular tourist destination, a relief from the surrounding Michigan flatlands. But on summer weekends when a racing event is scheduled at nearby

Michigan International Speedway it can be a major headache trying to get through this area. Try to avoid those weekends at all costs.

Walter Hayes State Park is situated on a lake in an especially scenic corner of the Irish Hills. Nearby are observation towers that have stood here since the dawn of automotive travel. They command a panorama of the surrounding countryside. Almost directly across the road is St. Joseph's Catholic Church, built by Irish settlers. As Rev. Lyster had foreseen, Irish immigrants were drawn here by the location's resemblance to the land of their birth. A stone chapel dates to 1854, and a small churchyard contains the graves of several pioneer families.

A panoply of tourist stops also has developed in the Irish Hills area. Since they are irrelevant to its history or character, they can be passed by with slight loss.

A Closer Look. Daniel Webster spent the night in this area. So did James Fenimore Cooper, who showed up with a pair of Native American guides. So did a mysterious guest who was found murdered the morning after his arrival. The Walker Tavern had rooms for them all.

It was the most famous inn on the Chicago Turnpike, an oasis of relief after days of jolting stagecoach travel from Chicago or Detroit. It stood on a slight hillock where the Chicago Turnpike, now U.S. 12, met the Monroe Pike, now Michigan 50, the main road from Lake Erie to Jackson, on the Grand River.

The Walker has been a museum far longer than it was a tavern. It opened in 1832 and shut down just 20 years later, as travelers deserted this route for the railroad. It served as a farmhouse for several years afterward and then stood deserted for decades. A Detroit clergyman, Rev. Frederick Hewitt, bought the place in 1921 and, after some restoration work, reopened it as a museum. That's what it has been ever since, an evocation of what traveling meant when this was a frontier highway.

The tavern is set up as if Sylvester Walker was preparing to welcome another stageload of travelers to his inn. Webster came through in 1838, on one of the perennial presidential aspirant's political swings through the West. Cooper arrived nine years later, with his wife and two daughters, two servants, and his guides. He was working on a novel about the Great Lakes frontier, which became *Oak Openings,* and he used the tavern as a base for conducting research. It is said that many farmers in the area would have been astonished to see themselves portrayed in the famed author's book . . . if they had been able to read.

Rev. Hewitt was an inveterate collector and stocked his tavern with everything he owned relating to the Michigan frontier. Other items were added later from the homes of Irish Hills families. They include Franklin stoves, bear traps, tableware, and four-poster beds. The original bar is still in place, too, bearing the scratches of its long years of service.

There are many stories surrounding the homicide that occurred here. According to most versions, the victim-to-be arrived one evening on his way west to stock a cattle ranch. While he did not identify himself, a few of his drinking companions could not help but notice a thick money-belt around his waist. On the next morning he either turned up dead or was missing, depending on which story appeals to you. One version says he was found in his bed, another that he was found on the ground beneath his shattered window. Still a third telling of the tale says that he disappeared completely and that his starving horse was found several days later, tied to a tree in the nearby woods. For many years, a dark stain on the floor of the room was pointed to as clear evidence of foul play here.

One of the biggest political gatherings in the young state's history was held on the grounds of the Walker Tavern during the presidential campaign of 1840. The rally attracted voters from three states who camped out in their wagons for several days to listen to the oratory. Those cheers were stilled long ago. But the tavern remains, at the side of the Chicago Turnpike, very much as it was.

Just beyond the Walker Tavern is the turnoff to Michigan International Speedway, where several major stock-car and Indy-style events run throughout the summer. You can see the grandstand directly to the north, and if you happen to be driving this way when a race or time trials are in progress, you will hear the sounds of the speedway much farther back along the road. As I already indicated, U.S. 12 is burdened with bumper-to-bumper traffic in both directions in the hours immediately before these races, as it is the major conduit of traffic from nearby metropolitan areas.

Many of Michigan's major rivers rise in the Irish Hills. Among them is the Kalamazoo, which is still barely a trickle as it passes through the town of Moscow. This place was a popular stop in the days before glas-nost, when travelers delighted in sending off a postcard to the folks back home with a Moscow postmark on it. It was a customary practice among pioneers to name new towns after foreign capitals, as a token of hope for future growth. In the 1830s, Moscow was a reasonable choice. Before being named Moscow, it was known as "the place on the Chicago Turn-pike at the Kalamazoo River," and mail was delivered there with those directions. So you can see why the settlers were eager to name it some-thing.

Another major river originating in the area is the St. Joseph, and the town of Jonesville grew up at a natural ford of that river. The Munro House in Jonesville, built in 1840 as the first brick building in Hills-dale County, is now a bed-and-breakfast. The Grosvenor House, built by a former lieutenant governor in 1872, is a museum of the town's Victo-rian period. After Jonesville U.S. 12 runs through Allen, noted for its collection of antique shops, which comprise virtually the entire center of town.

In Branch County, Coldwater, probably named for the chain of lakes that surrounds the city, grew up where the Chicago Turnpike inter-sected the main route north from Indiana. Location made Coldwater an important stop on the Underground Railroad, and many escaping slaves dispersed east and west to nearby Michigan towns from this point. In later years, the Tibbits Opera House was a measure of the town's pros-perity. Built in 1882, it is one of Michigan's grand Victorian theaters. It was rescued from a decline into a movie house and restored to its appear-ance when such luminaries as Ethel Barrymore and William Gillette trod its boards.

Bronson, also in Branch County, was a favored spot for Polish immi-grants in the 1870s, and the town celebrates its heritage each July with its Polish Festival. The founder of the place was a colorful old coot, Judge Jabez Bronson. He believed in competition between legal jurisdictions. To get himself more marriage trade he put out the word that ceremonies performed by the judge in neighboring Hillsdale County were not legal. The settlers, not altogether sure of their legal position, hedged their bets by getting married twice, to the profit of Judge Bronson.

The town of Sturgis lies at the interchange between the two great Native American trails through this area. We have been following the

Great Sauk Trail. The Nottawaseepe Trail led to the north and was used by the Potawatomi, whose homeland this was. The tribe managed to hold on to it until 1833, when it was overrun by settlers who coveted the fertile, well-watered territory. The tribe was transported to Kansas. The town of Nottawa, just north of here, is a shortened version of the name of the same tribal leader for whom the trail was named. It marks the center of Michigan's Potawatomi lands.

According to local lore, Sturgis got its name because of some exemplary biscuits. When Lewis Cass was a young surveyor working in the area, he enjoyed this treat in the house of the first settler here, John Sturgis. Years later, after Cass had been elected governor, the settlement petitioned to become a city. Cass insisted that it be named Sturgis, in tribute to the finest biscuits he'd ever tasted.

The town of White Pigeon recalls another chapter in the uneven relationship between Native Americans and whites in this part of Michigan. While the Potawatomi were still in possession of the land, several tribal leaders seriously considered attacking the white settlements on their borders, as a means of discouraging further incursions. One leader, Wahbemme, made his way on foot to this area to warn whites of the plan. In gratitude, they named the community for the English equivalent of his name. His grave was marked near the intersection of the Chicago Turnpike and U.S. 131 for many years.

Mottville prospered in the 1820s because of its position on the St. Joseph River at a time when most interior transportation was done by water. There are reports that there were wharves and warehouses along its waterfront, all of which disappeared when the railroad came through and bypassed the place.

The highway dips almost to the Indiana border, through rolling countryside, before reaching Niles. This town bills itself as the "Four Flags City," which confuses many casual historians. They know that France, England, and America controlled this area of Michigan in turn. But what country flew the fourth flag? It belonged to Spain. There is no great wonder why it isn't better remembered. It flew here only one day: February 12, 1781. The place that would become Niles was then Fort St. Joseph. The outpost was established by France in 1691 to protect the fur trade along the St. Joseph River. Britain took it over after the French and Indian War and maintained a light garrison here throughout the Revolutionary War. Seeing a chance to make some points with the local

Native American tribes and also pick up some booty, the Spanish commandant in St. Louis authorized an overland raid on the fort in January 1781. The party reached the fort one month later, accepted its surrender, declared that it had been annexed to Spain, and left the next day. The British troops then ran up their own flag, and no one ever saw the Spanish around here again.

The Fort St. Joseph Museum, in the middle of Niles, recalls that era. It also contains one of the more unusual Native American treasures, a piece of memorabilia from a great leader who lived many hundreds of miles away. When Sitting Bull decided to return from exile in Canada, where he had fled following the fight at the Little Big Horn in 1876, he was assured that he would not be punished for his role in the destruction of Gen. George Custer's forces (see U.S. 24). Instead, he was arrested and imprisoned for two years in Fort Randall, South Dakota.

The Hunkpapa Sioux leader, with much time on his hands, decided to take up drawing. The old warrior chose to illustrate the story of his life in a series of pictographs. It showed his military career, against other Native American opponents and the U.S. Cavalry, depicted with great color and energy. Sitting Bull befriended the fort commandant's daughter, Alice Quimby, and on his release in 1883 he gave her the drawings as a gift. She kept them for the rest of her life. She moved to Niles, where she left the drawings as a bequest to the museum at her death in 1947. Sitting Bull's saddle and rifle are also part of the exhibit.

This is Michigan's most bountiful fruit-growing region, and in early May the roads through Berrien County are a magnificent sight. The most intensive concentration of orchards is slightly to the north, but you can still get some sense of it along U.S. 12.

The road completes its journey across Michigan at New Buffalo, a resort town on Lake Michigan. Warren Dunes State Park, with its broad beaches and towering hills of sand, is just north of town. New Buffalo is surrounded by cottages and summer camps, and its downtown district is well stocked with souvenir stores. The area is very popular with visitors from Chicago, who make the swing around the bottom of Lake Michigan in an hour and a half. During the summer, the beaches here are almost an outpost of Illinois, rather than part of Michigan. Even local radio stations generally carry the games of Chicago's sports teams rather than Detroit's.

U.S. 12 crosses into Indiana just past the town of Michiana and becomes the Dunes Highway. It enters the eastern portion of Michigan City almost immediately (see U.S. 421 for a description of Michigan City's lakefront). At Potawatomi Park, the Great Sauk Trail ran a narrow course right along the lakefront. Most early explorers who came into the region passed through here. Fr. Jacques Marquette, for whom a nearby spring is named, was a visitor in 1675. In 1780, a French raiding party from St. Louis was overtaken here by British pursuers and scattered. Black Hawk met with Potawatomi leaders here in 1830 and tried to convince them, unsuccessfully, to join Sauk resistance to white settlers.

The park is now the home of the International Friendship Gardens. This collection of 65 varieties of gardens is meant to represent the horticultural styles of nations around the world. At their conception in 1934, the gardens were intended to promote peace in a world threatened by war. Among the leaders who donated plants were Benito Mussolini and Adolf Hitler. Things just didn't work out well on the global scale, but the gardens are lovely.

U.S. 12 now runs across downtown Michigan City. A local landmark is the Barker Mansion, built in 1900 by the owner of the country's largest manufacturer of railroad freight cars. John H. Barker intended his home to be a reproduction of an English manor. He stocked the 38-room mansion with antiques from across Europe and paneled it in the richest woods. It is now a community center, as well as a museum of how the good life looked at the dawn of the twentieth century.

The road continues into Beverly Shores. This was an upscale lakeside development that fell on difficult times during the Depression. To publicize the place, promoters brought in several buildings from Chicago's recently concluded Century of Progress International Exposition in 1933–34. You can still find a handful of them as you drive among the dunes on the lakeshore, including reproductions of Boston's Old North Church and the homes of Paul Revere and Benjamin Franklin.

Just to the west is the entrance to Indiana Dunes National Lakeshore. This is a 15,000-acre recreation and conservation area at the edge of the most intensive industrial development on the Great Lakes. The man who helped create that complex, Judge Elbert Gary, chairman of U.S. Steel, was instrumental in saving this tract of irreplaceable duneland from further spoilation. Gary, assisted by contributions from several

Chicago industrialists, persuaded Indiana to turn it into a state park in 1923. But after World War II, pressure mounted for construction of a deepwater port in this area. A group of local citizens formed the "Save the Dunes" committee and after a political battle that lasted almost 20 years, the Indiana Dunes National Lakeshore was created in 1966, preserving the dunes for the future.

The national lakeshore's visitors center is at U.S. 12 and Kemil Rd., about 3 miles east of Indiana 49. Here you can pick up maps and see displays about the unusual ecology of the dunes. This is really the birthplace of modern ecology, the site of pioneering studies by biologist Dr. Henry Cowles. The bog in which he did his historic work on plant distribution, in the eastern part of the park, is now named for him. Park rangers give walking tours of the area. There are also three beaches in the park from which the skyline of Chicago is clearly visible on most days.

Another historic feature of the national lakeshore is the Bailly House, built in 1822 as a trading post along the Great Sauk Trail. Joseph Bailly's descendants continued to occupy the dwelling until 1917. It is now restored to its appearance of frontier times, with a chapel and stagecoach tavern built by Bailly also on the grounds.

To the west lies the flaming furnace of the Calumet and the maw of an industrial giant. We'll end the trip here, in the lap of a gentler era on the southern Lake Michigan shore.

VISITING HOURS

Ypsilanti

Ypsilanti Historical Museum, at 220 N. Huron St. (313) 482–4990. Friday to Sunday, 10–4. Donation.

Cambridge Junction

Walker Tavern, at intersection of U.S. 12 and Michigan 50. (517) 467–4414. Wednesday to Sunday, 12–6, Memorial Day–Labor Day. Free.

Jonesville

Grosvenor House, at 49 S. Howell St. (517) 849–9596. Tours by appointment. Donation.

Coldwater

Tibbits Opera House, at 14 S. Hanchett St. (517) 278–6029. Monday to Friday, 9–6. Free.

Niles

Fort St. Joseph Museum, downtown, at Fifth and Main Sts. (616) 683–4702. Tuesday to Saturday, 10–4, and Sunday, 1–4. Donation.

Michigan City

International Friendship Gardens, east on Liberty Trail, in Potawatomi Park. No phone. Daily, 9–dusk. $2.50.

Barker Mansion, at 631 Washington St. (219) 873–1520. Tours Monday to Friday, at 10, 11:30, and 1, and on weekends at 12 and 2, June–October. Weekdays only, rest of year. $2.

Indiana Dunes National Lakeshore

Indiana Dunes National Lakeshore Visitors Center, at U.S. 12 and Kemil Rd. (219) 926–7561. Daily, 8–5. Free.

Bailly House, south from U.S. 12 on Babcock Rd. (219) 926–7561. Daily tours Sunday, 1–4, Memorial Day–October. Free.

U.S. 20

Oberlin, Ohio, to South Bend, Indiana

U.S. 20 is the longest of the old federal highways, running more than 3,000 miles, from
Boston to the Pacific coast of Oregon. In
much of its eastern portion, through Massa-
chusetts and New York, U.S. 20 retraces one of America's first overland
roads to the West, a route closely paralleled by the Erie Canal.

Many travelers on that road were bound for Ohio, and the look of the
towns on U.S. 20 in this state bear the unmistakable stamp of New England. This road was also the major connector between Cleveland and
Chicago before the construction of the interstates. It is still congested in
those cities, but for the miles in between it is a pleasant old road. It vis-
its many midsized towns bypassed by the interstates, including a liter-
ary landmark, a presidential retreat, and touchdown central, USA.

We'll pick up the road on the western side of metropolitan Cleveland. It does run through some interesting towns on the Lake Erie shore
east of that city, but passage through the city's suburbs is slow. Once
past Elyria, the road enters open country, so that's where we'll start the
ride. In fact, we'll fudge a little bit and begin in the college town of
Oberlin, a mile off U.S. 20. Since the original road used to run right
through this town, beginning here isn't that much of a stretch.

The New Englanders who chose to head west were, generally, an ide-
alistic lot. They were full of utopian ideas and plans to improve
humankind by education and right thinking, and they left a lasting
legacy wherever they settled. Oberlin College was one of their proudest
achievements. It was established in 1833 with two essential goals: to
educate women and to lead the fight against slavery. Its first class was
composed of 29 men and 15 women. It is hard to comprehend now what
a watershed that was. But the top Ivy League schools were still segre-

Home of Rutherford B. Hayes at Spiegel Grove, Fremont, Ohio. (Courtesy of Hayes Presidential Center.)

gated by sex 100 years later, when Oberlin was observing a centennial of granting equal degrees to women.

The college also decided that if it was serious about its abolitionist beliefs it should admit Black students, too. Other schools already had taken that step, but Oberlin was the first to make such admissions official policy. By the mid-1850s, one-third of its student body was Black. One of its graduates, John Langston, became the first African-

American to be elected to public office in America, as clerk of a nearby township.

Oberlin College continues to be among the country's most progressive institutions, with nationally recognized schools of music and art. The Music Conservatory, designed by Minoru Yamasaki and opened in 1964, is a campus landmark. The Allen Memorial Art Museum contains an excellent small collection, with a good representation of Dutch and Japanese works. Since the community grew up around the campus, it is an almost perfect integration of town and gown, with Tappan Square being the center of both classroom and commercial life.

Now head south from Oberlin on Ohio 58, follow it to its junction with U.S. 20 and turn west. We are entering the Firelands, a section of the Ohio Territory set aside for Connecticut residents who were burned out by British raiders during the Revolutionary War. Connecticut lost title to the land when the Northwest Territory was formed in 1787, but the Firelands grants were still honored. The problem was that not many claimants came forth. This was still a dangerous place to live then. The British refused to give up their base in Detroit, and it was their policy to encourage and arm local tribes to drive out American settlers. Only when these threats were finally removed, after the War of 1812, did the long-delayed immigration from Connecticut begin.

Many of the newcomers gave their settlements the same names as the towns they left behind. One of the most successful settlements was Norwalk. Its settlers built homes in the Greek Revival style. Many of them still stand, giving Norwalk a distinctive New England appearance. One of these dwellings, behind the public library, has been turned into the Firelands Museum, a regional facility that traces the history of the area and its ties to Connecticut and that depicts what life was like on the nineteenth-century Ohio frontier. Several fine old homes dating from the 1830s are on Main St. nearby.

Bellevue, despite the aristocratic sound of its name, was a railroad town. James Bell, who built the Mad River and Lake Erie line, the first in Ohio, between here and Sandusky, named the place after himself. A collection of nineteenth-century railroad cars and paraphernalia keeps this heritage alive at the Mad River and NKP Railroad Society Museum, just south of midtown.

Another peek at nineteenth-century life is preserved near Bellevue at

Historic Lyme Village. This complex contains several buildings moved here from other parts of the Firelands and grouped in a townlike setting. Besides an assortment of residences, there is a blacksmith's shop, a weaver's shop, an herb shop, and other businesses, staffed by costumed guides who explain their activities.

This is rich orchard land, featuring mostly cherries and some apples. The highway approaches Clyde, a town where a writer who knew some secrets about apples once lived.

A Closer Look. In his book *Winesburg, Ohio,* Sherwood Anderson wrote: "Into a little round place at the side of the apple has been gathered all its sweetness. One runs from tree to tree over the forested ground picking the gnarled, twisted apples and filling his pockets with them. Only a few know the sweetness of the twisted apples." For more than a century, the location of the real-life "Winesburg" was Clyde's town secret. Copies of Anderson's book were burned in the incinerator behind the Carnegie Library. The local newspaper treated him like a nonperson. His old friends would change the subject when his name was mentioned.

Children grew up and went through school in Clyde without ever learning that their little town was the model for one of the most famous places in American literature. Anderson's book is regarded as a twentieth-century classic and remains a staple of college American literature courses. It was a shaping influence on the young writers of the 1920s and one of the first American books to treat sex as a prime motivating factor in human behavior. That was a big part of the problem in Clyde.

There has always been some confusion over the identity of the fictional Winesburg, prompted in no small part by the fact that there actually is a Winesburg, Ohio. That village is located about 100 miles southeast of Clyde (see U.S. 62). Anderson said later that the coincidence was quite embarrassing and that he hadn't known of the real Winesburg's existence. But records of the paint company he once owned in Elyria indicate that he had frequent business dealings in the real Winesburg. Maybe he filed it, as writers do, in a subconscious list of promising place names.

To anyone familiar with Clyde, however, there was never any doubt that this was the place Anderson had in mind. Clyde's physical features, its street names, and the surrounding countryside are the same as those in the book. Anderson moved to Clyde as an eight year old in 1884 and grew up here, leaving for good after a stint in the Spanish-American War. The book appeared in 1919, almost 20 years after Anderson departed. But the town gasped when it read the stories.

Anderson swore that the characters—or "grotesques," in his own phrase—were drawn from people he had met in a Chicago rooming house. But that never washed in Clyde. The similarities were too strong. A downtown business block in the book is named the Heffner Block; it still stands along Main St. in Clyde. A nurseryman named John Spaniard appears in the book; in Clyde he was called John French. Clyde's town grocer was Skinner Letson; Winesburg's was Skinner Leeson. There is a Hern's Grocery in the book; in Clyde the store was Hurd's Grocery. The streets of Winesburg also ran through the heart of Clyde.

In 1919, however, those streets were a lot farther from big-city America than they are today. When Anderson wrote about the sexual longings that drove his characters to desperate acts, Clyde was shocked beyond words. While there were no one-to-one characterizations between the book's main characters and the populace of Clyde, there were still subjects that polite people didn't bring up. Sex was very much one of them.

The book caused a stir in New York as well. But that was because of Anderson's fresh use of language, his forceful repetition, and his refusal to wrench every short story into a dramatic climax. He belonged to "a small group that has somehow emancipated itself from the prevailing imitativeness and banality of the national letters," wrote critic H. L. Mencken in a laudatory review.

Anderson faded from critical favor in the 1930s, and at his death in 1941 he was regarded as a has-been. But his reputation underwent a posthumous revival, and *Winesburg* became regarded as a classic. Later critics detected the affection and sympathy with which Anderson treated his characters, his appreciation for a way of life that was about to be extinguished by the forces of standardization. Not until 1972, however, did Clyde hold a ceremony to honor its most famous son. Four years later, on Anderson's birth centennial, Michigan State University adjourned a conference on his writing and held its final day of meetings in Clyde. Then, in 1980, a local businessman, Robert Good, opened the

Winesburg Inn, a restaurant on U.S. 20 decorated with drawings of scenes from the book. "I was looking for a local history theme," Good explained to me, "and someone suggested Anderson. I asked about that Civil War general we got a monument to in the cemetery. They told me Anderson had him ten to one."

Most of the Clyde that Anderson wrote about is gone. But a few places from the pages of the book still stand. The Presbyterian Church, on W. Forest and Main, is there, with the tower from which its tormented pastor gazed down at the bare neck and arms of his neighbor. Anderson's old home is at 129 Spring Ave., one block west of Main and south of Cherry. The business district is also pretty much the same one Anderson saw.

But the hotel owned by the family of George Willard, the young reporter who is the book's central figure, was torn down in 1966. The fairgrounds, on which George shared a night under the immense starry sky with the banker's daughter, has disappeared. The railroad depot from which Willard left Winesburg for the last time is gone. The railroad doesn't stop here anymore. Even the sweet apples that were Anderson's symbol for the secret truths that Winesburg's citizens clasped to themselves are grown here no longer.

There is a good display on Anderson's life and works at the Clyde Public Library, at 222 W. Buckeye. Other than that, you can just walk around on a quiet spring evening and use your imagination to see the restless town of *Winesburg* lying just beneath the surface of the tranquil streets of Clyde.

The famous Civil War general from Clyde that Robert Good of the Winesburg Inn referred to in the preceding quote was James Birdseye McPherson. Unlike its response to Anderson, the town was proud to acknowledge this general. The local cemetery prominently features a monument in his memory and is named for him. So is U.S. 20 as it passes through town. McPherson's story is especially poignant. He was killed in action in 1864 while fighting against troops commanded by his West Point classmate and friend Confederate Gen. John Bell Hood. This cemetery is also the final resting place of Pvt. Rodger Young, who was celebrated in a song by Frank Loesser during World War II. Young was killed while charging a Japanese machine-gun nest, saving the lives of his platoon.

U.S. 20 proceeds from Clyde past Fremont, the home of Lt. Col. Rutherford B. Hayes, who was wounded in the arm during the Civil War but refused to leave his regiment. His heroism won him election to Congress in 1864, followed by three terms as Ohio's governor. When the 1876 Republican convention in Cincinnati found itself deadlocked for the presidential nomination, Hayes, the home-state favorite, emerged from the pack and won on the seventh ballot. He was called the "Great Unknown," and the voters apparently never got to know him either. Democrat Samuel Tilden won the popular vote and seemed to have the necessary margin in the electoral college too. But Republican operatives in three Southern states that were still occupied by Federal troops challenged the vote totals there. If they were upheld, the election would swing to Hayes. For months, the country teetered at the edge of a constitutional crisis. Outraged Democrats screamed that they were being cheated out of their prize. Eventually, an election commission, voting on straight party lines, awarded the disputed votes to Hayes, who kept his part of the deal by ending Reconstruction and removing troops from the South.

After this unpromising start, it was inevitable that Hayes would be a one-term president. When replaced on the 1880 ballot by fellow Ohioan James Garfield, he retired to his Fremont estate, Spiegel Grove. Hayes lived here until his death in 1893, receiving a steady stream of distinguished callers, many of whom left their names attached to trees planted on the grounds in their honor. There is an excellent presidential museum next to the family home, recounting the issues with which Hayes had to deal, mainly civil service reform. That issue so alienated powerful interest groups within his own party that it ended any last lingering chance he had of being renominated.

Fremont was also the scene of a rather unlikely battle during the War of 1812. American troops at Fort Stephenson, which is now in the heart of downtown, were besieged by a larger British force. But Maj. George Croghan kept shifting his lone cannon from place to place inside the fort, convincing the attackers that they were facing a well-armed and dangerous foe. The British withdrew, freeing the main American army under Gen. William Henry Harrison to provide unhindered land support for the critical Battle of Lake Erie, one month later. Croghan's remains are buried in a corner of the former fort, now a park in front of the city library. Nearby is Old Betsy, the cannon that won the battle.

The area around Woodville was famous as a breeding ground for blue heron, a fact memorialized in the name of the service plaza on the adjacent Ohio Turnpike. Some of the country's top tomato crops come from the fields of this rich farmland. Through the towns of Stony Ridge and Lime City you also get hints of the limestone quarries that were an important part of the area's economy.

At Perrysburg, the road enters the suburbs of Toledo and another scene of conflict in the War of 1812. Gen. Harrison built Fort Meigs here in the winter of 1813, on a bluff above the Maumee River. Its defenders were quickly besieged by a force of British and Native Americans. A group of Kentuckians sent to relieve them was ambushed a few miles downriver and cut to pieces; 660 of their number were killed. Still, Fort Meigs held out, frustrating British access to the Maumee and maintaining a threat to their rear. Finally, after a siege of six months, the British forces withdrew, having accomplished nothing. The fort has been reconstructed. Materials from the battlefield, personal effects of the garrison, and displays about the war in this region are exhibited in the blockhouses. Also on the site are a 61-foot-high memorial shaft and a marker to the victims of the relief-column massacre. The fort is on Ohio 65, just south of U.S. 20.

After crossing the river to Maumee (see U.S. 24), the highway divides. We'll take U.S. 20 Alt., the road that heads directly west out of the Toledo suburbs. This was the route of the old Western and Maumee Pike, a road so dismal and rough, even by nineteenth-century frontier standards, that it was reputed to be the worst in America. Things have improved, and the highway now makes a level run through the prosperous farmland that pioneers called the "Oak Openings."

The town of Wauseon, the seat of Fulton County, was named for a chief of the Potawatomi, whose ancestral home this was.

If you passed on visiting the Lyme Village restoration earlier on the road, you now get another chance to see a fine evocation of nineteenth-century Ohio. Sauder Farm and Craft Village re-creates the look of an agricultural community on the eve of the Civil War. Portrayers of the craftspeople who would have functioned then give demonstrations of their skills and how they fit into the life of the community. It is south of the highway from Burlington, on Ohio 66.

The two U.S. 20s reunite just east of the Indiana border and cross the state line together. Angola, Indiana, sits in the center of a recreational area, surrounded by lakes and hills. Once this was the core of Potawatomi tribal lands (see U.S. 27). Their presence lives on in the name of the Potawatomi Inn, at nearby Pokagon State Park.

Lagrange was platted by French land promoters, who named the town after the country estate of the Marquis de Lafayette. There was a craze for naming places after that Revolutionary War hero following his farewell tour of America in 1824. The Lagranges and Lafayettes that dot the national map are reminders of that enthusiasm.

The center of Indiana's Amish country lies just west of here. The group began arriving in 1841, moving steadily westward from their original American home in Pennsylvania. The Amish had split off from the Mennonite Church early in the seventeenth century in Switzerland. Still, the two groups often settled in close proximity to each other in the United States, although the Mennonites were considered far too worldly for Amish tastes. Shipshewana is a delightful, old-fashioned market town serving farmers who belong to both sects. The Menno-Hof Mennonite-Amish Visitors Center, just south of town on Indiana 5, is housed in a traditional barn, raised by the community. Exhibits explain the religious beliefs and culture of the groups. The town's name comes from a local Potawatomi chief, who was buried here in 1841 after being allowed to return from the tribe's deportation to Kansas.

Pills and trumpets built Elkhart, a medium-sized manufacturing town on the St. Joseph River. The pills came from Dr. Franklin Miles, a local physician whose popular home remedies grew into Miles Laboratories, founded in 1884. Within 24 years, one of its early investors was wealthy enough to build Ruthmere. This limestone mansion, owned by A. R. Beardsley, is a local landmark, with painted ceilings, silk wall hangings, and an Indiana limestone exterior. Built in the Beaux Arts style, it is a fine evocation of its times.

The company established by Charles G. Conn is still making music here too. More than half the band instruments used in the United States are made in its Elkhart plant. Conn was a cornet player in the local band but was not above getting into a good fight when the opportunity arose. In one such tussle, he suffered a bruise to his upper lip and could not toot his horn. Conn devised a soft rubber mouthpiece that enabled him to play. When word spread among musicians, he was inundated with requests for copies. His company went on to make the horns too and has dominated the wind instrument market ever since.

From Elkhart, the highway runs along the north side of the St. Joseph into South Bend. The St. Joseph was the river of destiny in northern Indiana. It was the route by which the first French explorers arrived, late in the seventeenth century. The place at which the St. Joseph made its southernmost bend was the start of the portage trail to the Kankakee River, which in turn flowed into the Mississippi. So the great bend in the river became a gathering place where the tribes met in peace. It was under an oak tree on this river bank in 1681 that Robert Cavelier, sieur de LaSalle, managed to sign a treaty with the Miami and Illinois. It bound them in an alliance with France against their common enemy, the Iroquois, who had terrified the local tribes with raids in the previous year. The Council Oak, now propped up with metal supports, still stands in Highland Cemetery.

South Bend was still a small trading center when Henry and Clement Studebaker arrived from Ohio in 1852. The brothers came to build wagons, and by the end of the century they were the most prestigious carriage makers in the country. Presidents Grant and Benjamin Harrison owned their products. Almost alone among the country's carriage makers, though, Studebaker understood the possibilities of the new automobile. In 1899 the Studebaker firm made the decision to transfer its know-how into the new field, making bodies for electric cars. Within three years, it was manufacturing its own vehicles in a local plant.

By the end of World War II, Studebaker was the last major auto producer in the country based outside Detroit. Its slogan, "More than we promised," typified its products. They were dependable, inexpensive, and tough little cars for the average consumer. Then in 1948 Studebaker struck gold. It hired packaging genius Raymond Loewey to design a new car for the company. He came up with the Hawk, one of the most distinctive vehicles ever made in America. Its front and rear ends were identical, its lines low and sporty. The country, with years of demand pent up by depression and war, rushed out to buy it. In 1951, Studebaker employed 21,000 workers in South Bend, the largest number in its history. But 12 years later the company was gone. It could not come up with new designs to match the Hawk, and it could not compete with the advertising and buying power of the three major automobile manu-facturers. A local group continued to make the Avanti sports car here until 1987. Then auto production finally ended in South Bend. The Studebaker National Museum traces the history of the company, from wagon days through the peak of the automotive years. It is also an exhi-bition of how Americans worked and lived in the early years of indus-trialization. Vintage vehicles are displayed in settings that reflect their history. The museum is located in the city's Century Center, on the banks of the St. Joseph.

To sports fans, however, South Bend is a dateline that means but one thing: Notre Dame football. The University of Notre Dame, located north of downtown, along Leeper Ave. (U.S. 31), is consistently ranked near the top of American academics. Its center for constitutional law is respected worldwide. But it is the Irish, in their golden helmets, with the richest tradition of any football team in America, that gets the juices flowing for the school's actual graduates and its "subway alumni," those who have never been anywhere near the campus but follow the team avidly. It has been this way since the 1920s, when coach Knute Rockne, aided by an adoring New York press, turned Notre Dame into a football powerhouse, innovative and tough. The battle cry "Win one for the Gipper" and the designations "Four Horsemen" and "Shock Troops" are all part of the lore, along with snappy shifts and dashing uniforms. Rockne masterminded it all and placed the university in a position it has never relinquished. Its 11 national football championships are more than any other school has won. The golden dome of the Administration Building and the religious mural of the Savior with uplifted arms, uni-versally referred to as "Touchdown Jesus," are national landmarks, as is the stadium. And though the stadium is small by major college stan-dards, with fewer than 60,000 seats, on autumn Saturdays the crowd is big enough to turn the streets of South Bend into a traffic-clogged car-nival.

Notre Dame was already 10 years old when the Studebakers arrived. The land belonged to the Diocese of Vincennes and was given to Fr. Edward Sorin in 1842 on the condition that he establish a university on the lake-dotted tract. This is not an overwhelmingly large campus (enrollment is around 10,000 students), so it is fairly easy to locate the Golden Dome, find a parking place, and walk around. The Art Gallery,

Grotto of Our Lady of Lourdes, and Hesburgh Library are major land-marks, and maps placed around the campus will help you find your way around. The Administration Building dates from 1879, and its murals of Christopher Columbus, painted by Luigi Gregori, the university's art director when the building was completed, are well worth seeing.

U.S. 20 continues on for several miles, becoming a divided highway as it rushes into the busy industrial belt of the Calumet. The best thing to do is end this ride the way we began it in Oberlin—on a college cam-pus, strolling amid the trees and thinking scholarly thoughts.

VISITING HOURS

Oberlin

Allen Memorial Art Museum, at 87 N. Main St. (216) 775–8665. Tuesday to Saturday, 10–5, and Sunday, 1–5. Free.

Norwalk

Firelands Museum, at 4 Case Ave. (419) 668–6038. Tuesday to Sun-day, 12–5, June–August. Weekends only, 12–4, April, May, and Sep-tember–November. $2.

Bellevue

Historic Lyme Village, 2 miles east on Ohio 113. (419) 483–4949. Tuesday to Sunday, 1–5, June–August. Sunday only, 1–5, May and Sep-tember. $5.

Mad River and NKP Railroad Society Museum, south of U.S. 20, on S. West St. (419) 483–2222. Daily, 1–5, Memorial Day–Labor Day. Weekends only, 1–5, May, September, and October. Donation.

Fremont

Hayes Presidential Center, Hayes Ave. at Buckland Ave. (419) 332–2081. Monday to Saturday, 9–5, and Sunday, 12–5. $4.

Perrysburg

Fort Meigs State Memorial, west on Ohio 65. (419) 874–4121. Wednesday to Saturday, 9:30–5, and Sunday, 12–5, Memorial

Day–Labor Day. Saturday, 9:30–5, and Sunday, 12–5, September–October. $4.

Burlington
Sauder Farm and Craft Village, south on Ohio 66, at Ohio 2. (419) 446–2541. Monday to Saturday, 9:30–5, and Sunday, 1:30–5, late April–October. $8.

Shipshewana
Menno-Hof Mennonite-Amish Visitors Center, north on Indiana 5. (219) 768–4117. Monday to Saturday, 10–5, April–December. Tuesday to Friday, 12–4, and Saturday, 10–5, mid-January–March. $4.

Elkhart
Ruthmere, north on Indiana 19. (219) 264–0330. Tours Tuesday to Saturday, at 11, 1, and 3, April–mid-December. $4.

South Bend
Studebaker National Museum, at 525 S. Main St. (219) 284–9714. Monday to Saturday, 9–5, and Sunday, 12–5. $3.50

Cambridge glassware. (Courtesy of Cambridge/Guernsey County Visitors and Convention Center.)

U.S. 22

Steubenville, Ohio, to Cincinnati, Ohio

Ohio likes to boast that it has more small cities than any other state—places not quite metropolitan but certainly bigger than towns. U.S. 22 samples several of these places, some of the most evocative small cities in the state.

U.S. 22 begins in Newark, New Jersey, runs across the width of Pennsylvania, and ends its overall run in Cincinnati. In Ohio the road runs from Steubenville to Cincinnati, meeting the Ohio River at either end of the journey, the only old road that pulls off that geographic stunt. It angles steadily southwest across the state, through countryside that varies from hilly to rolling. It runs for a time along the route of the National Road and Zane's Trace, the two earliest pioneer trails through the state.

Steubenville grew up at the heart of Ohio's coal belt, a section of the state that was an economic extension of neighboring West Virginia. Some of the landscapes in the area still carry the scars of the strip-mining that was used earlier in the century.

The coal provided fuel for the steel furnaces of Steubenville. With the collapse of that industry in the 1970s, however, the entire upper Ohio Valley felt the economic tremors. Steubenville was one of the places most severely shaken, losing almost half its population in the aftermath. The town had been an economic leader throughout its early history, trailing only Cincinnati and Marietta in population in Ohio for the first quarter of the nineteenth century. Its site, on a river plain and backed by hills, made it a strategic place for early settlement. A fort was placed here in 1786 to protect American interests in the Ohio country, an area then still hotly disputed by Britain and the Shawnee, as well as by the former colonies. Fort Steuben was named for the Prussian drillmaster who brought order to Gen. Washington's ragtag army. Within a decade, a city was established around the site of the military post, and Baron von Steuben's name was attached to a *ville* (village) rather than a fort.

Steubenville was a major port in the steamboat era and later became known for its woolen mills. Clothing made in Steubenville was a staple on the frontier. But in 1856 the place was transformed forever as the first rolling mill for steel opened on the riverfront and as the first coal mining shafts were sunk within the town limits. While the riverfront was taken over by heavy industry, the residential sections climbed the hills and opened out on magnificent views across the Ohio and into West Virginia. You can still get some sense of that by following one of the streets that wind upward from the business district into the hillside neighborhoods.

Many of Steubenville's downtown buildings have been decorated with murals that depict scenes from the city's past. A brochure outlining a walking tour of the murals, which are added to each year, can be picked up at the Chamber of Commerce offices, at 500 Market St. At the Jefferson County Historical Association Museum nearby are more historic displays and examples of the varied products that have been made in Steubenville over the years. Also exhibited is the desk of Lincoln's secretary of war, Edwin Stanton, who was born here. He was the man who murmured the valediction "Now he belongs to the ages" at the president's deathbed. Some historians have tried to implicate Stanton as a key conspirator in the plot on Lincoln's life, based on the supposition that he feared that the president's postwar policies toward the defeated South would be too mild. But these attempts at historic detective work are regarded, at best, as inconclusive. Stanton's statue stands on the courthouse lawn, at Market and Third.

A bit farther out Market St. is Union Cemetery, the resting place of the "Fighting McCooks," a family that answered the call in force to the conflict that Stanton oversaw. Sixteen of the McCooks, who lived in nearby Carrollton, served in the Civil War. One of them, Capt. Francis McCook, was the grandfather of a future president, Woodrow Wilson. The Stanton family plot is also in the cemetery.

The highway now enters Ohio's rugged hill country, running across lightly populated ridges and through stony valleys. A freeway route now makes this semimountainous drive much easier than it was before the 1970s. You can still see some of the evidence of strip-mining on the hillsides around Hopedale.

The road bypasses Cadiz (see U.S. 250) as a four-lane before narrowing and becoming a true old road through the hills. Just past Piedmont is a scenic overlook across Piedmont Dam, part of the Muskingum Watershed District. It impounds the waters of Stillwater Creek to form Piedmont Lake, a major water recreation resource.

The road enters Guernsey County, settled and named by families from that island in the English Channel. The group of 26 arrived here in 1806, on a grueling overland voyage from their American landing place in Norfolk, Virginia, to an intended new home in Cincinnati. But once they reached this area, the land looked so promising that they simply decided to stay, buy, and settle in. Subsequent residents came from another part of the British Isles. The towns of Londonderry and Antrim, also lying along this road, were built and named by people from Ulster, in Northern Ireland.

Just past Winterset, the highway passes an arm of Salt Fork Lake, another part of the Muskingum project, before entering the old glass-making town of Cambridge.

A Closer Look. Glass was one of the great luxuries of the era in which America was populated. Taxes in England were levied on the number of windows in a home, the supposition being that costly window glass was an accurate accounting of wealth in the household. Early exploration parties to Virginia and Massachusetts were urged to look for stands of timber; charcoal was essential as fuel in making glass, and there were fears in the early seventeenth century that England's natural supply was running low. Reports from Virginia also enthusiastically stated that the local sand seemed well suited for glassmaking. By 1608, the year after the Jamestown landing, a glassmaking operation was already functioning there, with experts imported from Europe to run it.

Glassware was the essential mark of wealth in the American colonies, when most drinking vessels were made from wood or clay. It was a true indication of the arrival of civilization when glassware appeared on a frontier table.

By the late nineteenth century, natural gas had replaced wood as the preferred heating agent in glass factories. With the discovery in the 1880s of vast fields of natural gas in Ohio, the industry quickly became centered in this state. Toledo developed into the country's top glass-maker. With impetus from the explosive demand for lightbulbs and automobile glass, the Ohio city came to dominate the industry.

In Cambridge, the emphasis was on tableware and novelties. The Cambridge Glass Co. opened in 1902, and over the next half century it turned out some of the most distinctive glassware in the country. Thousands of different items emerged from its blowing room before the place closed its doors in 1954. Its products developed a life of their own. Collectors have turned Cambridge into the country's top gathering place for glass. Each June they assemble here from across the country at the Cambridge Glass Collectors Sale and Show, to display rare items and exchange leads on the availability of other collectibles.

There are several museums dedicated to Cambridge glass in the area, and a few glassmaking operations keep the tradition alive. The Cambridge Glass Museum claims to have the largest collection of locally made glass in existence, with more than 5,000 items on display. This is the best place to compare the shades of difference in the unique colors that make Cambridge glass so highly prized.

The Degenhart Paperweight and Glass Museum exhibits the personal collection of M. Elizabeth Degenhart. Until her death in 1978, the family operated one of Cambridge's top glass producers. While Degenhart's interest was focused on her company's most distinctive item, decorative paperweights, she included glass products from across the entire Ohio Valley in her collection. Many of the old river towns in Pennsylvania, West Virginia, and Ohio had glass factories, each turning out a unique product in terms of shape and color. The Degenhart collection is among the best regional displays.

The Boyd family purchased the Degenhart factory shortly after Elizabeth's death and turns out products at Boyd's Crystal Art Glass. The Boyds continued several Degenhart molds, while adding many of their own. They are most noted for their glass dolls, as well as for fanciful bears, eagles, and mice. One of the most enduringly popular dolls, by the way, is named Elizabeth, for the former owner.

Mosser Glass, located east of town on U.S. 22, is known for its shimmering colored-glass birds and reproductions of fine antique tableware. Both Boyd's and Mosser give tours through the glassmaking operation and have extensive showrooms of their products.

There are several antique outlets along Wheeling Ave. (U.S. 22) in downtown Cambridge, between Sixth and Eighth Sts. Also look for the Hopalong Cassidy Museum, at 710 Wheeling. Cambridge was the hometown of actor William Boyd, who played the first of the great TV cowboy heroes in the late 1940s. Personal memorabilia from his long Hollywood career is displayed there.

As the road runs west from Cambridge, it joins U.S. 40. This is now a fast, four-lane highway. But when this route first was cut through the area, it was the extension of the National Road, the first federal highway to the West. Built by authorization of Congress in 1806, the road originally ran from Cambridge, Maryland, to Wheeling, in what was then Virginia. It reached the western terminus in 1818. There followed seven years of political and legal wrangling over a constitutional issue: whether the federal government had the right to sponsor such an internal improvement project. The U.S. Supreme Court's landmark ruling in *Gibbons v. Ogden* held that Congress could regulate interstate commerce, which gave it the power to extend the road. Construction resumed in 1825, and by the following year it had reached this area of Ohio.

For the first part of the route in Ohio, the National Road was built on the ruts of Zane's Trace. Far more primitive in its construction, this older road, the first overland track through Ohio, had been built from Wheeling (Virginia) to Maysville, Kentucky, starting in 1796. It was named for its contractor, Ebenezer Zane, regarded as the first permanent white resident in Ohio. Zane received land grants along the way as payment, much as the railroads were given incentives to extend their tracks into the West after the 1860s.

Zane's great-great-grandson grew up in the town that was built on one of these land concessions and named after its founder, Zanesville. Young Zane Grey studied dentistry and actually went into practice in New York City. But he was fascinated by his family history on what had then been the Western frontier. He was actually a frustrated writer who suspected that he had made a poor career choice. In 1904 Grey wrote his first novel, *Betty Zane,* which celebrated the heroism of his ancestor Ebenezer's wife (see Ohio 7). It enjoyed only a modest success, but enough to encourage Grey to make writing a full-time job. He felt that with the closing of the frontier, the country would be receptive to fiction about the last wild portion of the American West, Arizona and

New Mexico. In 1910 *The Heritage of the Desert* appeared, and with it Grey was on his way to becoming the best-selling American writer of his time.

His novels created the standard for the cowboys of fiction and film and were a tremendous influence on his contemporaries. Among them was Clarence Mulford, a writer from Maine. He created Hopalong Cassidy, whom we encountered a few miles back in Cambridge. A unique museum, which combines exhibits on both the National Road and Zane Grey, is located on the combined U.S. 22 and U.S. 40 between Cambridge and Zanesville, just west of the town of Norwich.

Ebenezer Zane selected the site of Zanesville (originally called Westbourne). A road builder like Zane was smart enough to know that a town situated at the junction of the Muskingum and Licking Rivers would prosper. He wasn't smart enough to cash in on it himself, though, selling off his landholdings in the area to his brother, Jonathan Zane. Three independent settlements grew up at the junction of the rivers. To connect the settlements physically and unify them politically, a bridge was authorized in 1812. It took the shape of the letter Y, with one arm leading to each settlement. It became Zanesville's landmark, and when the bridge was rebuilt in 1900, the shape was retained. The bridge still carries traffic across the water in the heart of town.

Zanesville was Ohio's state capital for two years, from 1810 to 1812. But on the day the legislature authorized the move here from Chillicothe, it also approved a resolution that the permanent capital had to be located within 40 miles of the state's geographic center. That excluded Zanesville by a distance of about 20 miles and cleared the way for Columbus to get the seat of government.

Zanesville, however, became the state's leading pottery maker. The industry is still an essential part of the city's economy, and examples of its beauty are exhibited at the Zanesville Art Center. The museum also emphasizes contemporary Ohio artists and craftspeople and collections of glass made in the Zanesville area. One of the area's largest potteries, the Robinson-Ransbottom Pottery Co., in nearby Roseville, gives tours of its factory. An adjacent museum, the Ohio Ceramics Center, displays even more varieties of the local products. The factory and museum are located 6 miles south of U.S. 22, by way of Ohio 93, from Moxahala Park.

U.S. 22 now bends southwest, away from the National Road and along the route of the original Zane's Trace. This section of the highway is designated a state scenic route, as it winds through some of Ohio's loveliest hill country.

The town of Somerset was the childhood home of the great Union cavalry general, Phil Sheridan. Superior Confederate cavalry dominated the early years of the Civil War, and the North looked desperately for an answer from among its leaders. Sheridan began the war working in the Quartermaster Corps in Washington. But his aggressive nature (he once was suspended from West Point for chasing another cadet with a bayonet) came to the attention of the president's chief of staff, Gen. Henry Halleck. With no previous experience, Sheridan was assigned to a cavalry command. He learned quickly and impressed Gen. Grant with the mobility of his forces at critical points in the Chattanooga campaign of 1863. He was transferred to Virginia and directed to wage a war of attrition against Southern supporters in the Shenandoah Valley. Sheridan's rapid strikes, so unlike the North's clumsy campaigns in the war's early going, demoralized Virginia. Inexorably, the advantage in the chief battleground of the war turned against the South. In one of the conflict's most dramatic incidents, Sheridan's force was mauled in a surprise attack at Winchester while he was off at a strategy conference in Washington. Riding desperately to the battle, Sheridan galloped into the midst of the Union retreat. The soldiers began to cheer, but Sheridan yelled: "God damn you, don't cheer me. There's lots of fight in you men yet. Come up!" His forces counter-attacked and drove off the Confederate troops.

Sheridan later was placed in command of U.S. cavalry in the Indian wars, starting in 1868. From his headquarters at Fort Hays, Kansas, he led the campaigns against the Cheyenne, Sioux, and Comanche on the Great Plains, always using his mounted forces to contain, build up a numerical advantage against, and then overwhelm the opposition. In 1883, he was named chief commander of the U.S. Army. Somerset remembers its hometown hero with a statue in the main square. It is, of course, an equestrian statue.

Just 19 miles away, is the home of another of the great leaders of the Union forces, Gen. William T. Sherman. Lancaster, on the Hocking River, was another site chosen by Ebenezer Zane for his land concessions. Mount Pleasant, a sandstone monolith that commands a view of the surrounding country, was a landmark to both Native Americans and settlers. It still stands in the city's Rising Park, on N. High St. But Lancaster's proudest monument is the prosaically named Square 13.

The town, which was laid out in 1800, three years after Zane's Trace reached Mount Pleasant, attracted many settlers from Lancaster, Pennsylvania. The new community was named for that town and was planned to include the sort of residential squares favored in the Middle Atlantic states. Square 13 was built up after the first decade of the town's existence, when prosperity began flowing into Lancaster. Nineteen of the structures in the square are listed as historic landmarks. The Federal and Georgian homes built here between 1811 and 1834 are regarded as Ohio's finest examples of early nineteenth-century domestic architecture.

Even without its associations with famous men, Square 13 would be worth seeing. But famous men did reside here. The house at 137 E. Main was the birthplace of two important Shermans: William T., whose march through Georgia is remembered as the most devastating campaign of the Civil War; and his brother, Sen. John Sherman, who gave his name to some of the most far-reaching legislation of the late nineteenth century. The Shermans were orphaned while still quite young, at the death of their father in 1829. They were adopted by a family friend, Thomas Ewing. His house also stands in the square, at 163 E. Main.

During the war, Gen. Sherman wrote frequent letters to his brother, three years his junior and already a senator, about the frustrations of his campaigns in the South. "No sooner do our forces pass through an area," he complained, "than the enemy returns, to be supplied by their sympathizers as if we never had been there." Gradually, the Shermans came to the conclusion that the only way to win the war in the South was through massive destruction. "It is about time the North understood the truth; that the entire South, man, woman and child is against us," the general wrote in 1863. "We can make war so terrible that they will realize its folly," he said in a letter to Grant in 1864. And in his most famous defense of his scorched earth policy on his march through Georgia, he stated to the 1880 convention of the Grand Army of the Republic: "There is many a boy here today who looks on war as all glory; but, boys, it is all hell." The effects of the grim campaign took their toll on

Sherman as well. Observers often commented that his face seemed sunken and that he looked much older than his 44 years.

John Sherman took a more peaceful path into the history books. The Sherman Antitrust Act, which he sponsored, was the first significant attempt by the federal government to break up the ruthless monopolies that were crushing competitors and squeezing suppliers into bankruptcy. He also backed the Silver Purchase Act, one of the great monetary reforms of the time, and served as secretary of state in President McKinley's first cabinet.

Another home in Square 13 that is open to the public is the Georgian, built in 1833 by the Reeves family in an echo of Southern domestic design.

Beyond Lancaster, U.S. 22 continues through rich, rolling farmland. Among the most ample products of these fields are pumpkins. The Pickaway County crop is reputed to produce the heftiest pumpkins in the world. Ever since 1903, the county seat, Circleville, has celebrated each October with its Pumpkin Festival. It is the biggest of its kind and has expanded to include locally grown squash and gourds, as well as the orange behemoths. The town got its name from a prehistoric round enclosure within which Circleville was laid out. Later excavations indicated that this had been a major village of the prehistoric Hopewell Culture (see U.S. 35).

Now the landscape flattens considerably, and the farms are more extensive too. This is stock-raising country, and the horse farms around Washington Court House are regarded as the finest in the state. Monthly auctions are held at the Fayette County Fairgrounds. The name of the community, which is among the longest in the United States, resulted from the enthusiasm early Ohioans had for honoring the country's first president. This Washington was one of four towns with that name in the state. So when a court of common pleas met here in 1810, it was decided to throw the words *court house* into the town's name to differentiate it from the others. The actual courthouse here shows off several murals by Ohio artist Archibald Willard, who painted the original *Spirit of '76.*

After Washington Court House, U.S. 22 runs through horse country into Wilmington. A Quaker institution, Wilmington College was founded here in 1870. It is now a small liberal arts school. The campus landmark is the Simon Goodman Memorial Carillon. More of the town's Quaker heritage is displayed at Rombach Place, the museum of the Clinton County Historical Society. Furniture, implements, and paintings—all part of the area's former Quaker community—are on display. So are items belonging to Gen. James Denver, who grew up here. He gave his name to Colorado's capital while serving as governor of that territory in 1858.

Just a short drive off U.S. 22, on westbound Ohio 350, is one of the most haunting reminders of the state's Native American history. Fort Ancient was erected by the Hopewell Culture (who built most of Ohio's mounds) in the final decades of their 1,000-year history here. By 600 A.D., the Hopewell people were severely threatened by invaders and were driven to build elaborate hilltop fortifications to protect their settlements. Eventually, they were either driven out or absorbed by the newcomers. Fort Ancient, on a bluff above the Little Miami River, indicates what the Hopewell were capable of building. It extends more than 3 miles, and the walls are more than 20 feet high in places. Its isolated location makes it all the more impressive.

U.S. 22 crosses the Little Miami at the town of Morrow and then enters the outermost suburbs of Cincinnati. It carries the name of one of them—it is called Montgomery Rd.—for the rest of its run into the big city. Instead of fighting your way through the traffic, a good place to end this ride is at the Montgomery Inn, at 9440 Montgomery Rd. Its barbecued ribs are famous throughout the Midwest. It is a poor old road, after all, that does not lead to a good meal.

VISITING HOURS

Steubenville

Jefferson County Historical Association Museum, at 426 Franklin Ave. (614) 283–1133. Wednesday to Saturday, 11–3, May–September. $1.

Cambridge

Cambridge Glass Museum, north on Ohio 209. (614) 432–3045. Monday to Saturday, 1–4, June–October. $2.

Degenhart Paperweight and Glass Museum, east on U.S. 22, at Interstate 77. (614) 432–2626. Monday to Saturday, 9–5, and Sunday, 1–5, March–December. Weekdays only, rest of year. $1.50.

Boyd's Crystal Art Glass, near downtown, at 1203 Morton Ave. (614) 439–2077. Monday to Friday, 8–3:30, and Saturday, 9–noon, June–August. Weekdays only, rest of year. Free.

Mosser Glass, east on U.S. 22, at Interstate 77. (614) 439–1827. Monday to Friday, 8:15–3. Free.

Hopalong Cassidy Museum, at 710 Wheeling Ave. (614) 439–3967. Monday to Saturday, 9–5. Free.

Zanesville

National Road–Zane Grey Museum, east on U.S. 22. (614) 872–3143. Monday to Saturday, 9:30–5, and Sunday, 12–5, May–September. Closed Monday and Tuesday, March, April, October, and November. $4.

Zanesville Art Center, north on Ohio 60, at 620 Military Rd. (614) 452–0741. Tuesday to Sunday, 1–5. Free.

Roseville

Robinson-Ransbottom Pottery Co., on Ohio 93. (614) 697–7355. Monday to Friday, 9–3. Free.

Ohio Ceramics Center, on Ohio 93. (614) 697–7021. Wednesday to Saturday, 10–5, and Sunday, 12–5, mid-May–mid-October. $1.

Lancaster

Sherman House, at 137 E. Main St. (614) 687–5891. Tuesday to Sunday, 1–4, April–November. $2.

The Georgian, at 105 E. Wheeling St. (614) 654–9923. Tuesday to Sunday, 1–4, April–November. $2.

Wilmington

Rombach Place, at 149 E. Locust St. (513) 382–4684. Tuesday–Sunday, 1–5, March–December. Donation.

Fort Ancient State Memorial, west on Ohio 350. (513) 932–2241. Wednesday to Sunday, 10–8, Memorial Day–Labor Day. Saturday, 10–5, and Sunday, 12–5, April, May, September, and October. $4.

Montgomery

Montgomery Inn, at 9440 Montgomery Rd. (513) 791–3482. Monday to Friday, 11–11, Saturday, 4–midnight, and Sunday, 4–9:30. No reservations on Saturday night.

U.S. 23 AND MICHIGAN 25

Mackinaw City, Michigan, to Port Huron, Michigan

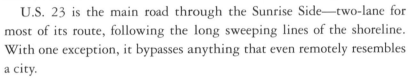

The Lake Huron coast of Michigan's Lower
Peninsula has been tagged the "Sunrise Side"
by travel promoters. Their hope is to build it
up as a less crowded and less expensive alternative to the intensive resort concentration on Lake Michigan.

U.S. 23 is the main road through the Sunrise Side—two-lane for
most of its route, following the long sweeping lines of the shoreline.
With one exception, it bypasses anything that even remotely resembles
a city.

Beyond Bay City, this drive retraces the route of what used to be U.S.
25. Numerical designations changed with the coming of the interstate
system, and U.S. 25 now doesn't start until the suburbs of Cincinnati.
But Michigan gave the state road the same number along its former
route around the edge of the Thumb.

The road begins practically beneath the Mackinac Bridge (see U.S. 2)
in Mackinaw City. You cannot help but notice the disparity in the
spelling of the bridge and city names. Over the last 300 years or so many
have noticed, but no one seems inclined to reconcile them. The names
are derived from the Algonquian word *Michilimackinac*. It means "at the
place of the big turtle" and refers to the famous resort island of Mackinac. When viewed from the lake, Mackinac Island resembles a turtle,
an animal with religious clan associations to many of the tribes who
lived in the area. *Mackinac* was the preferred French spelling, and it was
applied to the island, the strait, and the bridge. But when the British
arrived and fortified the southern end of the straits, they spelled the
word as it was pronounced, *Mackinaw.* That spelling is applied to the
heavy rainwear that originated among the traders and fur trappers who
worked here. It was also favored by Mackinaw City.

Fort Michilimackinac. (Courtesy Michigan Travel Bureau.)

A Closer Look. The French fortified the northern end of the Straits of Mackinac in 1681, at what is now St. Ignace (see U.S. 2). But 20 years later, the garrison was withdrawn to create a new settlement, which grew into the city of Detroit. The Straits remained without a European military presence until 1715. Then the French returned to build Fort Michilimackinac and garrisoned it for 45 years. The fort was abandoned during the French and Indian War and taken over by the British in 1761.

Britain's takeover led to the most violent episode in the area's history. Many of the tribes in the Great Lakes had friendly relations with the French. They were common enemies of the Iroquois, and French colonial policy, which stressed trade without permanent settlement, was satisfactory to the Native Americans. They were not pleased to see Great Britain, allies of the Iroquois and acquisitive toward tribal lands, come into the area. At this point Pontiac, one of the greatest of Native American leaders, emerged.

He is thought to have been born an Ottawa, although his tribal affiliation is a matter of dispute. Also disputed is his place of birth; according to some historians, it was in northern Indiana, while others say it was along the Detroit River, in Michigan. He fought for the French in the war with England and was quick to see that the arrival of a British garrison was a danger to the tribes of the entire region. Traveling from village to village, speaking to Potawatomi, Sac, Ojibwa, and Wyandot, he managed to construct a secret conspiracy. In May 1763, he struck. A series of brilliantly coordinated attacks routed every British garrison in the Midwest, with the exception of Detroit; and even it was besieged by overwhelming numbers and expected to fall. At isolated Michilimackinac, not a word of this trickled through. So in early June when the Native Americans approached the fort to play a game of lacrosse, there was no hint of danger. The relaxed soldiers wandered outside to watch the festivities, never noticing that even though the day was warm, the Native American women sat huddled under heavy blankets.

At a prearranged signal, the game moved toward where the women were seated. The blankets were thrown aside and concealed weapons taken in hand. The armed Native Americans rushed the soldiers (who still did not quite know what was going on) and attacked. Within minutes, the entire garrison was either dead, captured, or in flight. French traders living at the fort were left unharmed and hid a few of the soldiers. But the only survivor of the massacre was Alexander Henry, who was rescued by an Ojibwa leader, Wawatam. Henry later wrote a book about his experiences, the only surviving account of what happened here.

As the summer wore on and Detroit still held out, tribal solidarity began crumbling. When British reinforcements managed to reach the garrison, Pontiac's forces retreated. The rebellion had failed, but it came closer to stopping the white incursion into the Great Lakes than had any other uprising in history. Within a year, the British were back in control of Michilimackinac.

They remained here until 1781, when the garrison was moved to Mackinac Island, which was regarded as easier to defend from an anticipated overland attack from the south. The most notable visitor to Michilimackinac in the intervening years was Maj. Robert Rogers. He took command in 1766, still obsessed with his celebrated search for the Northwest Passage, the all-water route across the North American continent to the Pacific. He was convinced that the key to it was the Great Lakes area and that he would eventually control his own northern empire across the passage from Mackinac. When word of this scheme got back to the colonies, he was recalled, tried for treason, and financially ruined.

The abandoned fort, sitting on its isolated spit of land (several blocks west of the Mackinaw City business district), slowly fell into ruin. The state acquired the property in 1904, but not until 1959, after the bridge was built practically overhead, did reconstruction work begin. The fort has been returned to its appearance of 1763, with military quarters, the homes of French traders, a church, and several other structures rebuilt to the dimensions determined by archaeological research. Costumed guides play the roles of the fort's actual inhabitants during the summer season. Each Memorial Day weekend, a re-creation of the massacre is put on. There are also scheduled reenactments to mark the return of the voyageurs, a frontier wedding, and other fort activities.

The park that surrounds the fort runs right to the water's edge and features exceptional views of Mackinac Island. A short walk to its farthest end and then a few blocks south will take you into the heart of

Mackinaw City. The ferry docks to Mackinac Island are at the head of Central Ave., the main street, a wide boulevard lined with restaurants, souvenir shops, and stands selling fudge, the ubiquitous candy treat of northern Michigan. A small museum on S. Huron Ave. contains exhibits about the Woodland Native American tribes who occupied the area of the Straits before the arrival of Europeans.

Just south of town on U.S. 23 is Mill Creek State Historic Park. Discovered by a local history teacher and archaeology buff in 1972, the site was a small industrial complex that served the British fort. A sawmill, a dam, and several houses were located here. It is believed that this is where the lumber used in the construction of Fort Mackinac on the island was milled. The mill, the oldest ever found in northern Michigan, has been rebuilt, and demonstrations of its workings are given daily. Also, archaeological research is being conducted on the site, and visitors can observe the ongoing investigation.

Now U.S. 23 gets going in earnest, running along the Huron shore, with views of Mackinac Island and the big lake on the east. The larger island that soon comes into view is Bois Blanc, lightly developed and, when summer ends, populated only by a few families. Its school has received national media attention, because it contained just one student in the early 1990s.

The name of the first town on the route, Cheboygan, is subject to as many spelling and translation variations as the name Mackinac. The town name also appears in Wisconsin, where it is spelled *Sheboygan.* There is disagreement about what the word means. Some scholars say the Algonquian word refers to a pipe stem, used in religious ceremonies. Others insist it means a place of entrance, or a harbor. The town of Cheboygan fits the latter description. The Cheboygan River, one of the great nineteenth-century lumbering streams, passes through the middle of town and empties into Lake Huron. To connect Lakes Michigan and Huron across the northern tip of the Lower Peninsula, the Inland Waterway, a system of locks and linked lakes and rivers, was built in 1867. It runs from Conway, on the Lake Michigan side, to Cheboygan. Restored and enlarged, the waterway is still in operation and makes Cheboygan one of the top boating centers in the north.

This is also home port to the *Mackinaw,* the U.S. Coast Guard's prize icebreaker. Its ability to smash the ice jams that start to form on the lakes in late fall is credited with extending the Great Lakes shipping season a full six weeks. The boat may be toured when it is in port.

Like many old lumbering and mining towns, Cheboygan's pride is its opera house. Built in 1877, for the next 50 years its stage was the venue for performances by Annie Oakley, Mary Pickford, and other show business celebrities. Restored to its Victorian grandeur, it now puts on a season of theater and concerts each summer.

U.S. 23 makes an abrupt left turn in downtown Cheboygan, crosses the river, and heads south along the Lake Huron shore. This area of the lakeshore is light in population but heavy in trees. Most of the land is state forest. Only in the 1940s was a road cut through the area along the lakefront. There are several scenic turnouts and picnic areas along the way, and the beach on Hammond Bay is outstanding. According to legend, this was a ceremonial area for the Ojibwa, who encouraged those who were aged and no longer able to fend for themselves to feast and celebrate on the shore and then join their ancestors in the bay's deep waters. U.S. 23 curves past Forty Mile Point, named for its distance from Mackinaw City, then passes P. H. Hoeft State Park, with its beach, dunes, and woodlands.

Rogers City presents a commercial interruption in this almost unbroken line of beauty. Built as a lumbering town, it is now the world's leading limestone port. The quarry, worked since 1912, is an open pit, 3 miles long and 2 miles across. There is an overlook on the highway, and visitors can watch the mining operations going on in the vast hole. You can also see the loading of the lake freighters from this vantage point.

The highway soon arrives at Grand Lake. The narrow neck of land that lies between its waters and Lake Huron inspired the naming of both the county and the town there as Presque Isle, which is the French term for a peninsula. Signs along the county roads lead to Presque Isle Lighthouse. This is one of the most impressive and dramatic settings on the lakes, at the edge of a deep pine forest and overlooking the mouth of the Presque Isle River and Presque Isle Harbor.

There is a wonderful legend associated with the light. You may still see it repeated in tourist literature, although historians have debunked it repeatedly. The story goes that the first lighthouse, erected here in 1840, was built by Jefferson Davis, the future president of the Confederacy. The story is based on the flimsiest of evidence: the light was built by the U.S. Army, some of Davis's military service was spent in nearby Wisconsin as a young officer, and several stones on the site had "J. Davis" inscribed on them. Unfortunately, Davis was never an engineer, so he never served in the branch of the service that built the light. Moreover, he had left the army and was back on his Mississippi plantation when the light was built. Exactly who the J. Davis on the stones may have been has never been explained, but it certainly wasn't Jefferson.

The light was decommissioned in 1870 and stood abandoned for many years. Then a Lansing family bought it as a summer home and slowly restored it to its appearance of the Civil War era. It is now run as a maritime museum, with exhibits conveying how the lightkeeper and his family lived and with artifacts from some of the wrecks in the area.

Back on U.S. 23, the road cuts through more open land before reaching the metropolis of the Huron shore, Alpena. With a population of about 11,000, it is by far the biggest city on the lake north of Bay City. It traces it history as a lumbering town back to the 1850s, when the first sawmill was set up. At its peak, there were 20 lumber mills here, and hardwood panels are still manufactured locally, a vestige of that vanished era. The economy has broadened, though, to include limestone quarrying and recreation. The Thunder Bay area has become an underwater sanctuary, with more than 80 wrecks identified in its waters. Consequently, it is a top diving area on the Great Lakes. For those who prefer remaining atop the waves, the Alpena area is noted for its trout fishing and lake charter trips. Sportsmen's Island, in the northern part of town, has a wildfowl feeding area, a viewing stand along the road, and marked trails outlining nature walks through an adjacent sanctuary.

The Jesse Besser Museum, at Alpena Community College, is regarded as one of the finest in north Michigan, and its displays on local history are outstanding. There is also an art museum and planetarium in the complex. The entire facility is run at a level of quality unusual for the area, with none of the haphazard labeling and gaps in information that are so common in small-town museums.

The name Alpena sounds vaguely Native American, but the word is entirely concocted. It is one of several Michigan place names invented by Henry Schoolcraft, writer, historian, and Indian agent on Mackinac Island. Schoolcraft was the first white man to organize the legends of the Ojibwa. One of his books on the subject was read by Henry Wadsworth

Longfellow, who borrowed several of the tales for his *Song of Hiawatha* (see U.S. 2). When Michigan's north began to be explored and surveyed, Schoolcraft was invited by the state to come up with some "Indian-sounding" names for several of the counties and cities being organized. He obliged. The name Alpena is one example. The names of the next three counties you pass through on this road—Alcona, Iosco, and Arenac—are others. You will get spirited arguments from residents of those places that the names actually do have Native American meanings. But they did only in Schoolcraft's imagination.

The highway now runs along the shore of Thunder Bay and enters the village of Ossineke. The name of this town is the Ojibwa word meaning "image stones," and it refers to huge boulders that once stood on the lakeshore and were marked with the image of a deceased Ojibwa leader. They were believed to enclose his spirit. When raiders from another tribe tried to carry them away, the stones sank to the bottom of the lake, carrying the spirit molesters to their deaths.

The roadbed of the old Detroit and Mackinaw Railroad parallels the highway here as it bends inland through Alpena State Forest. It returns to the coast at Harrisville, another resort community and the hometown of baseball Hall of Famer Kiki Cuyler. A small state park and beach are just south of town. This built-up cottage country was within easy reach of a weekend drive from the Detroit area as far back as the 1920s. Many of the roadhouses and old inns in the area grew up then to serve this resort trade.

In Oscoda is the mouth of the Au Sable River, one of the state's great fishing and canoeing streams. In its greatest days, this was lumbering country, and pine logs floated like flotillas down the Au Sable to the lake. With the neighboring town of Au Sable, on the south shore of the river, the area had a population of almost 8,000 in the 1890 census. But the lumber gave out, and then a huge fire wiped out Au Sable in 1911. The community never recovered and is still largely a ghost town, while the total population of the area is around 2,000.

Oscoda lies at the edge of Huron National Forest. One of the top scenic drives in the area follows the southern bank of the river into the heart of this reforested landscape. The Lumbermen's Monument was erected in the midst of territory that once had been denuded of trees. It depicts a cutter, a riverman, and a surveyor, posed heroically above the

Au Sable, erected as a tribute to the men who cleared the land by several of their descendants. Paddlewheel boat trips up the river into the national forest aboard the *Au Sable River Queen* also leave from Oscoda during the summer months. You may also want to poke around the remnants of Au Sable, the largest community in the state to have gone entirely out of existence.

The Tawases, East Tawas and Tawas City, have become the area of top resort concentration in the area, with East Tawas the busier of the two communities. There is a pier, a beach, a few hotels, and a two-block-long shopping street—not much when compared to the corresponding Lake Michigan shore, but hot stuff for Huron. The towns face Tawas Bay, a sheltered arm of the lake with excellent fishing and boating opportunities. Perch, one of the true delicacies of the Great Lakes, is the fish of choice.

U.S. 23 can become pretty crowded south of here, into Standish. There are recurrent discussions about four-laning this strip or building a freeway up the interior to relieve some of the congestion. But nothing has been done, and when southbound on Sunday afternoons, you just have to resign yourself to a long haul.

Alabaster was named for the gypsum deposits found here in 1870 and still shipped from the port. Several miles south, the road bends sharply away from the lake, through the river resort towns of Au Gres and Omer. The highway joins Interstate 75 at Standish, a market town for the surrounding resort area. But instead of going into high speed, we'll continue south along Michigan 13, which is the old route of U.S. 23.

This is dairy country on the western shore of Saginaw Bay, and to Michigan's cheese-lovers the name Pinconning sets off bells. Wilson's is the largest of the cheese-making operations centered around this town, but you will find a wide variety of brands and styles in the community. Pinconning, incidentally, was named for the wild potatoes that once grew in the area.

At Kawkawlin watch for the turnoff to Bay City State Park. One of the best beaches in the area is here and is very crowded on summer weekends. Between the road and the beach is Tobico Marsh and Jennison Nature Center. Several trails with wildlife observation boardwalks lead through the area.

Michigan 13 now enters Bay City, the port at the mouth of the Saginaw River. This was the quintessential lumber town of the 1890s. Many tales are told of the wild nights of revelry along its waterfront and of the skull-whacking that went on along its long row of saloons. Bay City actually developed in the 1860s as a group of small settlements at the mouth of the river, and not until 1903 did all of them merge. There is still a slight jog at the Third Street Bridge where the competing business districts did not quite line up before consolidation. It is said that at its peak the river's flow was reduced to a narrow trickle here as stacked logs were piled up along both banks through the middle of town. Enormous fortunes were made here, and much of the capital that would finance Detroit's infant automotive industry came out of the Michigan forests. But the last of the lumber mills closed down in 1936, and the big industry in the area these days is the refining of beet sugar—not quite as exciting as milling lumber, but the pay is steadier.

Turn east on Michigan 25, which becomes Center St. after crossing the Saginaw. This is Bay City's showcase avenue, lined with the mansions of the timber barons. The Historical Museum, located just down the block from Bay City's Romanesque city hall, has exhibits that interpret the life of this once roistering community. The city hall itself is worth a look, for the view of the city from the top of its bell tower and for the unusual 31-foot-long woven tapestry that adorns the wall of the council chamber and depicts great events in the city's history.

Michigan 25 runs east from Bay City, through miles of table-flat country and beet fields. Sebewaing is one of the major sugar producers in the country. The refinery of the Michigan Sugar Co. dominates the skyline, and every July the town has a sweet old time with its Sugar Festival.

At Bay Port we're back in resort country. The sandy beaches on the west side of Saginaw Bay are the best on the Huron shore, and most of the small towns here cater to a cottage trade. This is the start of the Thumb, the distinctively shaped eastern corner of the Lower Peninsula. Mostly rural and lined with tiny resorts, it is an area within a short drive of the state's large population centers but maintaining the ambience of the North. No interstates run through it. No megaresorts draw the crowds. This is an area for solitude and gentle nostalgia.

Between Caseville and Port Austin are two state parks with first-rate beaches, and the road looks out on fine views of the bay. Veteran sunset-watchers swear that they will stack up those sites in Caseville against any other location in the state. But Port Austin is even better. Here, at the top of the Thumb, you can choose parks at either end of town and decide whether you prefer to watch a sunrise or a sunset across the water. The town's finest old home, believed to have once hosted James Garfield prior to his election as president, has been turned into an outstanding bed-and-breakfast and restaurant, the Garfield Inn. The town has been a resort area since the 1870s.

Grind Stone City is one of the strangest ghost towns in the country. For a good part of the nineteenth century, this village produced most of America's abrasive stones. When Carborundum was developed as a more economic alternative, the two plants here closed up. But many of the old grindstones are still found on the site of their manufacture, predominantly a resort area now.

Huron City, just down the road, is another ghost town, a relic of the lumbering days. But this one refused to disappear. The great forest fire of 1881 destroyed the lumbering industry in the Thumb. Since Huron City was built as a lumbering port, that did not leave it with much of a future. Its founder, Langdon Hubbard, who owned much of the devastated timberlands, found himself with a townsite that was essentially worthless. But he decided to spend his summers amid the shell of the community. By the 1920s, all that was left was a general store, a deserted hotel, a church, and the Hubbards' summer home, Seven Gables. His daughter married a young Yale University professor, William Lyon Phelps, who taught English literature and was also an ordained minister. On his vacations here, Dr. Phelps initiated the practice of giving a sermon in the old church to a small group of relatives and friends at 3 P.M. each Sunday. Word of the professor's eloquence and religious insights soon spread. By the mid-1920s, weekend drivers from Detroit would come up on the newly built road to hear him. The place became celebrated as the "visible church in the invisible town."

After Dr. Phelps's death in 1937, the next generation of Hubbards decided to turn their beloved town into a museum, celebrating a way of life that had disappeared and the career of Dr. Phelps. So Pioneer Huron City lives on. The surviving original buildings have been restored. Other historic structures from around Huron County, including a Coast

Guard rescue station, have been brought here. The church remains as it was when Dr. Phelps delivered his 3 P.M. sermon. And the Hubbards' summer home has become a museum of domestic life in the late nineteenth century.

The road now begins its trip south along the shore of Lake Huron. Port Hope was named by a party of sailors who managed to scramble onto its rocky shore from a shipwreck. Harbor Beach, with its small business district, was the birthplace of Frank Murphy, former mayor of Detroit, governor of Michigan, and justice of the U.S. Supreme Court. His leadership during the tumultuous days of the United Auto Workers' sit-down strikes at General Motors plants in Flint is credited with defusing a dangerous situation and restoring labor peace to the auto industry.

White Rock is named for a huge boulder that once stood on the shore here. It was such a prominent landmark that it was used to set the northern boundary of the Michigan Territory in the 1807 treaty with several northern tribes. Erosion long ago wore the rock away.

Port Sanilac is the most picturesque of the villages along this coast. A fine harbor and nearby lighthouse give it a pleasant waterfront, perfect for a short stroll. This part of the shore was once named Bark Shanty, after a rude dwelling set up along the beach by a group of early squatters. Unattractive though it was, the name stuck to the town. It was famous for its newspaper, the Bark *Shanty Times,* which functioned without editors or reporters. The proprietor simply put out large sheets of paper and pencils on a counter and invited any resident who wandered by and had something important to say to write it down. When the paper was full, it was filed away and another was set out in its place. Fortunately for journalists everywhere, the practice did not catch on.

A small local historical museum discusses the colorful history of the Bark *Shanty Times* and other Port Sanilac phenomena. Among them was the great storm of 1913. This November gale has been described as the worst in Great Lakes history. Ten ships went down and 235 sailors lost their lives, the highest toll of any disaster on the Great Lakes. Most of the loss occurred right offshore of Port Sanilac. Eight ships were caught in the blizzard and capsized here. The hull of one of the vessels could be clearly seen from this shore on the following morning. A historic marker on the bluffs south of town overlooks the site of the catastrophe.

Lexington is a resort town that won awards in the 1980s for restoration efforts on its Main St. and for its attempts to return the town to the charm of the previous century. It is another good place to stretch your legs and stop for a meal or a shopping break.

The highway becomes increasingly congested as it enters the northern suburbs of Port Huron. This is where Lake Huron narrows at the mouth of the St. Clair River, and at that point you will find the Fort Gratiot Light, the oldest operating beacon in the state. Cut over from Michigan 25 on Holland Ave. to reach it. This strategic site was first fortified by the French in 1686 to protect its fur traders from English marauders. The United States built Fort Gratiot on the same site 128 years later for exactly the same reason, during the War of 1812. The fort never figured in hostilities, although it was a processing center for federal troops heading for the Black Hawk War in Illinois during the 1830s. Port Huron developed around the fort, and the road that Michigan 25 follows the rest of the way into Detroit, Gratiot Ave., was built between the cities in 1826. The lighthouse was built three years later, although it was extensively remodeled in 1861. The fort was abandoned and subsequently dismantled, but the light shines on.

From this point south, Michigan 25 encounters the suburban sprawl of the Detroit area. So, much as began this ride far to the north, in the shadow of the Mackinac Bridge, we will end it here, in sight of the Blue Water Bridge to Canada.

VISITING HOURS

Mackinaw City

Fort Michilimackinac, at the Mackinac Bridge. (616) 436–5563. Daily, 9–6, mid-June–Labor Day. Hours vary from mid-May and to mid-October. Call in advance. $6.50.

Woodland Indian Museum, at 416 S. Huron St. (616) 436–7011. Daily, 7 A.M. to 9 P.M., May–October. $2.

Mill Creek State Historic Park, south of town. (616) 436–7301. Hours are the same as Fort Michilimackinac. $4.50.

Cheboygan

Icebreaker *Mackinaw*, at the mouth of the Cheboygan River. No Phone. Daily, 9–5, when in port. Free.

Opera House, at 403 N. Huron St. (616) 627–5432. Tuesday to Friday, 1–3. $1.

Presque Isle
Presque Isle Lighthouse, east of U.S. 23, on county roads. (517) 595–2787. Daily, 9–5, mid-May–mid-October. $1.50.

Alpena
Jesse Besser Museum, at 491 Johnston St. (517) 356–2202. Monday to Friday, 10–9, and weekends, 12–5. $2.

Oscoda
Au Sable River Queen cruises, leave from Foote Dam, 6 miles west on River Rd. (517) 739–7351. Times vary throughout summer and fall. Check in advance for schedule and reservations. $8 in summer. $10 for fall-color cruises.

Bay City
Jennison Nature Center, north of Michigan 13, in Bay City State Park. (517) 667–0717. Wednesday to Sunday, 10–4. $3.50 per vehicle.

Historical Museum, at 321 Washington Ave. (517) 893–5733. Monday to Friday, 10–5, and Sunday, 1–5. Free.

City Hall, at 301 Washington Ave. (517) 893–1222. Monday to Friday, 8–4. Free.

Huron City
Pioneer Huron City Museum, just east of Michigan 25. (517) 428–4123. Wednesday to Monday, 10–5, July–Labor Day. $10 to all buildings and Seven Gables. $6 for just the restoration.

Port Sanilac
Sanilac County Museum, at 228 S. Ridge Rd. (810) 622–9946. Tuesday to Friday, 11–4:30, and weekends, 12–4:30, mid-June–Labor Day. $3.

U.S. 24

Monroe, Michigan, to
Kentland, Indiana

U.S. 24 is a great river road, following the course of the Maumee through Ohio and of the Wabash in northern Indiana. Both streams played an important part in the early history of these states, and the towns along U.S. 24 reflect that past.

The road actually begins in the northwestern suburbs of Detroit. But its run through most of Michigan is a passage through franchise strips and urban congestion. Pick it up, instead, at Interstate 275, at the southern edge of the Detroit area.

U.S. 24 eventually winds its way across the Midlands, retracing portions of the old Pony Express route across Kansas, and ending high in the Colorado Rockies, a few miles west of Vail.

Monroe's tranquil setting is deceiving. This town in Michigan's southeastern corner carries memories of bloody clashes in the wars between the United States and Native Americans.

In the early days of the War of 1812, Detroit fell to the British without firing a shot. The British commander, Gen. Isaac Brock, threatened that he would be unable to stop an Indian massacre of the population unless the city capitulated. The Americans, under the leadership of Gen. William Hull, an aged veteran of the Revolutionary War, surrendered. His younger subordinates were mortified by his decision, which they regarded as cowardly. Hull was later court-martialed, and he was saved from conviction only by his distinguished record.

A relief column was quickly organized in Cincinnati and sent to drive the British from Detroit. But while encamped near the Raisin River, they were ambushed by a Native American force and annihilated. Reports that many wounded Americans had been slaughtered after surrendering enraged public opinion. In the following year, Detroit was

Peru Amateur Circus. (Courtesy of Circus City Festival, Inc., Peru, Indiana.)

retaken, and the British and Native American forces were pursued into Canada, where there was a retaliatory massacre of Native Americans near Thamesville. A memorial has been placed at the site of the Battle of the Raisin, just east of downtown Monroe. It contains displays relating to the battle and its place in the larger war.

At the time of the War of 1812, the tiny community was known as Frenchtown. But half a century later, when Elizabeth Bacon was growing up here, it bore its present name, honoring President James Monroe. Bacon married a dashing young West Point graduate named George A. Custer, and the couple made their home in Monroe briefly after the Civil War. But for most of their 12 years of married life, Elizabeth accompanied her husband on his campaigns. When he was sent to Fort Lincoln, North Dakota, in the spring of 1876, to deal with a Sioux uprising, Libby Custer went too. She rode with him from the fort to the first night's campground before turning back. It was the last time they saw each other. Custer and his command perished at the Little Big Horn less than one month later.

Mrs. Custer lived on for another 50 years, much of it in Monroe. She spent that time trying to rescue her husband's reputation. In the years immediately after his death, Custer was regarded as a national hero and martyr. But later he was described as a flamboyant, inept leader, a commander who took unnecessary risks. Later still, Native American historians depicted him as a near sociopath who reveled in slaughtering Native Americans. The truth lies somewhere in the middle. While he did divide his command at the Little Big Horn, his decision was based on tactics that were sound, given the numbers that Plains tribes usually put in the field. He had no way of knowing that an unprecedented concentration of 2,500 Native Americans was facing him. He also had been a key witness before Congress against crooked Indian agents in the Grant administration; he had denounced the practices that defrauded the tribes placed under such agents' care. Libby Custer was present when the heroic sculpture *Sighting the Enemy,* honoring her husband, was unveiled in 1920 in downtown Monroe. Just one block away, the Monroe County Historical Museum contains excellent displays about the Custers and their times, including many of the general's personal campaign items.

From here, the highway continues south through marshy country a few miles inland from Lake Erie, then over the Ohio border to Toledo. This border, so easily crossed, was one of the most hotly disputed in American history. Michigan claimed the northwestern tier of Ohio under boundaries drawn up by the Northwest Ordinance of 1787. The border between Ohio and Michigan was set on a line between the southernmost shores of Lakes Erie and Michigan. Unfortunately, the line was drawn wrong, and the Toledo area wound up being claimed by both states. When Ohio tried to swear in public officials and organize a local government there in 1835, Michigan Territory sent in a militia to chase them out. Eventually, the federal government had to intervene to prevent a full-scale war. Michigan reluctantly surrendered the Toledo Strip in return for the promise of immediate statehood and acquisition of the Upper Peninsula from Wisconsin. Since no one could then guess the mineral wealth that lay beneath the U.P. soil, this was regarded as poor compensation by Michigan. But some of the state's great fortunes were made in the iron and copper mines of that area, hundreds of miles north of Toledo.

U.S. 24 runs through the west side of Toledo as Detroit Ave., through mixed residential and commercial districts. It reaches the north shore of the Maumee in Toledo's southwestern corner and heads west as the Anthony Wayne Trail.

The town of Maumee is now a residential suburb, although its history goes back much farther than that of Toledo. The rapids of the Maumee were always regarded as the key site for controlling navigation on the river. The French fortified it in 1680, and the British erected a stronger outpost, Fort Miami, in 1764. Britain returned to the site of the old fort in 1813 and used it to mount an unsuccessful siege of Fort Meigs, the American outpost on the opposite bank of the Maumee (see U.S. 20). Only after the war was it peaceful enough for settlers to come into the area permanently.

Among the first was James Wolcott. He arrived from Connecticut in 1827, married a granddaughter of Little Turtle, greatest of the Miami leaders (we will encounter a memorial to him in just a few miles), and became a judge and mayor of the town. The home he built along the Maumee—the name is a variation of Miami—remained in the family until 1957. Now it is a museum of domestic life on this frontier, containing many Wolcott heirlooms passed on by the owners of the house through the generations.

Maumee has another museum of an altogether different nature, the Ohio Baseball Hall of Fame, which houses one of the best regional baseball displays in the country. Ohio has been a rich source of baseball talent. Many of the game's greatest players performed for the state's two major-league teams—the Cleveland Indians and Cincinnati Reds. Tris Speaker, Bob Feller, Nap Lajoie, Pete Rose, Johnny Bench, and Edd Roush are represented in the displays here, as are Rube Marquard, George Sisler, and Mike Schmidt, players who grew up in the state but played elsewhere. The museum is located on the grounds of the Lucas County Recreation Center, home of the minor-league Toledo Mud Hens. It is a must-see for baseball enthusiasts.

Maumee's biggest growth spurt came from the Miami and Erie

Canal, which connected Cincinnati to Lake Erie. Completion of this canal, in 1845, opened western Ohio to the markets of the East Coast and was a huge stimulus to economic development along the Maumee River. The Black Swamp, which had held back settlement in the area southwest of Toledo, was drained. Farmers poured into the region. Toledo became a major port. At its peak, more than 400 boats a year used the canal, and much of that business flowed through Maumee. But by 1856 the railroads had taken away most of the commerce. The state kept the canal running at a loss until 1912, but its days as an economic force were long over. Maumee preserves a portion of the old locks that once diverted traffic into the Maumee River, at Side Cut Metropark. There is also a scenic walk along the towpath at the water's edge.

High on a bluff overlooking Side Cut is the memorial to the battle that changed this region forever. The area just west of the locks was the site of Fallen Timbers, where Gen. Anthony Wayne shattered the tribal alliance under Little Turtle in 1794. The victory forced the British to turn over Detroit to the United States, 11 years after they had promised to do so in the treaty ending the Revolutionary War. The victory also cleared the way for settlement of northern Ohio and Indiana.

Little Turtle had unified all the tribes who had watched bitterly as whites edged onto their lands—Miami and Shawnee, Potawatomi and Ottawa. The alliance blocked any extension of American power into the region. Armies sent up from Cincinnati, at the behest of President Washington, had been wiped out. Little Turtle even succeeded in carrying the fight to the Americans and besieging their forts in southern Ohio (see U.S. 35). But Wayne was a different kind of general. A hero of the Revolutionary War, performing with gallantry at Stony Point, he won the nickname "Mad Anthony" for his daring tactics. He also understood the importance of terror. He began his campaign in the spring, marching north and methodically destroying Native American villages and cornfields along the way. Little Turtle's forces retreated before him, patiently waiting for the right time to fight. Finally, the armies met here, with the Native Americans aligned behind rows of trees felled by a recent tornado. Wayne's use of cavalry to get around the barrier, followed by a devastating bayonet charge, cleared the field of the enemy and left the Americans with an open path to Detroit. There are several memorials on the bluff, including tributes to the 33 Americans killed in action, to Little Turtle and his warriors, and to the Ohio settlers who died in the frontier wars of 1783–94.

Waterville is another old canal town with some nicely restored buildings in its business district. Between here and Grand Rapids, Ohio, on the opposite bank of the Maumee, there are rides on a restored passenger train, the Bluebird. This is an especially scenic portion of the river, with towering rock formations and islands. This rail trip is a pleasant way to take in the view without worrying about the road. But you can follow the same route on U.S. 24 and see it for free.

Near Grand Rapids is the Isaac Ludwig Mill, a nineteenth-century mechanism that demonstrates all the uses to which the pioneers put the water power at their disposal. It is just east of town, by way of Ohio 65.

At Napoleon, named by French settlers for their favorite conquering hero, turn off on Ohio 424 and follow it west. This is the original route of U.S. 24 and a lovely drive along the river. Watch for Girty's Island, named for a pair of infamous brothers who terrorized settlers from their base in Detroit in the years of the Revolution. The Girty family supposedly ran a trading post on the island.

Independence Dam is a local beauty spot, on the site of another old canal town, Independence. There are hiking paths following the canal bed and the river.

Defiance was one of the great crossroads of Ohio. The Auglaize River flows into the Maumee here. This also was where the Miami and Erie Canal linked up with the Wabash and Erie Canal, the two canals running as one the rest of the way to Lake Erie. Gen. Wayne fortified the place on his way to Fallen Timbers and gave a name to it. "I defy the English, the Indians, and all the devils in hell to take it," he proclaimed. So it was called Fort Defiance. This is where one of the greatest Native American leaders, Pontiac, probably was born. John Chapman, better known as Johnny Appleseed, made Defiance his home for 17 years too and tended his apple nurseries here.

The site of Fort Defiance is preserved in City Park downtown. It was never captured, but it was defeated by time. When William Henry Harrison arrived here with his forces during the War of 1812, he found that Wayne's fort was a crumbling ruin and built a new one across the Auglaize.

The traditional site of Pontiac's birth is just across the Maumee from Fort Defiance. This entire area was heavily populated with Native American agricultural villages early in the eighteenth century. It was in one of them that the future leader was born, in around 1720. He was part Ottawa, part Chippewa, and he was sympathetic toward the French, who did not seem to have any ambitions toward settling the region. But he was deeply suspicious of British designs. Immediately after the French and Indian War, in 1763, he organized a massive frontier rebellion against British rule, hoping to drive them out of the country forever before they had a chance to establish settlements. He almost succeeded, capturing most of the major forts in the West. But Detroit held out, and the French never sent him promised aid. He was forced to make peace with England and was later murdered after being exiled to Illinois. There is a marker to him here.

Just west of town is Auglaize Village, a collection of restored nineteenth-century buildings, grouped in a community setting. Museums examine the natural history and archaeology of the area too. Among the more interesting displays are the restored barbershop, doctor's office, and telephone exchange.

West of Defiance is the heart of the great swampland that once covered this part of Ohio and neighboring Indiana. Called the Black Swamp here, the Limberlost across the Indiana line, it was an enormous barrier to settlement and was completely cleared only in the early twentieth century.

Antwerp, an old Wabash and Erie Canal town, is the last settlement on U.S. 24 before the Indiana border. The Ehrhart Museum here is a testimony to the dedicated work of a local naturalist. Otto Ehrhart stuffed and mounted just about every kind of fauna that ever flew over or scampered through these parts. They are displayed in the museum in Antwerp's city hall.

The highway runs beside the Maumee and the bed of the Wabash and Erie Canal. Occasionally, you can catch a glimpse of one of the old locks along the road.

Fort Wayne, Indiana, where the St. Marys and St. Joseph Rivers meet to form the Maumee, is described more fully in the section on U.S. 27. But there are a couple of places here that relate more to this road. We encountered the nurseries of Johnny Appleseed back in Defiance, Ohio.

This strange figure from the American frontier is often regarded as a legend, a gentle myth to explain the profusion of apple trees in Ohio and Indiana, a Disney figure of fun, like Pecos Bill or Paul Bunyan. But John Chapman was very real and quite complex. He took his religious calling seriously. He was a Swedenborgian missionary, and he left religious tracts as well as apple seeds wherever he wandered. For more than 40 years he tramped up and down this area, wearing a flour sack for clothes so as not to submit to worldly enticements. He went unmolested by Native Americans, who regarded him as a holy man, and he was beloved by settlers. Many of his plantings still survive in remote corners of the Midwest. He died at the age of 70 near Fort Wayne and is buried here in a park named for him, just off the U.S. 24 Bypass, near the War Memorial Coliseum. Fort Wayne celebrates a Johnny Appleseed Festival each September to honor his memory.

In downtown Fort Wayne, a portion of the old Wabash and Erie Canal, which we followed west from Ohio, has been turned into a commercial development. The Landing has a nineteenth-century theme, and there are landscaped walkways beside the canal bed. It is on the 100 W. Columbia St. block.

For a few miles here, U.S. 24 has no river to follow. It becomes a four-lane expressway, as if eager to get to Huntington and the meeting with its next river route, along the Wabash. In fact, the route parallels a centuries-old Native American portage from the Maumee to the Wabash, one of the oldest trails through this region.

The town of Huntington was built near the Forks of the Wabash, where the greater river is joined by the Little Wabash. The Forks was one of the most important settlements of the Miami in the days of Little Turtle. It was also the place favored for the signing of treaties, by which Little Turtle's successors signed away their right to these lands. Huntington itself is a graceful sort of place, with several bridges crossing the Little Wabash as it winds through the business district. The Jefferson St. Bridge is known for the stores located right on the span, their back doors overhanging the river. This is also the hometown of former Vice President Dan Quayle, and a museum dedicated to that much-maligned official opened here in 1994.

The Forks are 2 miles west of town. The home of Richardville and his son-in-law, La Fontaine, last chief of the Indiana Miami, still stands here. La Fontaine was forced to sign the 1840 treaty that extinguished the last Miami claim to the land. The tribe was then transported to Kansas. But La Fontaine, who had been named chief as a teenager, could not bear to be away from this land. So he tried to make his way back alone to the Forks and the house his father-in-law had built there in 1833. He died before he could complete the journey. The legend is that he was given poison by his people, who felt he was deserting them. He was buried in Huntington's Mt. Calvary Cemetery.

U.S. 24 continues along the north bank of the Wabash. Lagro was named for a Native American leader named Les Gros (or Big Guy, to use the current vernacular). It was the site of a major tollgate on the Wabash and Erie Canal, and some of the gate remains are still visible in the middle of town.

The river that is the symbol of Indiana was given its name in this area. The town of Wabash is situated on the land once occupied by a Native American village called Oubache. The village name, which referred to the white stones in the riverbed here, was expanded by the pioneers to include the entire course of the river. It was also here that the Treaty of Paradise Springs, by which the Potawatomi signed away most of their lands, was signed in 1826.

But the brightest day in Wabash's history came 54 years later. On March 31, 1880, it became the first American city illuminated by electric lights. It is difficult now to grasp what that meant to Americans of that time. City streets had been lit by gaslight since the 1830s. But these systems were difficult to maintain and restricted in service. Only high-density urban areas could afford them. Moreover, the by-products of the gas had a disagreeable odor that made them inconvenient indoors. Ironically, when Thomas A. Edison formed his first electric company, in 1878, the major problem he faced was how to get electricity into homes and offices. The bright, dazzling light produced by his arc lamps could not be dimmed and was suitable only for streets. Nonetheless, when the lights went on in Wabash it was a stunning achievement, reducing the spectators into a "shocked, rigid silence," according to a witness. It would be another two and a half years before New York City's lights would shine. Wabash preserves one of its first electric lights inside the courthouse, near the area it originally illuminated.

Wabash is the home of the Honeywell Corp. The former lodge of the company founder, Mark Honeywell, has been turned into a community center, on the western edge of the business district. It is surrounded by rose gardens, contains a skating rink, auditorium, and dining rooms, and is furnished throughout with antiques. It is regarded as an especially fine piece of Art Deco architecture.

U.S. 24 now resumes its run alongside the Wabash to reach Peru.

A Closer Look. In the space of about eight years, two of the greatest show business attractions in history arrived in this Indiana town. Both started small, rose to international reputations, and, at the end, returned here to rest. One was the circus; the other was Cole Porter. Both called Peru home.

Ben Wallace, who owned the local livery stable, acquired a bankrupt traveling circus in the early 1880s. According to one inventory, it consisted of a camel, two monkeys, a one-eyed lion, some dogs and horses, and a bandwagon. But Wallace and his partners managed to build it into the second largest circus in America, after Barnum and Bailey. It toured America for half a century, with Peru as its winter home.

Porter arrived about eight years after the circus. He was born in 1891 in an upstairs bedroom of a house on E. Third St., the son of the town druggist. More to the point, he was the grandson of James Cole, one of the wealthiest and most influential men in town. His wealth would be put to good use when young Porter displayed musical talent and was sent off to preparatory schools and Yale University to develop it.

Cole Porter lived in Peru only through the eighth grade. It was long enough to have his first composition, "Bobolink Waltz," published, but he did not leave much more of a visible impact on the town. There is a marker in front of his birthplace, at 102 E. Third. The far more ornate home of his grandfather, who made his fortune in the California gold rush and then invested in West Virginia coalfields, stands one block away, at 27 E. Third. Cole detested his son-in-law, Samuel Porter, whom he regarded as an eccentric and weak-willed nonentity. You can see what an intimidating presence this patriarch must have been, with his great house just one block away from Porter's modest residence.

The Cole family also owned a country house, Westleigh, across the Wabash bridge from town, along the nearby Mississinewa River. Porter's mother, Kate, lived there until her death at 90. Its exterior was shown in the opening shots of Porter's film biography, *Night and Day.*

His grandfather's estate was also the inspiration for one of his earliest song hits, "In an Old Fashioned Garden." Porter, who had a keen ear for likely lyrics, also wrote a ditty about the mellifluously named river that flows nearby, "By the Miss-iss-iss-iss-iss-iss-iss-issinewa." You can catch a glimpse of Westleigh by following Indiana 124 east from the bridge and then making a right turn immediately after crossing the Mississinewa.

Some personal memorabilia of Porter's is displayed in the Miami County Museum, in downtown Peru, including several of his awards and the specially made divan that he used to prop up his legs after they were shattered in a horseback-riding accident. He was buried beside his wife, Linda, in Peru's Mt. Hope Cemetery in 1964.

Unlike Porter, the circus never really left town—at least not for long. Wallace's company, which became known as the Hagenback-Wallace Circus, began wintering on a tract of land across the Wabash in 1891. Soon those facilities were being used by several other circuses, among them Sells-Floto and Howes Great London. Railroad connections to Peru were good, and the vast barns built by Wallace made it convenient to store livestock there. Many of the performers also bought homes in Peru for the off-season and, when their traveling days were done, settled into town as retirees. Among those who lived here for a while were the famed animal trainer Clyde Beatty, the great clown Emmett Kelly, and trapeze artist Alfredo Cadona. Wallace sold out after suffering financial losses in the flood of 1913, which inundated the winter quarters. But the American Circus Corp., a syndicate formed by the new owners, continued to run five traveling shows from Peru. The operation was then sold to John Ringling in 1929. Just before World War II, he moved the winter quarters permanently to Florida.

But Peru never quite got the smell of sawdust out of its nostrils. In 1958, a group of local businessmen formed Circus City Festival, Inc., to revive the heritage. Assisted by big-top retirees, local teenagers were trained to put on a circus of their own. The idea was a smash, and the town decided to make it an annual event. Children were recruited in grade school to train in circus specialties, and the local performance, held each summer, quickly developed a professional gloss. By 1968 it had moved into its own arena, in a converted warehouse once used by a lumber company. This building is now the Circus City Festival

Museum, at the corner of Broadway and W. Seventh, filled with displays of circus memorabilia.

The big barn at the old winter headquarters still stands and was declared a National Historic Site in 1988. It is being transformed into the International Circus Hall of Fame, with planned exhibits of circus life and live performances. Auxiliary buildings that were torn down are being reconstructed according to original plans, so that the winter quarters will once again appear as they did when "the Greatest Show on Earth" made its home on this turf. The winter quarters are east of town on Indiana 124, then left past the Mississinewa Bridge.

The Peru area has a rich Native American heritage. Just a few miles away, a touching episode in the conflict between Native American and white cultures was played out. If you took the side trip to Cole Porter's former country home, Westleigh, you may have noticed that the highway you traveled was called the Frances Slocum Trail. Slocum was also called Maconaqua, the name she preferred as a member of the Miami tribe. She was carried off by Delaware raiders from her family's home in Pennsylvania in 1773, when she was four years old. Her family searched for her for the next 50 years, with her siblings persisting in the quest long after their parents had died. They didn't give up until 1826, when they finally were convinced that she had been killed.

But the child had been treated well by the Delaware and was taken with them to Indiana when the tribe moved there. She married a young Miami chief, Shepocanah, and moved to this area to raise her family. She lost the ability to speak English but never totally forgot the family of her birth. Finally, in 1835, she told her story to a white trader, who managed to locate her family in Pennsylvania. They were reunited two years later. Frances, then a woman of 66, spoke through an interpreter when she visited the Slocums at their Peru hotel. While she was initially reserved (in the Native American manner), the joy of the meeting overcame them all. She refused to accompany them back to Pennsylvania, though, fearing she would not be allowed to return. She lived out her days along the Mississinewa, passing away in 1847. She is buried in a Miami cemetery that bears her name. To get there, you have to follow the Frances Slocum Trail until the turnoff to the Mississinewa Reservoir, a distance of about 4 miles from Westleigh. A plaque at the cemetery gate tells her story.

Back on U.S. 24 once more, the Eel River flows into the Wabash at Logansport. The town is named for a Shawnee leader who fought with the Americans against his uncle, Tecumseh, in the War of 1812. There is a very pleasant little park along the Wabash at the east end of town, featuring an 80-year-old carousel with hand-carved wooden animals. The city is laced with bridges across its two rivers, giving it a very attractive business district.

Now U.S. 24 leaves the rivers and strikes out straight overland, across the flat fields of western Indiana. Although it appears unlikely, we are also close to one of the state's top water resorts. Lake Shafer, just north of Monticello, was formed when the Tippecanoe River was dammed in 1923 for a power project. Indiana Beach was developed along its shoreline. Located here are an amusement park, a swimming area, a boardwalk, a waterskiing show, and a paddle wheeler, the *Shafer Queen,* which cruises around the lake.

The little town of Wolcott was founded by a descendant of one of Connecticut's most prominent political families. Oliver Wolcott was a signer of the Declaration of Independence, and his son, Oliver, Jr., was secretary of the treasury in the John Adams administration and then governor of his home state. The younger Wolcott's son, Anson, settled here and built a three-story home in 1860. It is undergoing restoration.

The road then passes into the central time zone, heading due west with hardly a bend. Kentland was the birthplace of one of Indiana's best-loved writers, humorist George Ade. He helped develop the modern newspaper column on the *Chicago Record* in the 1890s. His *Fables in Slang* was a national best-seller in 1902, and he also wrote several popular stage hits. The football stadium at Purdue University, his alma mater, is named for him. But Ade just made it under the wire as a Hoosier. Barely 4 miles west of Kentland the highway crosses the state line into Illinois.

VISITING HOURS

Monroe

River Raisin Battlefield Visitors Center, east on Michigan 50, at 1403 E. Elm. (313) 243–7136. Daily, 10–6, Memorial Day–Labor Day. Donation.

Monroe County Historical Museum, at 126 S. Monroe St. (313) 243–7137. Tuesday to Sunday, 10–5, May–September. Closed Tuesday, rest of year. Free.

Maumee

Wolcott House Museum, at 1031 River Rd. (419) 893–9602. Wednesday to Sunday, 1–4, April–December. $3.50

Ohio Baseball Hall of Fame, north on Key St. (419) 893–9481. Wednesday to Saturday, 11–7, and Sunday, 12–5, April–September. Monday to Friday, 9–5, rest of year. $2.

Waterville

Bluebird Passenger Train, leaves from the Waterville Depot on U.S. 24. (419) 878–2177. Schedule varies through the year. Check in advance. $8.

Grand Rapids

Isaac Ludwig Mill, east on Ohio 65 and Ohio 578. (419) 832–8934. Wednesday to Sunday, 10–5, May–October. Free.

Defiance

AuGlaize Village, west of town, off Krouse Rd. (419) 782–7255. Daily, 9–6, June–Labor Day. $3.

Antwerp

Ehrhart Museum, at 118 N. Main St., in the city hall. (419) 258–8161. Thursday to Monday, 12–4. Free.

Huntington

Dan Quayle Center and Museum, at Warren and Tipton Sts. (219) 356–6356. Tuesday to Saturday, 10–4, and Sunday, 1–4. Donation.

Forks of the Wabash, 2 miles west of town. (219) 356–4218. Thursday to Sunday, 1–5, June–October. $2.

Wabash

Honeywell Center, at 275 W. Market St. (219) 563–1102. Monday to Friday, 8:30 A.M.–10 P.M. Free.

Peru

Miami County Museum, at 51 N. Broadway. (317) 473–9183. Tuesday to Saturday, 10–5. $1.

Circus City Festival Museum, at 154 N. Broadway. (317) 472–3918. Monday to Friday, 9–12 and 1–4. Donation.

International Circus Hall of Fame, off Indiana 124 and east of the Mississinewa Bridge. (317) 472–7553. Tuesday to Saturday, 10–4, and Sunday, 1–4, May–September. $2.50.

Monticello

Indiana Beach, north on W. Shafer Dr. (219) 583–4141. Daily, 11–11, mid-May–Labor Day. $1.50 park and beach admission. $9.50 for unlimited rides. $3 for cruises.

Miami University. (Photo provided by Miami University Applied Technologies.)

U.S. 27

Angola, Indiana, to Cincinnati, Ohio

Armies were the first to use this road. It was the main path from Cincinnati to the outpost of Fort Wayne, at the meeting of the Maumee, St. Marys, and St. Joseph Rivers. The struggle to secure northern Ohio, northern Indiana, and the Michigan Territory for the young American Republic was played out along what is now U.S. 27.

Two generations later, it was a major escape route on the Underground Railroad, as fugitive slaves were spirited northward to safety in Michigan and Canada. The road runs through Indiana's lake country, near the highest point in the state, and, finally, into the northwestern suburbs of Cincinnati.

U.S. 27 once began at the Straits of Mackinac. The highway that bears its number now originates south of Grayling, Michigan. But in Michigan, the route is entirely freeway. Only south of the Indiana line does it become an old road again. It continues on as a major route through the South, eventually coming to an end in downtown Miami, Florida.

The highway crosses the Michigan border as a captive of Interstate 69. But to get things off to a good start on this ride, exit the freeway at Pokagon State Park. This facility is in the midst of a small chain of lakes in Indiana's northeastern corner. It was once a favored hunting ground of the Potawatomi tribe, and the park is named for the last chief of the local band, Simon Pokagon. He was born near South Bend in 1830 and went on to attend Notre Dame and Oberlin. When he was an infant, his father, Leopold, had signed away tribal lands in this part of Indiana and near Chicago. Part of the purchase price was never paid, and for the rest of his life Simon fought to obtain justice from the federal government.

[79]

Finally, in 1888, he succeeded, and a sum of $150,000 was divided among members of the tribe. In recognition, this state park was named in his honor, and the lodge, built in 1926, is called the Potawatomi Inn.

Indiana 127 now follows the former route of U.S. 27, which is still caught up with the interstate at this point. The old road runs through the town of Angola (see U.S. 20) and heads south, east of and parallel to the interstate.

Classic car fanciers will recognize the name Auburn as one of the most elegant vehicles of the 1930s. For a time, the Auburn Automobile Co., located in the town of that name, also manufactured the legendary Cords and Duesenbergs. These were three of the most magnificent driving machines ever produced in America, the epitome of glamour and sophistication. The guiding spirit behind them was Jonas Cord. He joined Auburn as a salesman in 1926 and rose to head the company by advocating luxurious, high-performance cars. The Auburn was the first American-made stock car to be clocked at 100 miles an hour. Cord toured the country, asking attendants at service stations what they wanted to see in a car. He then incorporated what he learned to design the ultimate driving machine, one that was both quick and beautiful. The result was the Cord, introduced in 1935.

It had front-wheel drive and retractable headlights and could cruise at 110 miles an hour. Its looks were worthy of a Cole Porter lyric. But it cost $2,700, and in the middle of the Depression very few Americans had that kind of money to spend on a car. It failed and went out of production in 1937, dragging the rest of the company down with it. But in the former showroom of Auburn's hometown dealership, the largest collection of Cords, Auburns, and Duesenbergs in the world has been assembled. The museum is a must-see for anyone with a taste for Art Deco design and legendary automobiles.

Indiana 127 combines with Indiana 1 and then meets U.S. 27 as it enters Fort Wayne. This was the most important outpost in the northern half of the Northwest Territory. It lay on the main canoe route from Lake Erie to the Mississippi River. Long before the coming of Europeans, it was the largest settlement of the Miami tribe. French traders arrived in the 1680s and built a fort on the site. They held it for 80 years and secured control of the fur trade. It was turned over to Great Britain at the end of the French and Indian War and fell immediately to the forces of Pontiac in 1763. But the British survived that rebellion and struck a lasting alliance with Little Turtle, the most powerful of the Miami chiefs.

After the Revolutionary War, the Miami used the place as a base for raids on American settlements. They were egged on by their British allies, who still occupied Detroit despite having agreed by treaty to give it up. President Washington, realizing that the Northwestern frontier could never be secure with these outposts under hostile control, sent out three armies to take the Fort Wayne area. The first two were destroyed by Little Turtle. The third, commanded by trusted Revolutionary War veteran Gen. Anthony Wayne, managed to defeat the tribal alliance in 1794 at Fallen Timbers, Ohio (see U.S. 24.) This engagement opened the region to settlement and put Fort Wayne permanently in American hands, but not out of danger.

Reports of Native American activities sent from Fort Wayne first alerted Indiana's Gov. William Henry Harrison to the threat posed by Tecumseh and led to the Battle of Tippecanoe (see U.S. 231). The fort then survived a siege by the Miami and Potawatomi during the War of 1812. An American supply force was slaughtered near the fort, just around the bend of the St. Marys River, and Harrison had to hurry here with reinforcements to lift the siege. But with the end of the war, the British and Native American troubles were over, and the fort was decommissioned in 1819.

The old fort has been rebuilt as it appeared in its final days, following the original plans. Costumed interpreters play the roles of soldiers, Native Americans, traders, and fort employees, explaining their functions in the daily life of the outpost. Belongings of Little Turtle and Gen. Wayne are displayed in the museum. The fort is just east of the highway, in downtown Fort Wayne.

A few blocks east of U.S. 27, at 200 E. Berry St., is one of the great Lincoln collections in the country. The Louis A. Warren Lincoln Library and Museum is housed in a new facility opened in 1996. Thousands of items pertaining to the president are on display here, including rare photographs, manuscripts, and personal belongings. His law office in Springfield has also been reconstructed here.

South of here, the road runs beside the old Wayne Trace, the military route by which Wayne, Harrison, and their less fortunate predecessors marched their troops to Fort Wayne. The St. Marys River is just to the west.

In Decatur, the highway enters the Limberlost, a portion of Indiana that was once swamp. Its odd name came from a legendary hunter, Limber Jim McDowell, who wandered into the swamp one day and never came out. When the area was finally drained in 1913 most local farmers cheered. But a few naturalists and wilderness-lovers watched with sadness. Among these was Gene Stratton Porter, whose novels of life in the Limberlost were national best-sellers at the turn of the century. We'll come to her historic home in a few miles, but in Decatur she is honored with a statue on the courthouse lawn. She was married here in 1886 and made her home in Decatur for three years, before going on to fame in nearby Geneva.

This segment of the road links several Mennonite communities. The original settlers were Old Order Amish from Switzerland, many of them connected by family ties. They named their new settlement Berne in 1852 in honor of the capital of their former homeland. The Mennonites retain a strong influence. The First Mennonite Church, in the heart of Berne, at U.S. 27 and Main St., is the sect's largest house of worship in America. It has a seating capacity of 2,000.

Berne has also become noted for its furniture makers, who construct pieces using traditional designs. You'll see their showrooms as you pass through town on U.S. 27. Berne is a market center for Amish farmers in the area, and on trading days you'll see horses and buggies parked throughout the business district.

Echoes of Switzerland are also heard in the name of the next town along the road, Geneva. But memories of Gene Stratton Porter sound even louder. The Indiana-born novelist grew up on a farm along the Wabash River, developing an early fondness for wildlife and the natural beauty of the land. After her marriage to a local bank executive, she moved to Geneva. At the edge of the vast Limberlost Swamp, which stretched across this area for 13,000 acres, Stratton Porter began to write the novels that eventually would sell more than nine million copies. Best-known among them were *Freckles* and *Girl of the Limberlost*. A masterful storyteller, Stratton Porter incorporated a wealth of detail about nature in her books, and she was an early environmentalist in her pleas for preservation of natural landscapes. She did much of her later work in a cabin near Rome City (north of U.S. 6), after the federal government, bowing to agricultural pressures, drained the Limberlost and opened it to farmland. Stratton Porter was killed in an automobile accident in Los Angeles in 1924. The 14-room home here in which she lived until 1913 is preserved as a state historic site. Many of her personal belongings remain as they were when she worked here.

Portland was named for the type of cement that was made locally. It was also the birthplace of automotive pioneer Elwood Haynes, the inventor who devised the first clutch-driven vehicle (see U.S. 35). His success with his invention, in 1894, gave Indiana an early edge in that industry, and the state remained competitive until the 1950s.

Winchester is the seat of Randolph County, and on the courthouse square is an especially imposing Civil War monument. Completed in 1888, the bronze, 85-foot-high memorial is the second largest in the state, trailing only the 284-foot-high Soldiers' and Sailors' Monument in downtown Indianapolis.

South of Winchester, the countryside begins to roll perceptibly. Just past Lynn is the highest point in the state, an unnamed hill with an elevation of 1,257 feet. It lies east of the highway.

The road has been paralleling the old right-of-way of the Pennsylvania Railroad. But now we encounter a depot of an entirely different line. In Fountain City is the Levi Coffin House, for 20 years the busiest terminal on the Underground Railroad in Indiana. By one account, this place was the origin of the phrase describing the transport of escaped slaves to safety. "There must be an underground railroad running hereabouts," a frustrated Kentucky slave-hunter supposedly muttered, "and Levi Coffin is its president."

Coffin was a Quaker merchant who moved here in 1827 to enlist in the fight against slavery. Three major escape routes from Kentucky converged on this community, and Coffin is credited with rescuing about 2,000 fugitives. A master administrator who coordinated his secret system deftly, he ran what has been called the "Grand Central Station" of the railroad. He shut down the operation in 1847 to move to Cincinnati, so he could get even closer to the southern border. He continued his activities there, right up to the start of the Civil War. He also met Harriet Beecher Stowe, and he appears in *Uncle Tom's Cabin* as the Quaker abolitionist Simeon Halliday. The Coffin House in Fountain

City is a state historic site, restored to its appearance in the 1840s, at the peak of its underground days.

Richmond was another center of abolitionist ferment, also settled by Quakers. The religious group founded Earlham College in 1847 on the basis of opposing all wars. It still operates on the western edge of this city. Earlham began the first natural history curriculum in Indiana. It developed the Joseph Moore Museum, which is named for the course's first teacher at Earlham and houses a fine collection of dinosaur skeletons and fossils.

It was while speaking in Richmond in 1842 that Henry Clay, exasperated by Quaker petitioners demanding an end to slavery, told his audience that if they raised $15,000 they could buy his slaves. Otherwise, he advised them, mind your own business. The negative impact of his intemperate remarks is credited with being a decisive factor in his loss of the 1844 presidential election.

Richmond was the home of E. Gurney Hill, whose horticultural experiments made the city one of America's top rose-growing centers. The Richmond Rose, developed here in 1905, was the most popular hybrid in the country for many years. The Hill Memorial Rose Garden, in the city's Glen Miller Park, displays 73 varieties of the flower and more than 1,600 rose bushes. Hill Floral Products is still the largest producer of cut roses in the country and offers free tours of its facilities.

This entire area of Indiana left deep marks on Civil War history. Liberty, the next town on the route, was the birthplace of Union general Ambrose Burnside. He lived here until departing for the U.S. Military Academy in 1843. Burnside left a deep mark on men's hairstyles, because of his distinctive haircut, joining the beard with the growth atop the head. It was widely copied, and continuations of the hairline in front of the ears became known as "sideburns."

Burnside was better at fashion than war, however. He replaced the ever-delaying George McLellan as commander of the Army of the Potomac in November 1862. With President Lincoln imploring him to get moving, Burnside forced a battle at Fredericksburg. Unfortunately, as several Civil War historians have concluded, Burnside was a man of limited capacities, in far over his head as a commanding general. He attacked the well-entrenched Lee in a frontal assault, and his forces were annihilated. His subordinate, Gen. Joseph Hooker, wrote several years later: "It was a great slaughter pen. They might just as well have tried to take Hell." Burnside was relieved of command several weeks later. Nonetheless, they loved him in Rhode Island. After the war, Burnside served three terms as governor of that state and was in his second term as U.S. Senator at his death in 1881.

Another Liberty native went on to a softer sort of immortality. Mrs. Alice Gray was a local woman who is believed to have served as the model for James Whitcomb Riley's famed poem "Little Orphant Annie." That's the one that warns at the end of each stanza, "The goblins will get ya' if ya' don't watch out"—good advice in any age.

From Liberty, the road bends sharply east and enters Ohio and the college community of Oxford.

A Closer Look. The T-shirts in the university bookstore proclaim, "Miami was a university before Florida was a state." That is true enough. In fact, Miami was a university before its home, Oxford, was even a town. The Ohio legislature created the school in 1809 and only then got around to finding some land on which to place it. A local surveyor suggested available property here, and 15 years after the legislature mandated it, Miami University opened its doors. Oxford grew up around it.

For a while, five schools functioned in Oxford, including two of the first women's colleges in the Midwest. All were eventually absorbed by Miami. Then, for a while, there was no college at all. Miami shut down after the financial panic of 1873 and was closed for 12 years, until the state revived it with funds. But today it is almost the ideal blend of town and campus. Robert Frost called it "the prettiest college that ever there was." With its red-brick Georgian classrooms and bordering streets lined with fraternity and sorority houses, the Miami campus looks like the set for a movie musical, ready for the big dance number to break out anytime.

Leave your car near the corner of Campus and High, where the college meets the edge of Oxford's business district. On either side of this intersection are headquarters of national fraternities. Even before Miami became famous on the sports page as the "cradle of coaches" in football, it was known in academia as the "mother of fraternities." At one time, it was estimated that one-sixth of all members of Greek-letter organizations in America belonged to groups that had originated at Miami. Five of them maintain national offices in Oxford.

On the southwestern corner, in a castlelike structure modeled after the Governor's Palace in Williamsburg, Virginia, is the headquarters of Phi Delta Theta. The fraternity was founded at Miami in 1848. Its headquarters occupies the site of the home of Dr. John Witherspoon Scott, president of Oxford Female Institute. That pioneering women's college opened in 1849 and merged with Miami in 1928. Scott's daughter, Caroline, was born in the house that once stood here, and she attended her father's school. She married a member of Phi Delta Theta's charter class, who became the country's twenty-third president, Benjamin Harrison. The fraternity headquarters was erected here in 1948, at the birthplace of the wife of its most illustrious member.

Diagonally across the intersection is the national house of Beta Theta Pi, the oldest of the Miami fraternities. It was founded here in 1839, six years after this house was built by Oxford pioneer Zachariah DeWitt. The fraternity has occupied it since 1898.

Sigma Chi, perhaps the best known of the Miami-based fraternities, was started in 1855. But it no longer maintains a local headquarters, and its house is a bit removed from the path of an easy walk. Besides, the renowned song about its sweetheart was not written here, but at the chapter at Albion College in Michigan.

Now walk east along High St., across from the campus. At the corner of University Ave., at 220 E. High, is the home of Lottie Moon. One of the most romantic figures of nineteenth-century Oxford, the beautiful Ms. Moon, daughter of a Virginia family, was known as a heartbreaker. She was also a spy. As a student at Oxford Female Institute she made the acquaintance of a young man from across the Indiana border— Ambrose Burnside—and accepted his marriage proposal. But she changed her mind at the altar and left her perplexed groom standing there as she fled the church. The legend goes that on the next occasion Lottie assayed marriage, her groom went through the ceremony with a pistol pointed at her side. When the Civil War began, the Moon family made no secret of its Confederate sympathies. Moving to Cincinnati, Lottie made frequent trips in a variety of disguises to the Southern lines, transmitting any information she thought would be of value. Finally apprehended by Union forces, she was taken before the district's commanding officer. As luck would have it, this was her old beau Burnside, who was now a general. He threw her into prison, but she served only three months before being released. Lottie eventually made her way to New York and, after the war, became Paris correspondent for the *New York World.*

One more block east will bring you to Lewis Place. This mansion, called "the most beautiful house in Oxford" by Frank Lloyd Wright, has been the official residence of Miami University's president since 1903. Built by Romeo and Jane Lewis in 1839, the house was noted for combining elements of New England and Southern architecture. The couple came to Oxford from Connecticut, by way of Florida, where they were among the founding families of the state capital, Tallahassee. Oxford served as a geographic compromise for the pair, and their house, with its blend of Federal and Greek Revival elements, did the same for domestic arrangements. Jane occupied the dwelling until 1880, and the 17-room house was purchased by the state for the university in 1925.

Continue along High St. until you are opposite the Beta Bell Tower, a gift to the university from Beta Theta Phi on its 1939 centennial. Cross the street and enter the campus, with the tower on your right and Roudebush Hall, the administration building, on your left. Once past Roudebush, angle toward the left. In a few steps, you'll find yourself at the Hub, the center of Miami's campus. The area is decorated with stones sent by alumni from all 50 states, each one pointing in the direction from which it came. Here you are surrounded by Miami's history, with some of its most venerable and distinguished buildings all around.

Walk to the west. This is the oldest part of the campus. Elliott Hall, the building facing you on the right, dates from 1828 and was Miami's first residence hall. Stoddard Hall, on the left, came seven years later and was a residence for upperclassmen. Both were extensively restored by the Works Progress Administration in 1937.

Once past a short flight of steps, you will have the pillared bulk of King Library right in front of you. Turn left on the walkway that runs between Alumni Hall, the domed structure on the left, and Irvin Hall, headquarters of the foreign language department.

Just across Spring St. is a small house once owned by one of the most influential educators in American history. William Holmes McGuffey came to Miami two years after it opened, in 1826, as professor of ancient languages and moral philosophy. While living in this house, which he built in 1833, he worked on the textbook series that gave him lasting fame. His *Eclectic Readers* introduced five generations of American schoolchildren to the joys of language. True to McGuffey's area of scholarship, they went heavy on moral philosophy. The lessons were intended to teach right behavior, both civic and private, along with reading. They were also intended to be read aloud as training in rhetoric, regarded as the most important of nineteenth-century language skills. They helped shape the American mind as much as any other book for nearly a century.

The McGuffey Readers began to be phased out in the 1920s and were relegated to the realm of nostalgia by the end of the Great Depression. They still are fondly recalled, however, by educators alarmed at the way reading has become more of a chore than a pleasure to students. It was estimated that the Readers have been reprinted more often in America than any book but the Bible. The house contains many of the professor's belongings, including his traveling lectern and bookcase, as well as a collection of early Readers.

Continue along Spring St. to Campus St. and then turn right, heading back to High St. and the start of this walk. If you feel energetic, turn left on High for a stroll through Oxford's business district, which is loaded with bookstores, restaurants, and student hangouts. Four blocks up, at the corner of College St., is Oxford College Hall, the main building of the former women's school. Built in 1849, it is thought to be the oldest surviving structure associated with a women's college in America. Retrace your steps along High to Campus to return to the point where the stroll began.

U.S. 27 runs through Oxford as High St. On the way out of town, though, take a short jog left on Bishop St. This is the access road to Yager Stadium, the university's football field. As I already mentioned, Miami is famous as the "cradle of coaches." A disproportionately high number of great football coaches began their careers here. Among them were Paul Brown, Woody Hayes, Ara Parseghian, and Bo Schembechler. A room under the grandstand pays tribute to these legendary figures, as well as to other athletes associated with the university.

The highway now dips south, as Patterson Ave. At the far southeastern corner of the campus is the Miami University Art Museum, a facility worth a stop. Its five galleries feature works from the university's permanent collection as well as exhibits from national loan shows. It is noted for its paintings by American artists. The museum building was designed by Walter Netsch, architect of the Air Force Academy Chapel.

The road now heads for Cincinnati. It enters the northwestern suburbs and then the city itself as Colerain Rd. Watch for the turnoff on the right to Mount Airy Forest, one of the Midwest's loveliest urban parks. The land was acquired by the city in 1913. On a bare hillside here, the first municipal experiment in reforestation was initiated. Now it is a Cincinnati landmark, with more than 1,000 acres planted in hardwoods and conifers and laced with hiking trails. Mount Airy Arboretum is noted for its spring displays of lilacs and rhododendrons. This shady oasis on the regal heights above the Queen City is a perfect place to end the drive.

VISITING HOURS

Auburn

Auburn-Cord-Duesenberg Museum, south of downtown, at 1600 S. Wayne St. (219) 925–1444. Daily, 9–6. $6.

Fort Wayne

Historic Fort Wayne, at 211 S. Barr St. (219) 424–3476. Friday to Sunday, 10–5, Memorial Day–October. $3.50.

The New Lincoln Museum, at 200 E. Berry St. (219) 455–3864. Monday to Friday, 9–5, Saturday, 10–5, and Sunday, 1–5. $2.99.

Geneva

Limberlost State Historic Site, at 200 E. Sixth St. (219) 368–7428. Wednesday to Saturday, 9–5, and Sunday, 1–5, April–December. Donation.

Fountain City

Levi Coffin House, south of town. (317) 847–2432. Tuesday to Sunday, 1–4, June–mid-September. Weekends only, 1–4, mid-September–October. $1.

Richmond

Joseph Moore Museum, on the campus of Earlham College, west on U.S. 40. (317) 962–6561. Sunday, 1–5, September–June. Free.

Hill Floral Products, at 2117 Peacock Rd. (317) 962–2555. Daily, 9–4. Free.

Oxford

McGuffey House, at Spring and Oak Sts. (513) 529–1809. Call ahead for hours. Free.

Miami University Art Museum, south of campus on Patterson Ave. (513) 529–2232. Tuesday to Sunday, 11–5. Free.

Cincinnati

Mount Airy Arboretum, at 5083 Colerain Ave. (513) 352–4080. Daily, 6 A.M.–10 P.M. Free.

U.S. 31

Carp Lake, Michigan, to Ludington, Michigan

U.S. 31 is an exceptionally scenic drive along the northern Lake Michigan shoreline, through the most highly developed resort area in the upper Midwest. There are wonderful views over the lake from roadside turnouts, as well as a succession of vacation communities, ranging from the rustic to the luxurious to the bustling streets of Traverse City.

South of Ludington, freeways take up most of U.S. 31's path. In fact, for most of its run to Mobile, Alabama, it is seldom far from an accompanying interstate. But in this most northern portion of the road, except for peak summer weekends when traffic can be heavy, U.S. 31 is a drive into pure delight.

The road once started right in Mackinaw City (see U.S. 23), but the approach to the Mackinac Bridge from Interstate 75 has taken over that section of its route. So U.S. 31 now begins a few miles south of the Straits of Mackinac, branching off the interstate near the resort town of Carp Lake.

Shortly after we get underway on our road, we come to an interesting side trip. At Levering, head west on Michigan C66. It leads across a range of hills and rocky northern farmland to Cross Village, on a bluff high above Lake Michigan. There has been a cross on this site for centuries. According to legend, Fr. Jacques Marquette erected the first one on his voyage of 1675. The French called the place Crooked Tree (L'arbre Croche), from another landmark that once stood atop this bluff. This was an Ottawa community for centuries, and many of the town's residents are still Native Americans. Its biggest draw is Legs Inn, a restaurant built entirely of native stone, where the cuisine is predominantly Polish.

Lake Charlevoix. (Courtesy Michigan Travel Bureau.)

Cross Village's greatest appeal is the road that begins there and travels along the lakeshore, Michigan 119. This is a narrow, winding byway
leading south. It follows the lakeshore through country so thickly
forested that it has been nicknamed the "tunnel of trees." This is repeatedly cited as Michigan's most scenic drive. There are few turnouts,
though, and it is slow going.

The road emerges in Harbor Springs, a resort community that also
originated as an Ottawa settlement. This tribe was renowned as a tribe
of traders, middlemen between more powerful groups such as the
Ojibwa and Sioux. Driven south into Michigan's Lower Peninsula, they
thrived on the lakeshore and built stable communities there. Even after
Michigan became a state, in 1836, the Ottawa retained rights to their
lands for another 40 years. But the pressures of lumbering interests were

too great, and the tribe was forced to sign away their rights in 1875, opening this land to white settlement. Within a decade, Harbor Springs grew into one of the premier resorts on Little Traverse Bay. Some of the fine Victorian summer homes built in those years can be seen by following the bay's shore south from downtown through the Wequetonsing Association. Harbor Springs also has a lovely harbor and marina, and on summer afternoons you can see artists sketching the town and its hilly backdrop from the pier.

A vestige of the older Harbor Springs is the Holy Childhood of Jesus Church, located one block west of the business district. The original mission to the Ottawa was established on this site in 1827 by Fr. Peter de Jean. The church that stands there now was built in 1892 but incorporates two earlier structures within it. The church school served the Native American community until the 1970s but now is used by the general community. One of this school's first students was Andrew J. Blackbird. Although born a Sioux, he became an Ottawa leader and educator and helped secure tribal rights during the early years of statehood. His home, at 368 E. Main St., is now a museum of Ottawa history in this area.

Michigan 119 continues along the shoreline of Little Traverse Bay and rejoins U.S. 31 just north of Bay View. This is the oldest cottage community in northern Michigan, established by the Methodist Church for summer conclaves in 1876. Hundreds of its old homes are lovingly maintained by summer residents. The graceful nineteenth-century architecture and the pastel shades of the houses make a charming picture as the road winds through the center of the community. While the grounds are private, visitors can park and walk through the area.

Petoskey was named for an Ottawa chief. The name means either "Rising Sun" or "Between Two Swamps," depending on which Algonquian translation you accept. It is another venerable resort, with extensive parkland along the bay. Travelers flock to the bluffs here on summer evenings to watch some of the finest sunsets on the Great Lakes. In Waterfront Park there is a small museum of the Little Traverse area, housed in a former railroad station. The town has a rich history, savoring its associations with Ernest Hemingway, who was a frequent visitor as a young man; his family owned a cottage at nearby Horton Bay. Much of Petoskey's Victorian downtown has been restored to form the

Gaslight District, an area of exclusive shops, most of them locally owned. Some stores show off Petoskey stones—rocks with fossils embedded within them, which are found on the nearby lakeshore and are Michigan's official state stone.

The highway now swings around the southern shore of Little Traverse Bay, past some exclusive resort communities, then along the water. This drive between Petoskey and Charlevoix is beautiful. A large rest area at about the midpoint allows travelers to walk down to the water's edge and take in the view of the bay's entire sweep.

A Closer Look. There has been a bridge across the Pine River Channel almost since the settlement of Charlevoix in 1853. It remains the symbol of life in this lovely resort town, regulating time and traffic on both road and water. The bridge goes up on the hour and the half hour as long as the lakes are navigable. When it does, everything on U.S. 31 and the rest of Charlevoix comes to a halt. Cars, bikes, pedestrians—everything stops to watch the spectacle of the boats making their way back and forth through the channel between Lake Michigan and Lake Charlevoix.

Charlevoix's main thoroughfare is, in fact, named Bridge St., and the drawbridge defines its northern limit. It is probably the most beloved bottleneck in the state. "It would be hard to imagine life in Charlevoix without the bridge," a local restaurant owner told me a few years ago, adding: "When it goes up, northbound traffic always backs up through downtown. People get a chance to stop and look around. Maybe they like what they see and decide to park and look a little bit more. The bridge is part of the flavor of this town—a little inconvenient, maybe, but indispensable."

Charlevoix has one of the most beautiful settings of any town in the Michigan north. On one side of Bridge St. are shops in structures that date mostly from the Victorian era. On the other side is a city park and Round Lake, the town harbor, filled with every imaginable sort of pleasure craft. That leads, in turn, to Lake Charlevoix, the third largest inland lake in the state, with narrow, hill-rimmed arms that demand to be explored.

Charlevoix was not always such a restful place. Originally named Pine River, this was a freewheeling fishing and lumbering town. There were frequent conflicts with the Mormon settlement on Beaver Island, in Lake Michigan, to which this is the nearest port. In one major dustup, Mormon deputies trying to arrest some local fishermen were chased back to the island in a gun battle fought between boats that lasted most of the day. When the Mormon colony collapsed after an invasion from the mainland, Charlevoix emerged as a commercial center. The channel to the big lake was completed in 1876, turning the port into the busiest lumber shipper on northern Lake Michigan.

By the end of the century, however, a different industry was developing here. A group of wealthy vacationers organized the Chicago and Belvedere Clubs, private associations filled with enormous summer homes. The two clubs still face each other from opposite heights of Round Lake. That sort of elegant rusticity still defines the place.

To get a taste of it, walk east on Dixon St., one block north of the bridge. This wonderfully evocative street is lined by fine old homes with lots of shade trees and big front porches. On your right, you can catch an occasional view of Round Lake from the bluff. After two blocks, you will be adjacent to the grounds of the Chicago Club. You can make out some of the rambling houses, and if you take a quick walk through the grounds, no one will be upset. Follow this street all the way to Depot Park, on Lake Charlevoix. The town's former rail station is here, and the adjacent ground has been turned into a beach and picnic grounds on the lake. The waters here are slightly warmer than in the big lake, so it is a favored place for swimming. (The sun, however, is stronger on the Lake Michigan beaches.)

Retrace your steps back to U.S. 31 and cross over to the south side of the bridge. A flight of stairs leads to a walkway that runs along the Pine River Channel, from the bridge to the pier. This is the best place to get a close-up view of the boat traffic. If you are really lucky, you may see a lake freighter maneuvering through the narrow channel, a sight akin to watching a hippo dance the polka. The *Beaver Islander,* a car and passenger ferry that makes the two-hour run to the island twice a day, also may be passing through. The view from the pier takes in a vast sweep of lake frontage, extending to the dunes that run to the north of town. The beach is right next to the pier.

Now walk back to Bridge St. and stroll the shopping district and the park across the way. The sidewalk cafés here are where Charlevoix gathers on warm summer nights, to devour ice cream cones and ogle the passersby. There are several excellent restaurants on the street, many of them specializing in whitefish taken just hours before from the local waters.

Be sure to get a good vantage point when the bridge goes up. It is the town's biggest spectacle. Bells ring, lights flash, cameras click, and Charlevoix glows in the summer sun.

U.S. 31 continues on its southern course, running inland from the lake a mile or so. Just south of town is the turnoff to Fisherman's Island State Park, the best beach in the area, on a lightly populated stretch of coastline.

The countryside rolls as the road heads on. Every once in a while, you can see the big lake to the west, as it narrows to form the head of Grand Traverse Bay. The body of water was named by French explorers who saved many miles of paddling by carrying their canoes across its narrow neck. The hills of the Leelanau Peninsula rise across the water.

The road runs through the resort town of Torch Lake, named for the Native American practice of spearing fish at night by torchlight. The long, narrow lake lies just to the east of the road. Beyond that is Elk Lake, and the highway occupies a narrow isthmus that runs between the inland body of water and Grand Traverse Bay. Elk Rapids is another old lumbering town that made the conversion to resort status late in the nineteenth century.

The highway is lined with produce stands through this area. The waters of the bay exert a moderating influence on the northern climate, allowing even wine grapes to be cultivated in this area. There is some evidence that apple orchards were cultivated here in the eighteenth century, possibly by French trappers. In the 1880s local farmer B. J. Morgan began growing red tart cherries here. This variety, perfectly suited for filling pies, thrived in the area. Early plantings were concentrated on the Old Mission Peninsula, the narrow finger of land that divides Grand Traverse Bay into its eastern and western arms. By the first decade of the twentieth century, cultivation had spread along both shores of the bay. Many of the old orchards have fallen victim to the population growth of this area since the 1960s. But the annual Cherry Festival, held in Traverse City each July, is one of the country's major agricultural celebrations. And as you can see by the roadside stands, plenty of fruit remains. Amon's Orchards, just north of Acme, offers tours of its plantings and pick-your-own trips through the grounds. This area is especially lovely in May, when pastel blossoms color the rolling landscape.

In Acme, orchards have been replaced by one of the upper Midwest's finest golf facilities. Grand Traverse Resort was among the first places to prove that championship courses could be profitable in the comparatively short outdoor season of northern Michigan. The success of the golf program here touched off a boom in the 1980s that transformed the region into the top golfing concentration in the Great Lakes, enhancing its appeal as a resort.

Past Acme the road slides right alongside the bay for a spectacularly scenic entrance into Traverse City. This is Michigan's Riviera, the largest mix of urban area and resort land in the state's north. The highway is lined for miles with beachfront hotels and condominiums. Thousands of full-time residents have moved up from the big cities in the southern part of the state for a more relaxed pace of life. Consequently, real estate prices have soared, and this has become one of the great boom areas of the Great Lakes.

A small state park with a beach and a camping area is wedged among the hotels on the eastern arm of the bay. On the western arm is Clinch Park, the city's playground on the water. Featured here are excellent beaches, a miniature steam train that makes a circuit of the grounds, and a zoo exhibiting wildlife native to the northern Great Lakes. Traverse City has a bustling downtown area, which begins right across U.S. 31 from Clinch Park. It is anchored by locally owned Milliken's Department Store, founded by the family of a former governor of the state. There are also many fine apparel shops and restaurants.

From Traverse City, U.S. 31 heads south into the state's interior. Instead of going that way, take Michigan 72 west and then turn north on Michigan 22, following it around the edge of the Leelanau Peninsula. This area, the "little finger" of Michigan's mitten-shaped Lower Peninsula, is almost European in its blending of natural beauty and enjoyment of the good life. There are several country inns and fine restaurants scattered among its rolling hills and lakes, along with a few larger resorts discreetly tucked away on back roads. A traveler could do worse than spending several days wandering those roads. For our purposes, however, stay on Michigan 22.

Views immediately open across the western arm of the bay to the Old

Mission Peninsula, with the waterfront of Traverse City in the near foreground. The first community on the route, Suttons Bay, is one of the great fruit-shipping ports in the area. It is now a top antiquing town as well, and there are several offbeat shops along Main St.

The old Native American settlement of Peshawbestown now operates a gambling casino, giving a measure of prosperity to the once impoverished Ottawa-Ojibwa community. Several of northern Michigan's tribal communities have gone into gambling since the 1980s, and this casino, in the midst of the state's prime resort country, has been one of the most successful.

Omena takes its name from another of those Algonquian words that has a wide disparity in translations. According to one version it means "he gives to him," while another insists it is a colloquial expression that means "Is that so?" Rev. Peter Dougherty established a mission church here in 1858, and it is now the oldest Protestant congregation in northern Michigan. (Yes, that's so.)

Turn west onto County Road 626 at the main crossroads at Omena and follow the signs to the Leelanau Wine Cellars. This is the most northern of Michigan's wineries. It offers tours of its vineyards and tastings.

Continue west on County Road 626 until you encounter Michigan 22, making its way back on the southbound leg of its journey around the Leelanau. Turn left, and in a few miles you will come to Leland, the tiny commercial center of the peninsula. The old fishery area has been turned into a shopping area called Fishtown, with lots of craft stores and galleries. A mill still turns on the site of the original sawmill built on the Carp River in 1853. Boat trips to the Manitou Islands leave from the end of the Fishtown parking area. Both islands, which are part of Sleeping Bear Dunes National Lakeshore, contain vast wilderness areas and stands of forest. They are popular destinations for day-trip backpackers. The Leelanau Historical Museum in town contains displays on the development of the peninsula and folk art. One of the north's shrines for whitefish fanciers, the Blue Bird, is also located here; reservations are essential for dinner in summer.

The road continues along the shore of Lake Leelanau. Past the village of Glen Arbor, it enters Sleeping Bear Dunes National Lakeshore. Turn on Michigan 109 to reach the dunes. This mountain of sand, towering

480 feet above Lake Michigan, has been formed by thousands of years of prevailing westerly winds depositing sand on the cliffs left by retreating glaciers. To the Native Americans, the immense dune resembled a mother bear in repose. According to legend, she and her two cubs fled a fire on the Wisconsin side of the lake and swam to the far side. The mother made it, but her children drowned. The Great Spirit marked the spot of their deaths with the Manitou Islands, while the mother waits for eternity on the far shore.

You can explore the dunes either by climbing them yourself, an excursion recommended only for the young and hearty, or by motoring to the summit on Pierce Stocking Scenic Dr. This road commands breathtaking views of the lake and the dunes, which continue to shift every year, as well as of Glen Lake, an inland body of water cut off from the big lake by the barrier of sand. The road is open from mid-April to mid-November. The former Coast Guard station at nearby Glen Haven is also part of the national lakeshore and displays exhibits on the maritime history of the area.

The road continues on to Empire, a land's-end sort of village. The Friendly Tavern at the town's main intersection is celebrated across the state for its hamburgers. The visitors center for the national lakeshore is also located in the middle of town, with exhibits on dune formation and other information.

U.S. 31 then runs along the shores of two more scenic lakes, Platte and Crystal, with the dunes towering off to the west. Take the marked turnoff to the Point Betsie Light. It occupies a highly photogenic site and is also one of the state's oldest lighthouses, dating to 1858. The name is French and is probably a derivation of *bec scie,* the term for the spoonbill ducks that inhabited the nearby river.

Frankfort has one of the best harbors on the lake, and for many years a car ferry made the crossing to Kewaunee, Wisconsin, from here. But the service was discontinued in the 1980s, a victim of superhighways and changing travel patterns. Frankfort is still an evocative port town, with many charming shops situated along its single main street, opposite the water.

Michigan 115 from Frankfort will take you back to U.S. 31 at the town of Benzonia. The name is another exercise in odd linguistic derivations. It is the seat of Benzie County, which is a variation of the same

French words that named Point Betsie, as I already explained. The learned settlers of this town, a mission of clergymen from Oberlin College, decided to give their new community the Latinized version of this name. So you have the name Benzonia.

This was the boyhood home of Civil War historian Bruce Catton and is now the site of the studio of Gwen Frostic, an artist well known for her wildlife prints. The studio is located in the midst of a sanctuary on the Betsie River, just west of town. You can watch presses making prints of the original blocks.

The highway enters Manistee County, passes through the resort of Bear Lake and finally reaches the lumbering town of Manistee. This was a legendary port city during Michigan's great lumbering era. The fortunes that once were made here live on in the Victorian heritage that the town proudly shows off in its residential and commercial districts. Manistee calls its wooden mansions "the painted ladies" for their pastel hues. The streets off downtown are lined with them. Its entire business area is a national historic district, with immaculately restored buildings, including an 1880s firehouse painted raspberry red. It is the oldest in the state.

The centerpiece of the downtown restoration is the Ramsdell Theatre. Built by one of the lumber tycoons and opened in 1903, the Ramsdell was decorated in grand Victorian style. As the town's economy declined, the theater resorted to showing movies to stay open, and for a few years in the 1950s it closed altogether. A civic project refurbished the place, starting in 1972, and a season of live theater was produced every summer. The comeback of the theater sparked the overhaul of downtown, using a Victorian theme in everything from facades to lampposts. The handiwork is regarded as a model for other aging northern communities. The curving main street follows a bend of the Manistee River, and a boardwalk runs along the water's edge. The former waterworks, built in 1882, has been converted into a museum that tells the story of the lumbering era and the town's time as a brawling port city.

The highway runs through forest to the next lumber town on the route, Ludington. There is more of a resortlike feel to this place, with its broad sandy beach right at the end of the main downtown street. Ludington is thought to be the place at which Fr. Jacques Marquette was buried in 1675, when he fell sick and died on the way back to St. Ignace from his voyage of exploration to the upper Mississippi Valley. Native Americans from his mission retrieved his remains the following year and reinterred them at St. Ignace, where he had expressed a desire to spend his eternal rest (see U.S. 2). A cross on a hill near the beach marks the place where his first grave was traditionally believed to be located.

Ludington is home harbor for the last remaining car ferry across Lake Michigan, which runs to Manitowoc, Wisconsin. This is also one of the top fishing ports on the lake, with coho salmon being especially prized in local waters. Just south of town is White Pine Village, a collection of historic buildings from around Mason County, many of them associated with the lumbering era. The structures also are meant to reflect everyday life in the 1880s and include an ice cream parlor, a blacksmith's shop, and a school.

Once south of Ludington, U.S. 31 turns into a superhighway for most of the remainder of its run through Michigan and Indiana. It is better to leave it here on the Ludington beach, with the scent of the north still in our lungs.

VISITING HOURS

Harbor Springs
Andrew Blackbird Museum, east of downtown, on Michigan 119. (616) 526–7731. Monday to Saturday, 10–5, and Sunday, 12–4, Memorial Day–Labor Day. Donation.

Petoskey
Little Traverse Regional Historical Museum, in Waterfront Park. (616) 347–2620. Monday to Saturday, 10–4, May–Labor Day. Closed Monday, Labor Day–October. $1.

Acme
Amon's Orchards, north on U.S. 31. (616) 938–1644. Daily, daylight hours, May–February. Free.

Traverse City
Clinch Park Zoo, on the waterfront of Grand Traverse Bay. (616) 922–4904. Daily, 9:30–7:30, Memorial Day–Labor Day. Daily, 9:30–4:30, mid-April and May–October. $1.50.

Omena

Leelanau Wine Cellars, west of town, at 12693 E. Tatch Rd. (616) 386–5201. Daily, 12–6, July and August. Daily, 12–5, rest of year. Free.

Leland

Leelanau Historical Museum, at 203 E. Cedar St. (616) 256–7475. Tuesday to Saturday, 10–4, and Sunday, 1–4, mid-June–Labor Day. Friday to Sunday, 1–4, rest of year. $1.

Sleeping Bear Dunes National Lakeshore

Sleeping Bear Point Maritime Museum, west of Glen Haven, on Michigan 209. (616) 326–5134. Daily, 10–4, June–August. Weekends only, May and September. Free.

Sleeping Bear Dunes National Lakeshore Visitors Center, on Michigan 72, in Empire. (616) 326–5134. Daily, 9–5. Free.

Manistee

Ramsdell Theatre, at Maple and First Sts. (616) 723–9948. Times vary with performance schedule. Call in advance. Donation.

Old Waterworks Museum, at 540 W. First St. (616) 723–5331. Tuesday to Saturday, 10:30–4:30, mid-June–Labor Day. Donation.

Ludington

White Pine Village, south at 1687 S. Lakeshore Dr. (616) 843–4808. Tuesday to Sunday, 11–4:30, mid-June–Labor Day. $4.

U.S. 35

Michigan City, Indiana, to Gallipolis, Ohio

U.S. 35 tracks a long diagonal from Lake Michigan to the Ohio River, angling southeast across Indiana and Ohio. It passes through a town adjudged as America's most typical and another town that is one of America's most ancient. Aside from passing right through the heart of Dayton, it avoids most large cities. The highway eventually enters West Virginia and ends a few miles outside the state capital, Charleston.

In its northernmost segment, U.S. 35 runs close to the Michigan Road (see U.S. 421), the pioneer route that once connected Madison, Indiana, to Lake Michigan. The highway leaves Michigan City (see again U.S. 421) heading southeast, through farmland, past the shores of Pine Lake, and into La Porte. This town name means "the door," and to the French explorers who first passed this way it was regarded as the great entryway to the Great Lakes. La Porte occupied the site at which the central Indiana woodlands opened out to the prairies around the big lake, a dramatic change in landscape that deeply impressed the French traders.

Its proximity to Chicago and national transportation links make La Porte a surprisingly diversified industrial city, with several major corporations located there. They make everything from baby buggies to boilers to rubber goods. It also rates high in quality of life, with seven small lakes located in or just outside of the city. Take a walk around the town's central square to get a feeling for La Porte, which may typify the stability and charm of Indiana's smaller cities better than any other. If you fancy antique firearms, you might peek in at the La Porte County Historical Museum, which has one of the best collections in the Midwest.

In the next several miles, U.S. 35 runs through country drained by

Hopewell Culture mounds. (Courtesy of the Ohio Division of Travel and Tourism.)

two of Indiana's most historic rivers. Just south of Kingsford Heights is the Kankakee, the oldest route through this area. The Kankakee was used by seventeenth-century French traders headed for the Mississippi, and it was used for centuries before that by Woodland tribes on their way to the same destination. The voyageurs would follow the St. Joseph River to its great south bend, then portage to the Kankakee to complete the journey west. This section of northern Indiana became a vital part of French colonial policy. Its design was to try and form alliances with local tribes against France's implacable enemy, the Iroquois Confederacy. The plan had only limited success. But France did manage to control this part of North America from the arrival of Robert Cavalier, sieur de la Salle, in 1679, to the end of the French and Indian War, 86 years later.

A bit farther down the road is the Tippecanoe River, which figured prominently in the American conquest of this region (see U.S. 231). Between the two rivers are a succession of state wildlife areas, built on marshy land off the highway. The largest and most significant is Kanka-kee. It is located 5 miles west of the highway, by way of Indiana 8, just north of Knox. The tract was donated to the state by local farmers in 1927. They found it impossible to cultivate but perfect for wildfowl. Bird-watching continues to be one of the great attractions on this 3,300-acre preserve. There is also canoeing, hunting for mushrooms, and berry picking, in season.

Beyond Knox, U.S. 35 passes along the western shore of Bass Lake, which has a public beach operated by the state.

Winamac is named for a Potawatomi leader who fought with the tribal alliance against the Americans at the Battle of Tippecanoe in 1811. The town site, near the Tippecanoe, was a Miami and Potawatomi village, before being ceded to Indiana in 1832 and opened to white settlement.

U.S. 35 continues steadily on its southeastern course, through Star City and Royal Center, crossroads that never quite lived up to the expectations of their grand names. The highway bypasses Logansport (see U.S. 24) and runs across rich farmland to one of America's most mellifluously named communities, Kokomo.

The Miami leader for whom the town was named was actually called Kokomoko. But the settlers who named the place in 1844 thought that last syllable was a bit too much. Kokomo's rippling name has figured in the title of several popular songs, of which the most recent, a hit for the Beach Boys, placed it somewhere in the Florida Keys. But Kokomo is solidly in Indiana.

Its leading attractions relate to Elwood Haynes. He was employed here in 1887 as a pipeline inspector in the surrounding natural gas fields. While making his tedious rounds, he felt there had to be a better way of getting around quickly. It took him seven years of planning and experimentation to build his driving machine, but on Independence Day in 1894 he was ready for the test. He took it out to Kokomo's Pumpkin Vine Pike and turned it loose. The first gasoline-powered, clutch-driven vehicle to travel on an American road did just fine. It is regarded as the direct antecedent of the motor car.

Haynes's death in 1925 was front-page news, even in Detroit, where the industry he founded had grown to maturity. He was never memorialized with his name on a car, so Haynes is not nearly as well remembered as Ford and Olds and a few others who built on what he began. Nonetheless, the debt to him was always acknowledged by other automotive pioneers. Haynes started his work by ordering a marine motor from a company in Grand Rapids, modifying it right on the kitchen table of his Kokomo home. He fitted it on the chassis of a buggy and rigged it out with steering and gears that increased its weight to about 820 pounds. The machine attained speeds of about 8 miles an hour on its test run.

He formed the Haynes Automobile Co. and publicized his contraption by making the first journey by car from Kokomo to New York. But when he tried to run it along Michigan Ave. in Chicago, a policeman flagged him down and told him to "get that thing off the streets." Haynes also did major innovative work on the electric ignition and the use of aluminum alloys to cut down on engine weight.

The site of Haynes' historic road test is just east of the city, off U.S. 35. In town is the Haynes Museum, the home he occupied for the last 10 years of his life. It exhibits models of his driving machine and other inventions he worked on, as well as family memorabilia.

Not as significant historically but a Kokomo landmark nonetheless is Old Ben. He is a stuffed Hereford steer revered as the largest of his breed anyone around here has ever seen. He stood six-foot-four, weighed 4,720 pounds, and has been mounted in Highland Park since 1919 to be admired by the passing throngs. Nearby is another huge Indiana native: the stump of a sycamore measuring 51 feet around at its base, into which 24 people can fit. It is a suitable companion for Old Ben.

Greentown was a glassmaking center during the natural gas boom in this area, from 1894 to 1903. The Indiana Tumbler and Goblet Co. was in business then, and many of its best pieces, including its distinctive chocolate and golden agate colors, are displayed in the Greentown Glass Museum.

The surrounding gas fields gave this whole area its economic push. That resource is vividly recalled in the name of Gas City, which may not be as pretty as Kokomo but certainly imparts more information. This was an 1880s boomtown when the gas fields came in, and it managed to survive as a small industrial city after the boom petered out.

The boom had an even more profound effect on Muncie. U.S. 35 angles its way into this city after running for a few miles with Interstate 69. The highway actually bypasses central Muncie, but by following Indiana 3 south you will come to the heart of town.

Muncie was a small community of about 6,000 people in 1887, when the first gas well came roaring in. Within three years, it more than doubled its population. Manufacturing firms flocked here to be closer to the fuel source. Among them was Ball Brothers, a thriving company from Buffalo and the leading maker of glass jars in the country. The Balls had a virtual monopoly on preserve containers. In an era before widespread refrigeration, when most families stored fruits for the long winter, it was a huge business. The natural gas supply gave out in 1900, but by then the Balls were established as a Muncie fixture. Their philanthropy turned the nearly dormant Eastern Indiana Teachers College into Ball State University. Ball Corp. remains Muncie's biggest employer, although the trademark jars are now made elsewhere.

The university is in the northwestern part of the city, along a branch of the White River. The campus is abundantly landscaped, and its Christy Woods Arboretum serves as an outdoor laboratory for its biology department. Plantings there are labeled so strollers receive a self-taught lesson in botany as they walk. Christy Woods also contains the Wheeler collection of rare orchids, one of the largest of its kind at any university.

The Ball Corp. operates a museum of its products near company headquarters. Most prominent among the displays is one tracing the development of the Ball jar. The corporation has diversified, however, so that glass containers are only a small part of its present operation.

Muncie occupies a rather significant niche in the history of American social science. This was "Middletown," the "typical American community" exhaustively studied by Robert and Helen Lynd in their pioneering sociology work of 1929. The first systematic examination of how social dynamics function in the United States, the book *Middletown* caused a tremendous stir at the time. Many readers, in Muncie and elsewhere, thought that its conclusions on social stratification amounted to an attack on the democratic ideal. The Lynds returned to Muncie eight years later to chart the effects of the Depression on the city and write *Middletown in Transition.* For years Muncie wasn't sure whether to be pleased or offended at its designation as the country's most typical town. Yet even today, this section of the Midwest is used frequently by national corporations to test new products. The assumption is that its consumers are the closest thing to a cross section of the national market. Dayton, Ohio, which lies a few miles farther along this road, is the metropolitan area most commonly used in these tests.

For the remainder of its Indiana run, U.S. 35 parallels the old right-of-way of the Chesapeake and Ohio Railroad. There is an odd echo of the distant past as it passes the town of Losantville. The original name given to Cincinnati in 1788 was Losantville. It referred to the Native American term for the Licking River. That stream emptied into the Ohio River from the shore opposite Cincinnati, in Kentucky, and seemed to offer the most promising commercial possibilities for the new town. The name was changed two years later by Gov. Arthur St. Clair, who wanted to honor the Cincinnati, a society of Revolutionary War officers, of which he was a member. This village in Indiana apparently liked the first choice better and stuck to its variation of the name.

Near the Indiana border, U.S. 35 passes through the old Quaker community of Richmond (see U.S. 27). At that town's eastern city limits, it enters Ohio.

Ohio's Gov. St. Clair had better success at naming cities than he did as a military leader. Under his command, American forces sought to dislodge the tribes allied with the British from northern Ohio and Indiana. St. Clair built a series of forts on the road from Cincinnati toward the strategic Native American settlement at present-day Fort Wayne, Indiana. But in 1791 he was outmaneuvered by the brilliant Miami leader Little Turtle, and his force was routed, suffering losses higher by percentage than in any American engagement in the Revolutionary War. St. Clair was exonerated by a board of inquiry, but it took three more years before his military successor, Gen. Anthony Wayne, was able to clean up the mess. One of St. Clair's forts, which was named for him, is right outside Eaton. It was also one of his more successful installations. Fort St. Clair was built two months after his crushing defeat. It was intended to protect settlers, but instead it was itself attacked by Little Turtle in November 1792. The defenders managed to hold out and ended the Native American threat to this part of Ohio. Fort St. Clair is a state memorial, with markers relating the history of the place and the battle. It is just west of Eaton, on Ohio 122.

The road now heads straight east to Dayton. This is the route of the Dayton and Western Turnpike, a private road built in competition with the federally financed National Road. That highway ran north of Dayton, along the line of present-day U.S. 40. Promoters of the Dayton alternative were hoping to divert traffic through their community. But they ran out of money at Eaton, and their road show folded in 1840.

The highway enters Dayton as W. Third St., turning south on the west side of the city to pick up the freeway route across the Great Miami River. Drive a few blocks beyond the turnoff to the freeway, then turn left at Paul Laurence Dunbar St. (formerly Summit St.). You are heading to the home of the man for whom the street was named. The first African-American poet to win a popular following, the Dayton-born Dunbar was a sensation in the 1890s, lionized by the most powerful critics in the East. Unable to attend college despite sweeping his high school's scholarship awards, Dunbar worked on his poems while running an elevator in a Dayton office building. They were written in black dialect, a departure from the academic language favored by Dunbar's predecessors among African-American poets. A local church helped underwrite publication of his first volume, *Oak and Ivy.* His second book, *Lyrics of Lowly Life,* published in 1896, went through 11 printings. He was sent on a tour of the major eastern cities and England, his work hailed as a major achievement.

But when he tried to write other poems in conventional English, he was rejected by critics and the public. "Every time I send them something not in dialect they send it right back," he reflected with bitterness, concluding, "If it's Dunbar it has to be dialect, that's all." He suffered from tuberculosis, and to ease his coughing seizures doctors prescribed whiskey. He soon developed a problem with alcohol, his health continued to fail, and he died at the age of 34. Dunbar bought his house on Summit St. in 1900 with the earnings from *Lowly Life,* and this is where he died six years later. His mother continued to occupy the home until her death in 1934. Afterward, it became a state memorial. Displays relating to Dunbar's life and work and family memorabilia are displayed here.

Past Dayton, U.S. 35, alternating between freeway and two-lane road, bypasses Xenia and Washington Court House (see U.S. 22), angling steadily southeast toward Chillicothe.

A Closer Look. When the first white settlers reached southern Ohio, they were baffled by what they saw. Throughout the area were groups of earth mounds. Some were almost 70 feet high. Others sheltered vast interior spaces, as much as 250 feet wide. Still others were shaped into fantastic forms, long coiled snakes and birds. The European pioneers didn't know what to make of them. So they fabricated theories of a vanished race of brilliant people, possibly related to the Aztecs, whose glorious Mexican empire had fallen to Spain. It never occurred to them that the real builders of these monuments were the ancestors of the Native Americans who still remained on the land. To the newcomers, these tribes were an annoyance, an impediment that had to be removed. They were incapable of seeing them as builders and artists.

What made this confusion doubly odd was that European explorers had encountered Mound Builders within historic times. Extensive accounts of the Natchez, visited by French traders in Mississippi before they were wiped out in the eighteenth century, had been published. But the English-speaking world either was ignorant of them or chose to ignore them. Almost until the start of the twentieth century, there was widespread disagreement about the origin and significance of the mounds.

It is known now that the Ohio mounds were the work of a people who have been named the Hopewell Culture. Their real name is unknown. Hopewell was the farmer on whose land the first of the mounds was systematically excavated. The Hopewell appeared in southern Ohio in about 200 B.C. They quickly developed trade routes that reached to Michigan's Upper Peninsula, the Rockies, and the Atlantic and Gulf coasts. They created a complex system of rank within their community and felt it was vitally important to perpetuate that rank after death, in burial mounds. Many objects placed in these mounds were crafted of rare materials from 1,000 miles away—copper, obsidian, shark teeth. The higher the rank of the deceased, the more precious the pieces interred with him.

Along the Scioto River, a major Hopewell ceremonial site grew up. The place was important to them for the same reason that Chillicothe,

the pioneer city that was built nearby, was made Ohio's first state capital. This is where the major roads met. The Hopewells, much like today's interstate traveler, made their way across the continent on a well-established system of trails. The settlers built their roads on these same trails, and Chillicothe was at their nexus. There are many other important Hopewell sites in Ohio. But the concentration of burials and the wealth of material found in the 23 mounds here mark them as especially significant. Formerly known as Mound City Group National Monument, since 1992 it has been designated as the central unit of Hopewell Culture National Historical Park.

While the mounds have been preserved, this entire site is a reconstruction. It was first excavated—and raided for burial items—in the 1840s. But so little appreciated were the mounds that at the start of World War I many of them were leveled to make room for Camp Sherman, a military training base. Only in 1923 did they come under federal protection. The place was meticulously rebuilt, and many items were returned to the mounds in which they were found. The Mica Grave Mound was spared destruction, and most of the pieces shown inside the exhibit area there were uncovered in 1921. The mica for the carvings has been traced to sites in the Great Smoky Mountains.

Other mounds in this grouping are the Death Mask Mound, in which 13 burials were discovered, and the Mound of the Pipes, in which 200 ceremonial items were found. Pipes were an important part of the burial ritual. It is thought that their smoke was believed to be a way of communicating with the spirit world.

By about 500 A.D., the Hopewell Culture was in decline, and within 200 years it had been overrun by invaders. Mound building continued to flourish in North America, but its center shifted to the lower Mississippi Valley. In Ohio, only the silent hillocks were left behind, to astonish the Europeans who entered the land 1,000 years after the Hopewell disappeared.

The visitors center at the park headquarters shows off a wide variety of artifacts recovered here and also places the mounds in a historical perspective. You may also take a short walking trip around the mound area. The park is just north of U.S. 35, at the Ohio 104 exit.

U.S. 35 bypasses Chillicothe (see U.S. 50) and then heads toward the hills of Wayne National Forest.

More evidence of the area's early inhabitants is seen near Leo. The Leo Petroglyphs State Memorial preserves figures—some animals and some geometric forms—cut into a sandstone ledge. The natural beauty and isolation of the site adds to the sense of mystery and awe conveyed by the ancient carvings. Watch for the turnoff on a county road.

Jackson was settled by one of those accidents of fate that seemed to occur so often on the frontier. A group of Welsh immigrants was heading west on the Ohio River in 1818 when their boats were stolen at Gallipolis. Showing a certain amount of grit and flexibility, the men in the party decided to scrap the original plan. Instead, they got jobs on a gang cutting the road between Gallipolis and Chillicothe. When they got to the hilltop that is now downtown Jackson, they liked what they saw and settled in. The six original families sent reports back home about the promise of the land, and more Welsh settlers poured in. Many of them were ironworkers and helped build up a thriving industry in Jackson that lasted for almost a century. There was also a good deal of coal mining in the area, another endeavor with which the Welsh were well acquainted. Those enterprises have faded, and the area around Jackson is now better known for its apple orchards and fields of mushrooms, many of which find their way into Campbell's soups. The town holds its Apple Festival each September.

On the courthouse lawn is a memorial to Jackson's most adventurous son. John Wesley Powell served in the Civil War, losing an arm in the conflict and attaining the rank of major. The lost limb did not deter him from embarking on one of the great voyages in American history. He led the first expeditions down the Colorado River, in 1869 and 1871, and became the first European to see the Grand Canyon from the water. Powell later became head of the U.S. Geologic Survey and a leading advocate for a national water-resources policy. He realized, correctly, that this was a crucial ingredient for settling the Southwest. The lands he helped to open up are a long way from Jackson, but his hometown appreciates what he accomplished.

This road changed the lives of a lot of people. It took Jackson's Welsh immigrants to a new home, and right after it was built, Nehemiah Atwood opened a tavern on it. That made him wealthy. He used part of his fortune to endow a college in his hometown of Rio Grande. It opened in 1876 and is still operating. Rio Grande College is most fondly recalled by basketball fans as the home of the legendary 1950s player Bevo Francis.

No one fared better on this road than Bob Evans. The owner of a small café in Gallipolis, Evans stumbled into a rare bit of luck in 1946. West Virginia passed a law prohibiting double-trailer trucks from its highways. Several trucking companies asked Evans if they could use his property to reload their vehicles before crossing the state line. Evans didn't see the harm in that. Before the truckers went on their way, they usually stopped in for a big country-style meal, featuring sausages made by Evans' wife, Jewel. Word of her cooking spread, and soon the restaurant became a mandatory stop, even after West Virginia repealed its law. Evans opened a branch in Chillicothe in 1968 and then decided to franchise the idea. The rest has become a part of American roadside lore.

Evans always considered himself a farmer first and a restaurant owner by necessity. He owned land near Rio Grande, and as his restaurants made him wealthy, he kept adding on to the place. Bob Evans Farms, located just south of Rio Grande, is now a recreational complex, with a thickly nostalgic country theme. There are animal exhibits, a farming museum, crafts, festivals throughout the year, horseback riding, canoeing—it's a rural Disneyland built by sausages.

The road continues its run through hill country to the river town of Gallipolis (see Ohio 7), then passes over the bridge to West Virginia.

VISITING HOURS

La Porte

La Porte County Historical Museum, in the county building, at Michigan and State Sts. (219) 326–6808. Monday to Friday, 10–4:30. Free.

Knox

Kankakee State Fish and Wildlife Area, west on Indiana 8. (219) 896–3522. Daily, mid-December–mid-October. Free.

Kokomo

Elwood Haynes Museum, at 1915 S. Webster St. (317) 452–3471. Tuesday to Sunday, 1–4. Free.

Greentown

Greentown Glass Museum, at 112 N. Meridian St. Tuesday to Sunday, 10–12 and 1–5, Memorial Day–Labor Day. Weekends, 1–5, rest of year. Free.

Muncie

Christy Woods Arboretum, on the campus of Ball State University. (317) 285–5341. Schedule varies. Call in advance. Free.

Ball Corp. Museum, at 345 S. High St. (317) 747–6100. Daily, 9–5. Free.

Eaton

Fort St. Clair, west on Ohio 122. (513) 456–4125. Daily, 8–8, April–October. Free.

Dayton

Paul Laurence Dunbar State Memorial, at 219 N. Paul Laurence Dunbar St. (513) 224–7061. Wednesday to Saturday, 9:30–4:30, Memorial Day–Labor Day. Weekends only, Labor Day–October. $2.50.

Chillicothe

Hopewell Culture National Historical Park, north on Ohio 104. (614) 774–1125. Daily, 8–5. $2.

Leo

Leo Petroglyphs State Memorial, north on a county road. (614) 297–2630. Daily, daylight hours. Free.

Rio Grande

Bob Evans Farms, east on Ohio 588. (614) 245–5305. Daily, 8:30–5, Memorial Day–Labor Day. Free, except during the Farm Festival, in October.

U.S. 36

Uhrichsville, Ohio, to Dana, Indiana

The National Road was the first transportation project funded by the federal government, the main artery to the pioneer West. Its route lives on as U.S. 40. Running parallel to that road is U.S. 36, serving the string of smaller towns that lay just north of the nation's main stem. Most of U.S. 40's route was usurped by the interstates and four-laned long ago. U.S. 36, however, still cuts and darts its way across the less-traveled countryside of Ohio and Indiana. Along this road are memories of long-ago tragedies, canal towns, college towns, and America's most intensive concentration of covered bridges. U.S. 36 shadows the wider highway all the way to the Colorado Rockies and finally ends up at the resort town of Estes Park, at the base of Rocky Mountain National Park.

U.S. 36 starts its run in the Tuscarawas Valley, one of Ohio's earliest places of white settlement. From the junction of U.S. 250 near Uhrichsville, the road heads west, following the course of the Tuscarawas River through a deep, wooded valley. One of the ugliest episodes of the American Revolution took place in this lovely setting.

The Revolutionary War was a vicious affair on the Western frontier. Far from the courtesies that marked much of the campaigning in the East, the battles in the wilderness settled into a cycle of massacre and retribution. Ohio lay on the edge of white settlement in the 1770s. In fact, Parliament's attempt to halt any further settlement beyond Pittsburgh raised sentiment for war in the West.

David Zeisberger, a Moravian missionary from Pennsylvania, arrived in Ohio in 1772. He had been invited by the Delaware tribe to establish a mission in their country. But the tiny settlement was surrounded by the Shawnee, who were bitterly opposed to any white presence in their

Covered bridge. (Courtesy of Parke County, Inc., Rockville, Indiana.)

lands, a policy supported by the British. Within a few years, Zeisberger and his little community of Christian Native Americans found themselves in a dangerous and untenable situation, surrounded by the hostile forces of three cultures—Native American, British, and colonial. He returned east with many of his converts in 1776.

But some of the Delaware stayed on the land, in a place the Moravians had named Gnadenhutten (which means "tents of grace"). In 1781, with the Shawnee raiding Pennsylvania and colonial militia retaliating throughout Ohio, the Delaware abandoned their imperiled settlement and moved west, to the Wyandotte country. Crops were poor in the new place, however, and in the winter of 1782 a group of Delaware returned to Gnadenhutten to see if they could salvage any food remaining in their former fields. While they were there, colonials searching for Shawnee found them instead. They disarmed and imprisoned the Delaware, who included women and children. The following morning they began to execute them. A total of 90 defenseless Native Americans, all of them Christian noncombatants, were slaughtered.

A church and cabin have been rebuilt as a memorial on the site of Gnadenhutten. A museum here contains Native American artifacts and relates the history of this terrible incident.

U.S. 36 runs through Port Washington, a stop on the Ohio and Erie Canal, which was extended through here in 1830. Still running along the Tuscarawas, the highway crosses Interstate 77 and enters Newcomerstown. This odd name is the echo of a love triangle from the 1750s. Mary Harris was a white woman captured in New England by Native American raiders and eventually married to a Delaware leader, Eagle Feather. She rose to a position of respect in the tribe. The place where she lived was in fact called White Woman's Village. But then her husband decided to take another wife, which ended the domestic tranquility. Harris resented the arrival of the woman, whom she referred to disdainfully as "the Newcomer." After weeks of acrimony, Eagle Feather was found murdered one morning and the Newcomer was gone. She was pursued to a Delaware village that then occupied the site of Newcomerstown, captured, and executed, although the evidence against her was slight and circumstantial. Mary Harris's scornful nickname for her rival in love lives on in this place. In later years, the town was famous as the birthplace of Cy Young, the greatest baseball pitcher in the nineteenth century and winner of the most games in major-league history—511.

Near the turnoff to Isleta, look for the road to the Old Stone Fort. Some local historians believe this is the oldest building standing in Ohio. The walls are almost two feet thick, and it was obviously intended as a defensive structure, but its exact date of construction is open to argument. Some sources date it as early as 1760, others as late as 1806.

Past the turnoff to West Lafayette, the road becomes a scenic drive. It ascends Hardscrabble Hill, with overlooks across the junction of the Tuscarawas and Muskingum Rivers. Coshocton lies at the meeting of these two rivers with the Walhonding. The town's name, in fact, means "river crossing." Coshocton is a small manufacturing center, boosting itself as the birthplace of specialty advertising. J. F. Meek opened a novelty plant here in 1887, and the town still turns out promotional doodads there.

Coshocton's brightest memories, however, are the years in which it was a port on the Ohio and Erie Canal. This waterway, which was completed in 1827 and ran from Portsmouth to Cleveland, transformed the economy of eastern Ohio. It brought the agricultural riches of the state to eastern markets and turned Cleveland into the leading port on the Great Lakes. The canal packets ran until the eve of the Civil War, carrying passengers and cargo at about 2 miles an hour.

Those canal days are re-created at Roscoe Village. Built along the actual route of the canal, in the northwestern part of town, the village is a living museum, with shops and craftspeople operating just as they would have in the 1830s. An inn and several restaurants in the village are housed in historic buildings, some of them original to the site. The Johnson-Humrickhouse Museum, which was moved here from another location in Coshocton, is noted for its displays of Native American basketry, Eskimo art, and oriental porcelains. Historic festivals are held at the village throughout the year, and visitors can ride aboard a horse-drawn canal boat, the *Monticello III*.

Now U.S. 36 follows the course of the Walhonding. The name means "ravine," and the stream flows through rugged canyons in rolling hill country. Near the town of Nellie is Mohawk Dam, which impounds the water of the Walhonding for flood control. There is a scenic overlook, worth a turnoff.

Gambier is just south of the highway, by way of the Ohio 308 turnoff. This is the home of Kenyon College, one of Ohio's finest liberal arts schools. With a population of just 2,000, there isn't much more to Gambier besides Kenyon. President Rutherford B. Hayes was an alumnus, and the college has been noted through its history as a training place for lawyers. Kenyon was founded in 1827 through the efforts of two British noblemen, Lord Gambier and Lord Kenyon. They intended to establish an Episcopal seminary, but the first building on the campus was built with such thick walls that a rumor spread that it was intended as a fort in a dark plan to reclaim Ohio for England. The two nobles left their names on the college and the town, but British claims never went any farther than that.

True to its billing, Mt. Vernon, named for George Washington's estate, sits on a hilltop. It also is seriously dedicated to preserving the colonial ambience of its Virginia namesake. Many of its well-kept old homes were built in Greek Revival style, popular in the South in colonial times; the Chamber of Commerce publishes a walking tour of them. The town's public buildings also were planned with a colonial look in mind.

But the town's Southern roots go deeper than its name. This was the birthplace of Daniel Decatur Emmett, the composer of "Dixie." He worked at the local newspaper before running off to join the army as a fife player and then to tour the country in minstrel shows. He wrote "Old Dan Tucker," and by 1859 Emmett was one of the best-known musicians in show business. That is when "Dixie" was written for Bryant's Minstrels as a "walk-around," a number during which the entire company paraded around the stage.

There are at least a dozen explanations as to how the word *Dixie* came to stand for the South. Some historians trace it to the Mason-Dixon line of 1767, which delineated the southern border of Pennsylvania. Others find its origin in a French coin, the dixe, or 10-cent piece, which circulated in Louisiana. One source tracks it all the way back to Manhattan Island and farmland owned by a Johaan Dixie. Historian J. C. Furnas claimed it didn't come into general usage until the bitter debate over the Missouri Compromise of 1820, when a term was sought to describe the slave-owning region as separate from the rest of the country. By the time Emmett wrote his song, the name Dixie was well established. Within two years, "Dixie" had been adopted as the official marching song of the Confederacy. But it was tremendously popular in the North, and as it was written it was intended to be sung by a Black freedman longing for the region of his birth. One of the best-loved Abraham Lincoln stories recalls that as a gesture of reconciliation the president asked the band at the celebration of the South's surrender to play "Dixie." Emmett never made much money from the song. He returned to Mt. Vernon, eking out a living by selling copies of his compositions. He died in 1904.

The topography flattens considerably as U.S. 36 approaches the center of the state (marked by passage through the town of Centerburg). The rugged hills that characterize eastern Ohio now give way to the level fields of the true Midwest. The highway widens to four lanes as it crosses the lake formed by the damming of Alum Creek. An active boating center, Alum Creek Lake also contains a state park, just north of the highway.

Delaware is another of the state's historic college towns. This one holds the campus of Ohio Wesleyan University, established in 1840 to educate the children of the state's Methodist ministers. Prior to that, Delaware was a spa. Mineral springs along the east side of the Olentangy River were developed, and a grand hotel, the Mansion House, was built in 1833 to put up the anticipated hordes of visitors. They never showed, though, and when Ohio Wesleyan opened, the hotel, renamed Elliot Hall, became its first classroom building. It still stands at the center of the campus. President Hayes, whom we met as a student at Kenyon College a few miles back, courted his future wife, Lucy Webb, when she was a coed here. According to local lore, he popped the question at the old sulphur spring. On campus, Gray Chapel, with its rare Klais organ, is worth a look.

We are running just beyond the northern suburbs of Columbus here, through countryside that still retains a rural appearance. The Japanese automaker Honda emphasizes that look in many of its ads. The town of Marysville was chosen for Honda's first American plant. The Accord, the most popular auto export manufactured in the United States, is made here. The town was named for the daughter of one of its first settlers, Samuel Culbertson.

At the center of Urbana is Monument Square, built around a sculpture of a Civil War veteran's homecoming. The sculpture was the work of local resident John Quincy Adams Ward, whose heroic civic pieces enjoyed a vogue in the late nineteenth century. One of them, *The Indian Hunter,* stood in New York City. A copy of it was used as his monument when Ward died in 1910 and was buried in Urbana's Oakdale Cemetery. It is on the south side of the highway.

The road crosses the Mad River, named for the swiftness of its descent into its valley. The name of the nearby town of St. Paris exemplifies the vagaries of naming communities in frontier days. The town's settlers wanted to call it Paris. (Naming new settlements after European capitals was taken as a sign of bold optimism.) But they were told that name was already taken in Ohio. So they tried New Paris. That was being used too. Finally, someone remembered that there had been a St. Paris. So the town settled on that, which is how a rather obscure fourth-century bishop wound up with a town being named after him in Ohio.

The site of Piqua, situated on the Great Miami River, was favored by Native Americans for centuries before the Europeans arrived. The fertile soil and strategic location made it close to ideal. The Miami believed that the first man of their nation arose from the ashes of a campfire here. The name Piqua means "risen out of ashes" and is a shortened form of the Native American name for the place, Pickawillany.

Pickawillany became a major trading center, a place where tribes could carry on commerce in peace. The Miami saw no reason why they could not extend such privileges to the British, whose traders began moving through this area in the 1750s. But that was dangerous policy in the years of European colonial rivalry. The French, who had been allies of the Miami, sent a punitive expedition from Detroit in 1752 to express their displeasure at this trade. They killed several tribal leaders and British traders. The disheartened Miami abandoned the spot and retreated into Indiana. But Pickawillany had so many natural advantages that the Shawnee too, migrating westward, settled here. Their alliance with Britain also proved disastrous. American forces under George Rogers Clark burned them out during the Revolutionary War in 1780.

Seventeen years later, the first white settlers arrived and called the place Washington. But in 1816 the Ohio legislature restored the name to a shortened version of that by which it was known to the Miami and Shawnee. Piqua became the country's leading producer of linseed oil, which was carried by flatboat down the Great Miami to the Ohio and then to market in New Orleans. When the Miami and Erie Canal arrived in 1836, connecting Piqua to Toledo and the Great Lakes, it became a prosperous port and industrial center.

The Piqua Historical Area recaptures a portion of the town's greatest eras. The Indian Museum displays artifacts of the tribes who inhabited Pickawillany in the eighteenth century. There is a working farm of the 1820s, with demonstrations of crafts and historic implements. Canal boat rides along the actual bed of the old Miami and Erie waterway are given aboard the *Gen'l Harrison.*

Resuming the westward drive on U.S. 36, look for the turnoff to

Bear's Mill, an operating 1849 flour mill along Greenville Creek, near the town of Gettysburg.

Greenville stands on the site of a fort built by Gen. Anthony Wayne at the start of his decisive campaign of 1793–94 against the Native American alliance (see U.S. 24). This is where Wayne trained his troops for the rigors ahead. The stockade was named for his former comrade-in-arms in the Revolutionary War, Gen. Nathaniel Greene. After defeating Little Turtle at the Battle of Fallen Timbers in August 1794, Wayne returned to Fort Greenville to await offers of peace from his shattered opponents. In June 1795, delegations from the various tribes arrived here to sign a treaty that, in effect, opened northern Ohio to American settlement and drove the British out of Michigan. The place at which the treaty was signed is marked by a memorial in front of Greenville's civic building.

While Wayne's frontier troops were known for their marksmanship, they couldn't compare with Greenville's best-known daughter. This was the hometown of Annie Oakley, who became an American heroine while touring with Buffalo Bill's Wild West Show from 1875 to 1901. Her rivalry and romance with Frank Butler was the basis of the musical show *Annie, Get Your Gun.* Her surefire aim, often performed while on horseback, was legendary, and it astonished audiences in America and Europe, since accuracy with firearms was thought to be a male preserve. Her trick of shooting playing cards several times as they fluttered through the air was so well known that complimentary passes, which were perforated in advance, came to be known as "Annie Oakleys." After suffering career-ending injuries in a train wreck, she returned to Greenville and lived here until her death in 1926.

This was also the birthplace of journalist Lowell Thomas. He was the narrator for Fox Movietone News throughout the 1930s and the writer who first broke the story of the exploits of Lawrence of Arabia during World War I. Personal articles belonging to both Oakley and Thomas are displayed in the town's Garst Museum, which is housed in a historic railroad inn built in 1852.

Another reminder of the late eighteenth-century Native American wars lies just south of the highway, on Ohio 121, at Fort Jefferson. This outpost was built by Wayne's unfortunate predecessor, Gen. Arthur St. Clair, in 1791. Moving north from his base in Cincinnati, St. Clair put up a string of forts to mark his progress north. Fort Jefferson was occupied for a brief time, and then St. Clair moved on to the next outpost, Fort Recovery. There he was ambushed by Little Turtle, and his forces were annihilated. He had to seek refuge back at Fort Jefferson to save what was left of his shattered command. The site is now a park, with markers explaining the significance of the fort's remains.

U.S. 36 enters Indiana and, at the old railroad town of Lynn, passes just north of the state's highest point, an elevation of 1,257 feet. A few miles beyond is the turnoff to the birthplace of a man who made it up far higher than that. Wilbur Wright was the son of a traveling minister—later a bishop—of the United Brethren Church. He and two older brothers were born near the town of Mooreland in 1867. His younger brother, Orville, came along after the family had moved on to Dayton, Ohio. While running a bicycle shop in that Ohio city, the Wrights began working on the ideas that led to the first flight of a motor-driven aircraft, in 1903. Each man made two flights on that historic December day, at Kitty Hawk, North Carolina. Orville was at the controls for the first flight, and Wilbur made the longest one, a trip of 852 feet that lasted 59 seconds. Shared credit marked their entire collaboration, one's ideas advanced by the other so seamlessly that it was impossible to say where any concept had originated. But with the 1903 tests, the brothers knew that they had solved all the major problems with powered flight—all that remained was refinement. Wilbur saw relatively little of the revolution in travel he helped bring about. He died of typhus in 1912. But Orville survived until 1948, long enough to witness all the uses, in trade and war, to which his invention would be put. The Wright homestead here has been reconstructed and furnished with pieces appropriate to the period.

Back at the start of this drive, in Gnadenhutten, we saw one of the darkest chapters in Native American history. In the town of Pendleton is a reminder of the time when justice slowly began to right itself. In 1823, three white men were arrested and tried for the murder of nine members of the Miami tribe. This was only a decade after Native American warfare had swept across Indiana, and most residents of this town had firsthand recollections of the fighting. But early the next year, the judgment of the court was carried out when the men convicted of the crime were hanged. It is believed to be the first time in American history that whites were executed for murdering Native Americans. A memorial marks the place in Falls Park, on Pendleton Ave., beside the cascade that gives the park its name.

The highway now dips south through Fortville, named not for a frontier stockade but for its founder, Cephas Fort.

As the highway nears Indianapolis, watch for the Post Rd. turnoff, and follow it west to Fifty-sixth St. for a short side trip to an actual fort—Benjamin Harrison. This U.S. Army base was established in 1903 and contains one of the more offbeat military museums in the country. The U.S. Army Finance Corps Museum traces the development of currency and military scrip issued by federal forces, from the American Revolution to the Persian Gulf War. There are also exhibits of military money issued by enemies and allies of America. It is a fascinating lesson in one of the lesser known functions of the military.

Continue west on Fifty-sixth St. to Interstate 465. The original route of U.S. 36 through Indianapolis is hopelessly obscured by a tangle of freeway construction and new roads, so the best way out is to simply take the beltway, southbound Interstate 465, to westbound Interstate 70. This highway runs through the central part of the city. Exit at northbound Holt Ave., which will lead you to westbound Rockville Rd. and the continuation of U.S. 36.

The old road now resumes its accustomed position as a rural highway running north of U.S. 40. Its route parallels that of the old Cleveland, Cincinnati, Chicago, and St. Louis Railroad as it heads west from Indianapolis. Once past Danville, the highway narrows to two lanes, running through level farmland. Beyond Morton it crosses Cecil M. Harden Lake, a major recreation area created by the damming of Raccoon Creek. The reservoir lies just over the Parke County line. Among Indiana's counties, Parke may not be quite as celebrated for its scenery as Brown. But among fanciers of covered bridges, it is the very top of the line.

A Closer Look. In the American popular mind, covered bridges are associated most closely with New England. In all probability, they did originate there. In that part of the country, familiarity with the principles of shipbuilding would have been an invaluable aid to the construction of these bridges. In recent years, however, the covered bridges of the Midwest have moved to the forefront. The best-seller *The Bridges of Madison County,* used Iowa's covered bridges as a plot device. But Parke

County has the most intensive concentration of these bridges in the country, a total of 32.

The legendary "kissing bridges" of romantic lore actually served a far more utilitarian function than their nickname suggests. The covered top protected the planking on the road from the wear of rain and snow. The covering evolved from basic solutions to bridge-building problems. It was discovered that trusses raised perpendicular to the roadway strengthened the bridge. But the trusses were subject to wind pressure in winter storms, so that the roadway became uneven. To solve this problem, transverse braces were added. Once they were in place, it was a simple matter to add the roofing, much like raising a miniature barn. By the eighteenth century covered bridges were a familiar part of the roadway in the Northeast and Pennsylvania. As settlers from these states moved west, they brought the style of bridge with them.

It wasn't until the mid–twentieth century that the people of Parke County began to appreciate their bridges as attractions. Even then, the authoritative WPA Guide to Indiana, which was published in 1940 and hardly misses a landmark or a view, briefly mentions only one covered bridge as an attraction in the area. Now Rockville's annual Covered Bridge Festival, held on the second weekend of October, has become the signature of Parke County. To really enjoy the bridges as they should be seen, though, I strongly recommend that you make your visit at any time other than the festival. The narrow county roads become so crowded on that weekend, and parking so difficult at the major bridges, that a lot of the fun turns into frustration.

U.S. 36 runs right through the heart of Rockville, the county seat. Just east of town is Billie Creek Village, an early twentieth-century community, assembled from historic structures brought here from all over the county. It is a living museum, a re-creation of a farm town your grandparents may have known, with crafts, a museum, and mule-drawn wagon rides. Three of the county's covered bridges are located here— Leatherwood Station, Beeson, and Billie Creek, which is the oldest, dating from 1895. All three are of the Burr arch type. This laminated wooden arch was developed by Pennsylvania architect Theodore Burr, who used it in 1815 to build the country's longest covered bridge, extending 360 feet across the Susquehanna River, in Pennsylvania.

Two of the county's most picturesque bridges are southeast of

Rockville, in the towns of Mansfield and Bridgeton. Take Indiana 59 south from the town of Bellmore to reach Mansfield. This is an old mill town, and the gristmill here, dating from the 1820s, is a national historic landmark. Just a few yards away is the 247-foot-long covered bridge built across Big Raccoon Creek in 1867. Adjacent buildings in the village have been turned into shops.

Even more spectacular, and a bit more remote, is the covered bridge at Bridgeton. From Mansfield, continue south on Indiana 59 to westbound County Road 720S, and follow the signs. En route you will pass the Conley's Ford Bridge, built with white pine in 1907. Bridgeton itself has been declared a national historic district, and the double-span bridge there is perched atop a dam and gristmill. Both the Mansfield and Bridgeton bridges were designed by local architect Joseph J. Daniels.

Return to Rockville along County Road 80E, which will take you past three more bridges, including the oldest in the county, Crooks Bridge, dating from 1855. The Parke County Convention and Visitors Bureau, housed in an old rail depot on the eastern edge of Rockville, has maps and directions for suggested scenic drives to all the covered bridges.

U.S. 36 resumes its run west, passing through Montezuma, an old canal town on the east bank of the Wabash River. The place was named by early settlers who were convinced that the large Native American encampment they saw here was somehow related to the Aztec Empire. The old Wabash and Erie Canal bed, built through here in 1848, is still visible.

There is still one more stop to make, after the highway crosses the Wabash and just before it enters Illinois. The town of Dana was the birthplace of America's most celebrated war correspondent, Ernie Pyle. His dispatches from the battlefields of World War II for the Scripps-Howard newspapers perfectly captured the outlook of the ordinary soldier in the front lines. They made Pyle as much a hero as the men he wrote about. One of the few reporters brave and resourceful enough to get to these hot spots, he was acutely conscious of his role as a voice of the guys who were doing the fighting. Other correspondents stayed behind and talked to the generals. Pyle was in the trenches. He adopted a fatalistic attitude toward the risk, always assuming that he would not come out of it alive. Showered with awards and honors, he was given the option of changing assignments when the focus of the war shifted to the Pacific. But he insisted on being sent there and was killed by a sniper during the battle for the island of Ie Shima, in April 1945. "No man in this war better told the story of the American fighting man the way the American fighting man wanted it told," said President Harry Truman in tribute. The farmhouse in which Pyle was born, in 1900, is filled with family memorabilia and exhibits relating to his journalism career.

VISITING HOURS

Gnadenhutten

Gnadenhutten State Monument, 1 mile south of town. (614) 254–4143. Monday to Saturday, 10–5, and Sunday, 12–5, June–Labor Day. Weekends only, Labor Day–October. Donation.

Coshocton

Roscoe Village, north of town, on U.S. 36, at its junction with Ohio 16 and 83. (614) 622–9310. Daily, 10–6. $6. Canal boat rides are given daily, 1–5, Memorial Day–Labor Day, but on weekends only in May and Labor Day–mid-October; fare is $4.50.

Johnson-Humrickhouse Museum, in Roscoe Village. (614) 622–8710. Daily, 12–5, May–October. Tuesday to Sunday, 1–4:30, rest of year. Donation.

Delaware

Gray Chapel, at Ohio Wesleyan University, on Sandusky St. (614) 369–4431. Times vary. Free.

Piqua

Piqua Historical Area, north of town, on Ohio 66. (513) 773–2522. Wednesday to Saturday, 9:30–5, and Sunday, 12–5, Memorial Day–Labor Day. Weekends only, Labor Day–October. $4 (includes canal boat ride).

Gettysburg

Bear's Mill, south on Arcanum–Bear's Mill Rd. (513) 548–5112. Saturday, 9–5, and Sunday, 11–5. Donation.

Greenville

Garst Museum, at 205 N. Broadway. (513) 548–5250. Tuesday to Sunday, 1–4:30. Closed in January. Donation.

Fort Jefferson State Memorial, south on Ohio 121. (614) 297–2300. Daily, dawn to dusk. Free.

Mooreland

Wilbur Wright State Memorial, south of U.S. 36 on a county road marked "Millville." (317) 332–2513. Monday to Saturday, 9–12 and 1–5, and Sunday, 1–5, April–October. Closed Monday and Tuesday at other times. $3.

Indianapolis

U.S. Army Finance Corps Museum, in Fort Benjamin Harrison, Bldg. 1, at Post Rd. and Fifty-sixth St. (317) 542–2169. Monday to Friday, 8–4:30. Free.

Rockville

Billie Creek Village, east on U.S. 36. (317) 569–3430. Daily, 11–4, except Christmas week. $3.50.

Dana

Ernie Pyle State Historic Site, north on Indiana 71. (317) 665–3633. Tuesday to Saturday, 9–5, Sunday, 1–5. Free.

U.S. 41

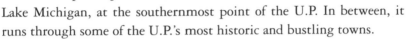

Copper Harbor, Michigan, to Menominee, Michigan

U.S. 41 is the perfect Upper Peninsula sampler. It runs from Michigan's most remote mainland community, at the tip of a spectacular Lake Superior peninsula, to the shores of Lake Michigan, at the southernmost point of the U.P. In between, it runs through some of the U.P.'s most historic and bustling towns.

U.S. 41 is an important north-south road in the old federal system. It was the main stem from Chicago to Miami, and most of its route now is made up of freeways and passages through big cities. But you'd never guess that from its quiet beginnings in Michigan.

When songwriters wrote the song "Let's Get Away from It All," they must have been thinking of Copper Harbor. This is truly the end of the road, hundreds of miles from any place that even resembles a city. It is almost 600 miles from here to Detroit, the metropolis with which it shares a state but little else. The Keweenaw Peninsula, on whose edge it sits, is arguably the most beautiful piece of land in the Midwest. Surrounded by Lake Superior and rimmed by green hills, it is as magnificent as any place between the Appalachians and the Rockies.

But what lay under the land determined its fate. The Keweenaw is copper country, the site of the biggest and richest strike in American history, during the 1840s. They found gold in California during the same decade. But more miners rushed to Michigan to strike it rich than ever made the trip to the California diggings. For a brief time, Copper Harbor was the main port of shipment from the mines. When reports of the copper strikes came in, Congress hurriedly concluded a treaty with the Ojibwa, who still had title to this land. To make sure the peace was kept, Washington also sent a garrison of 105 men from the U.S. Fifth

Copper Harbor. (Courtesy the *Detroit* News.)

Infantry in 1844. They built Fort Wilkins (named after the secretary of war), just outside the port.

The Native Americans were mostly indifferent, and any damage done to the miners was inflicted primarily by other miners. So the soldiers didn't stay long. Within two years, war with Mexico had broken out, and the garrison was withdrawn to fight there. After the Civil War, the War Department, as if suddenly recalling that it owned a fort way up here, sent in more troops. But they were recalled in 1870, after just three years. The only enemies they ever faced were cold and boredom. The fort never fired a shot in battle, and in 1923 it was acquired by the state as a historic recreation area.

Twelve buildings at Fort Wilkins, including the officers quarters, have been restored and contain displays on what life was like at this far northern outpost. Costumed guides are on the grounds in summer to talk about its brief history. There are also splendid seasonal displays of wildflowers here.

Copper Harbor itself is a tiny place, whose population swells with summer vacationers then drops to under 100 during the long, snowy winter. It is the closest jumping-off point in Michigan for boat trips to Isle Royale National Park in Lake Superior. The island is actually much closer to Minnesota and Ontario. But during the peace talks following the Revolutionary War, American negotiators, alerted to the possibilities of massive copper deposits on the island, insisted on its inclusion on their side of the border. The British wearily gave in, sighing that if they didn't, "they'll be wanting Ireland next." As it turned out, the Native American copper workings there were ancient and minimal. But the island has been maintained as one of the country's great natural habitats for northern wildlife.

Just outside of Copper Harbor is the entrance to Brockway Mountain Dr. This is regularly voted the most scenic drive in Michigan, if not the entire Great Lakes region. It climbs to a height of more than 700 feet and features several turnoffs with breathtaking views over the lake and harbor. Try to make the trip just before sunset if possible, when the light across the water is a sight you will remember always.

Stay on the drive for its entire 10-mile length. It joins Michigan 26 at the lakeshore. This road is a scenic alternative to U.S. 41, which runs down the center of the peninsula.

Eagle Harbor was another old copper port, developed in 1845 by the mining company of the same name. There is a photogenic old lighthouse here, built in 1851, as well as a marker to Justus H. Rathbone, a local teacher who wrote the ceremony adopted as the official ritual of the fraternal group the Knights of Pythias.

Eagle River, a bit farther down the shore, is the county seat of Keweenaw County. Its courthouse is the oldest in Michigan, and since the business transacted there is minimal, it doesn't get much wear. The town also has a monument to Douglass Houghton, an amateur geologist. His survey in 1840 was the first to indicate the scope of copper deposits in this area. He was drowned off Eagle River five years later, when his canoe was caught in a sudden storm during another surveying trip.

From here, Michigan 26 curls back to rejoin U.S. 41 at Phoenix. This was the site of the second oldest mine in the Keweenaw, opened in 1845. But the mine was never one of the major producers, closing temporarily in 1905 and permanently, after years of working with a skeleton crew, in 1936.

At Cliff, the next town, was the oldest and one of the richest mines in copper country. Its vein of almost pure copper touched off the great mining rush to the area in 1844 and brought in major investors from New England. The success of the Cliff Mine proved that there was big money to be made here. While it was only an outcropping of the primary vein and was played out by 1880, the Cliff made possible all that happened here later.

One deserted mining camp after another, named for the companies who operated them, line the road all the way into the community that sat atop the mother lode, Calumet.

A Closer Look. Everything that occurred in the copper country before 1864 was only a prelude to the success at Calumet. By that time, mining had been established for 20 years in the Upper Peninsula. But the taking of copper from this ground was far older than that. Copper artifacts found in the mounds of the Hopewell Culture in Ohio (see U.S. 35 and U.S. 50) have been traced to Native American diggings in this region. Tales of boulders made of solid copper had fascinated French explorers as far back as the early seventeenth century. They sent several expeditions to western Lake Superior, trying to find it. When the British took over the area, they, too, got the copper bug. A book written in 1770 by Jonathan Carver caused a sensation in London when it repeated all the old copper legends, and a syndicate was formed to exploit the wealth. But while some prehistoric diggings were uncovered, the major vein still eluded the searchers.

All this was almost forgotten by 1837, when Michigan received the Upper Peninsula as a consolation prize for giving up its claims to Toledo. This distant country, as remote then as the moon, was regarded disdainfully as a bad bargain by the rest of the state. But Douglass Houghton, a Detroit physician, was convinced that he had seen evidence of copper there on a mapping expedition in 1830. Although he was not trained as a geologist, Houghton convinced the governor to grant him $3,000 to conduct mineral surveys. Houghton issued his report in

1840, and it was a sensation. Deliberately understating his find so as not to cause a stampede, Houghton described taking two tons of ore with a single dynamite blast and finding copper masses of up to 40 pounds. More than that, he had located the legendary copper boulder, on the Ontonagon River.

The boulder, which weighed two tons, eventually was taken to Washington, D.C., and displayed at the Smithsonian Institution. It was headline news across the country, and once more excited investors began looking to this far corner of Michigan. In 1844, the first major mine, the Cliff, came in, and the rush was on in earnest. Five hundred shares in the Cliff, offered for $9,000 when the mine opened, would return $255,000 in dividends in 14 years. By the start of the Civil War, Michigan was producing 15 million pounds of copper a year, almost 90 percent of the national total. Then Detroit investor Edwin Hulbert struck the vein that would become the Calumet and Hecla Mine.

For the next 50 years, this was the capital of the copper kingdom. Wealth beyond anything imagined by Jonathan Carver, or even Douglass Houghton, rolled out of here. The mine paid $200 million in dividends, 57 percent of all the dividends paid by all the copper mines in Michigan. The Calumet and Hecla and its branches mined almost 50 percent of all the copper taken from the U.P. The district around Calumet swelled into a city of almost 60,000 people by 1900. Its opera house was a showplace. Its downtown streets were the first in all of Michigan to be paved. Each ethnic group competed to build the most elaborate churches. The greatest financial institutions in America opened offices here.

Then it ended. The returns from the Calumet and Hecla began dwindling. New copper strikes in Montana and Arizona shifted the center of the industry to the West. A bitter and violent strike in 1913 resulted in the shutdown of some mines. From an annual production of 266 million pounds, the total dwindled over the next 30 years to 43 million, less than 4 percent of the national figure. The mine finally closed in 1968. By that time, only small shifts still worked there. Area population had fallen to barely 1,500 full-time residents. A way of life had ended. "King Copper" was dead.

But its ghost is fairly lively. Calumet refused to disappear. The old Calumet and Hecla company offices have been turned into a museum of the industry, Coppertown U.S.A. The main business area of the Calumet district, which was known as Red Jacket, has revived and become a showcase of the city that was thriving here in 1900. Older people who once moved away to find work have come back home to retire, which is keeping the population constant and returning a measure of prosperity to the town.

The Coppertown complex is on U.S. 41, at the southern end of Calumet. The company offices have been left just as they were when the owners walked away for good, after 104 years of operation. Museum exhibits show the evolution of mining equipment and represent the incredible assortment of ethnic groups who flocked here from all over the globe to look for copper. The complex also features a simulation of a mine entrance, which will give you a sense of the dark and dangerous conditions the miners faced daily.

The Red Jacket business district begins just two blocks from Coppertown. In its heyday, this was essentially a company town, the largest in America. Calumet and Hecla controlled most aspects of community life. It was, in general, a benevolent employer, providing amenities that were not available within hundreds of miles at that time. But as financial pressures grew and militant unions demanded a greater share of the profits, the good feelings ended in bitterness and, eventually, tragedy.

The steeple of Ste. Anne's Church, which served the town's French Canadians, guards the entrance to downtown. Its soaring Gothic lines and exterior of red sandstone (the material used for most of the U.P.'s finest buildings) make a stirring gateway into town. The church was built in 1900. Like four of the five Catholic churches that once functioned here, Ste. Anne's has been deconsecrated and is now privately owned.

From the church, walk one block west to Sixth St. and then turn right. This was the main business street of the old town. So many of its structures, built to serve a community 40 times this size, look oddly out of place, misproportioned in the village that exists here now. The two sandstone buildings at Scott St., with businesses on the ground floor and apartments upstairs, were put up in 1898 as a matching set. Even then they were regarded as pretentious, and deliberately so. They were built to impress visitors and show off the wealth of this northern metropolis.

Two blocks up, at the corner of Oak St., is the old Vertin Brothers

Department Store. At its opening in 1899, it was the largest commercial emporium north of Detroit, and not even many there could challenge it. The repetitious rows of windows on the upper floors make a powerful visual statement. The bank buildings at this intersection were also completed in the same year.

The next block, between Oak and Elm Sts., was the heart of Red Jacket. Now filled with tenants who sell copper souvenirs and rely on the tourist trade, it was once the civic center. The main attraction remains as it was. The building that served first as a town hall and then was remodeled as an opera house in 1898 was Calumet's pride. The greatest stars of the American stage and opera were brought here, at incredible expense. Here Caruso sang, Houdini made his escapes, Lillian Russell looked glamorous, and John Philip Sousa led his band. As the town declined, the theater shifted to showing movies and then closed completely. Fully restored to its rococo splendor and reopened in 1976, the old opera house now mounts a schedule of live productions, except during the winter months. It is also open for tours.

The fire station across the street is another of the town's monuments. It hasn't answered a fire bell in 50 years and now rents its space for a variety of uses, including storing scenery used at the opera house.

Turn left on Elm and walk one block to Seventh. Near the northwestern corner is the site of Calumet's greatest disaster, a vicious tragedy that tore the town apart. During a bitter strike in 1913, the miners and their families gathered in the Italian Hall at this spot for a Christmas Eve celebration. At the height of the party, with the building jammed with women and children, someone shouted "Fire." In the ensuing panic, people were trapped in narrow halls and stairwells, and 72 were trampled to death or suffocated. The union's later accusation that company spies were involved was never proven, and no one was ever prosecuted for the deaths. Woody Guthrie wrote a ballad about the incident, "Copper Country 1913 Massacre." The building was torn down in 1984 as a safety hazard.

Now walk back to Fifth St and turn right. This was Red Jacket's financial district, and many of the imposing structures, dating from the 1890s, are still used as banks. Look, especially, at the Detroit and Northern offices, at 330 Fifth. This is one of the oldest buildings on the street, built in 1888 as a candy store. D&N took it over 92 years later, imported historic fixtures from old banks around the area, and turned it into a contemporary version of a nineteenth-century bank. The company was honored with a state restoration award for its work. At the end of Fifth St. is the turn back to Coppertown and the start of this walk.

Just to the east of U.S. 41 is another of the Calumet communities, the town of Laurium. At the entrance to its center is a small fountain and memorial to the town's most famous son and greatest athlete, George Gipp. He was already in his twenties when a Notre Dame recruiter visited Gipp here and persuaded him to play for the school. He was locally celebrated as a gifted athlete who excelled at everything, from pool to baseball. But when Knute Rockne saw his speed and power, he immediately made him a football player. As Notre Dame's tailback in 1917–20, Gipp set records that stood for 50 years, and in 1919 and 1920 his team went undefeated. After his death from pneumonia in his senior year, Rockne called him the greatest athlete he had ever coached. Gipp was returned to his hometown for burial, but the story, of course, lived on. According to most accounts, it was during halftime of the 1928 Army game that Rockne gave the famous "Win one for the Gipper" speech to his trailing team, insisting that it was Gipp's dying wish. It has become college football's most famous moment, and because of it Gipp is remembered decades after his contemporaries faded into obscurity. Gipp's persona eventually blended completely with that of President Ronald Reagan, who portrayed him in a 1940 movie and used the "Gipper" reference repeatedly in his political career.

U.S. 41 now continues to the base of the Keweenaw. Just north of Hancock is the entrance to the Quincy Mine (the names of the town and mine reveal the Massachusetts origins of the major investors). The mine was nicknamed "Old Reliable" because from its opening in 1867 until 1921 it never missed paying a dividend. But the ore also was found at ever deeper levels and was more difficult to extract. The solution to this problem can be seen at the mine. The Quincy steam hoist was the marvel of the industry. Designed by engineer Bruno Nordberg in 1920, this 60-foot-high machine was capable of raising 10 tons of ore to the surface at a rate of 40 miles an hour from more than a mile below the earth. But the very necessity of running this behemoth was an indication of the Quincy's problem. The hoist operated for only 11 years, and the mine closed for good in 1944. But at Shaft Number 2, this technical wonder is still in place. Be sure to take in the view of the Hancock-Houghton area from the grounds of this hillside mine.

Copper Country drew immigrants from across Europe. In Hancock, they were predominantly from Finland and Cornwall. The Finns remain a major cultural presence here, and Suomi College, opened in 1896 by the Finnish Evangelical Lutheran Church, is the only such institution of its nationality in the country. The Cornish bequeathed to the U.P. a treat called the pasty. This well-seasoned meat pie was taken underground by the miners as a filling midday meal. It is now a staple of local restaurants, who outdo each other in claims for the originality and scrumptiousness of their recipes.

The twin towns of Hancock and Houghton were laid out by a pair of mine owners on either side of Portage Lake, which narrows to the width of a river here and defines the southern end of the Keweenaw. A canal was cut through in 1873, making the towns the leading copper ports in the state. Houghton's waterfront is still a bustling place, and its main thoroughfare, Sheldon St., is lined with fine nineteenth-century buildings. It is about the only flat street in town, the rest of Houghton being built on a range of hills. It is now essentially a college town. Michigan Technological University was founded in 1885 for the pressing local need of training mining engineers, and it is still a leader in that field. It is east of downtown, on U.S. 41. An exceptional display of copper ores and unusual minerals found in the area is in the school's Seaman Mineral Museum, in the Electrical Energy Resources Center.

The road runs south from Houghton along the shore of Portage Lake, which widens into Keweenaw Bay, in Lake Superior. This is a beautiful drive, placing the sparkling waters of the big lake on your left. Near the town of Keweenaw Bay, you can look across the inlet to the ruined towers of Pequaming. This was a company town built by Henry Ford in 1923 as a processing point for his mining and timber interests in the area. It was abandoned in the 1940s, but the deserted old works make an evocative picture.

At Assinins, you are entering the home ground of Bishop Frederic Baraga. A remarkable figure in the nineteenth-century U.P., he was called the Snowshoe Priest for his tireless work ministering to Native Americans in this vast wilderness. Baraga, who was born in Austria and, according to some accounts, had Hapsburg relatives, arrived here in

1843. For the next 25 years, he refused reassignment, compiling an Ojibwa dictionary and establishing several missions among the Native Americans. Assinis was the first of them, dating from the year of his arrival. Just beyond the town of Baraga, at the southern end of Keweenaw Bay, there is a shrine to the bishop, with a statue and meditation garden overlooking the water.

Past L'Anse (the name of which means "the bay"), the road heads south, away from the lake. To the east are the Huron Mountains, the highest range in the state, amid some of Michigan's wildest country. Mt. Arvon, at an elevation of 1,979 feet, is the highest point in Michigan— although no one will swear to that. For several years, the high point was thought to be the summit of Mt. Curwood, at 1,980 feet. But a resurvey of the area in the 1980s showed that Curwood's height had been overestimated, and Arvon emerged as the new champion. The area can only be approached on foot.

Alberta is another town founded by Ford, an experimental self-sufficient community set up in 1936. It now has a just a handful of residents.

The road turns east, through the forests at the southern edge of the Huron Range. When it reaches Michigamme, on the lake of the same name at the Marquette County line, it passes from copper to iron country. This metal's history stretches back almost as far as copper in U.P. lore. The first find was made in November 1844, just as the Cliff Mine was starting up in the Keweenaw. William Burt was a government surveyor working in this largely uncharted area. Reaching a hillock about 25 miles east of here, Burt found that his magnetic compass refused to respond. It was being deflected by 87 degrees. He thought that someone had placed an ax handle too close to the instrument, but when he found that was not the case, he started digging into the soil with his boot. He found outcroppings of iron.

America's steel industry was then in its vigorous youth in the Ohio Valley, but there were concerns that the country was running out of iron deposits. When news of Burt's find reached southern Michigan, Philo Everett, a resident of Jackson, immediately embarked for the area. In the spring of 1845, he hit the vein that became the Jackson Iron Co., the first of the major U.P. mines. So for the second time in five years, the rush was on for metallic riches. The Michigamme Mine closed in 1905, after producing nearly one million tons of ore, and the area is now resort country. Van Riper State Park, near the eastern end of the lake, has a beach and picnic facilities.

Champion is another of the old iron towns. It had a population of 2,500 when its mine closed in 1910. Residents now register only in double figures.

U.S. 41 continues east, into the town of Ishpeming. One of the most populous places in the iron range (it has 7,500 residents, down from a peak of 10,000), Ishpeming's name means "high place" in Ojibwa, and it is so named because it is situated on the divide between lakes Superior and Michigan. While iron made the town, it was the ironworkers who gave Ishpeming its distinct flavor. The Cleveland-Cliffs Co., owner of Ishpeming's biggest mine, concentrated on recruiting labor in northern Europe, figuring that only the heartiest could stand up to the U.P. winters. So Ishpeming became a strongly Norwegian community.

One of the newcomers was Carl Tellefsen, who immigrated here in 1888 to work in a local bank. The previous year, a group of his countrymen who missed their favorite sport had organized America's first ski-jumping competition here at nearby Suicide Hill. Tellefsen, a top jumper in his old hometown of Trondheim, immediately took over leadership of the local club and began making plans for a regional association of ski jumpers. This was the first version of the sport to enter the United States. Downhill skiing didn't become popular until the 1930s, when instructors from Austria began to move to America.

In 1904, Tellefsen's United States Ski Association held its first national tournament in Ishpeming. Special trains ran up from the major cities of the Midwest, and the meet received countrywide attention—or, at least, the attention of that part of the country in which it snowed. The association eventually moved to Denver when that city became the center of downhill skiing. But the sport's Hall of Fame was placed here in 1954, at its roots. The Hall of Fame embraces all forms of the sport, but its warmest memories are reserved for the jumpers, who still make the U.P. their particular province. There are displays on the evolution of equipment, an old lift car, grooming equipment, and mementos of the greatest figures in the sport. Suicide Hill remains in use, at the eastern end of Ishpeming, with five jumping runs in operation.

It was near Negaunee that Philo Everett made the find that became the Jackson Mine. The town grew up around the workings. The memorial to that discovery sits right in the middle of town, in Jackson Park, on Iron St. It is a 12-foot pyramid of iron ore blocks.

There is still some open-pit mining going on at sites on the Marquette Range, but iron has pretty much joined copper in the U.P. history books. The Michigan Iron Industry Museum, just south of Negaunee, recounts the colorful story of its mining here. There are historic exhibits, audiovisual displays, and an original hauling locomotive from the Jackson Mine.

It was 12 miles from Negaunee to the ore docks in Marquette. Each of those miles was an ordeal for the early mine owners. They used sled dogs for the first few winters, then mule carts. A plank road was finally laid down in 1855, over the route now followed by U.S. 41, and two years later the railroad was built. But the greatest advance, which also came in 1857, was completion of the first locks in the canal at Sault Ste. Marie. Before that, all ore shipments had to be unloaded to pass around the rapids of the St. Marys River and then put on another set of ships for transport to the industrial centers of the lower Great Lakes. When the U.S. Congress debated funding for the canal, there were hoots of derision on the floor of the House. Even as astute a man as Henry Clay said he could find no reason to support such a remote project. But the completion of the canal at the Soo helped transform America into an industrial giant, with an assured steady supply of steel.

The trip to the Soo began in Marquette, the port that was created in 1849 to serve the iron range. Its ore docks, at the western end of town, are still an incredible sight, even though the flow now is only a trickle of what it was. The adjoining Presque Isle Park is a beautiful place from which to watch a Lake Superior sunset or take a quick dip in the chilly waters. The Maritime Museum, on the lakefront near downtown, recounts Marquette's great days as a nineteenth-century port, with historical displays on both the ore freighters and the fishing craft that sailed from here.

This is now the largest city in the Upper Peninsula, with a population of 23,000. It is the home of Northern Michigan University, founded in 1899 and situated on a modern campus in the western end of town. Many of the state's regional administrative facilities are located here, making it Michigan's unofficial second capital. The U.S. Olympic

Committee also maintains a training facility on the Northern Michigan campus, one of three in the country. It is located under a huge wooden dome, at the Great Lakes Sports Training Center.

From Marquette, U.S. 41 runs briefly east along the Lake Superior shoreline, then begins to angle south for its long continental run in that direction. It passes through lightly populated forestland, following the West Branch of the Whitefish River between Kiva and Trenary. Then it heads due south to its junction with U.S. 2, on Lake Michigan's Little Bay de Noc, at Rapid River. U.S. 41 and U.S. 2 then proceed together from Rapid River to Escanaba (for a description of this portion of the route, see U.S. 2).

From Escanaba, U.S. 41 continues west with U.S. 2 for a distance of 22 miles before dropping south to Menominee. To take a much more scenic route, follow Michigan 35 south from Escanaba to Menominee. It gets you to the same place but runs along the western shore of Green Bay, which makes the drive much nicer.

Ford River was once a shipping port for lumber but is now the start of a resort district that stretches south along the lakefront. Just a few miles south of town is a pleasant turnoff with a view across the bay to the Garden Peninsula.

Cedar River is renowned as a fishing port, and right outside of town is J. W. Wells State Park, with a beach and other water recreation facilities on the bay.

The southernmost beach in the U.P. is in Henes Park, just north of the city limits of Menominee. The Door Peninsula of Wisconsin is directly opposite the park, and the enclosed waters here may be marginally more temperate than Green Bay's usually frigid conditions.

Menominee is the Ojibwa word for "wild rice," one of the food staples of that tribe. It was so important an item in their way of life that cities are called by that name in every state in the northern Great Lakes region. Michigan's town by that name is the oldest, dating from 1797, when a fur trader opened a post here. But lumber built the town. By the late nineteenth century, it was the greatest port for white pine in the world. In recent years, Menominee has become a diversified city of light industries and, as you might expect from its proximity to Wisconsin, a leading producer of milk and cheese. The city has restored its old waterfront district, which runs along First St. between Fourth Ave. and

Tenth. Many of the buildings here were erected at the peak of the lumbering boom of the 1890s and are now filled with specialty shops. Across the road is the marina and city park, with waterfront views and fine recreational facilities.

U.S. 41 has rejoined us here and crosses the bridge over the Menominee River to Marinette, Wisconsin. Midway in the stream is Stephenson Island. This is properly part of Wisconsin, but the Historical Logging Museum in the island park is part of the history of Menominee too. It makes a logical final stop on this trip down U.S. 41.

VISITING HOURS

Copper Harbor

Fort Wilkins, east of town. (906) 289–4215. Daily, dawn to dusk, mid-May–mid-October. $3.50.

Calumet

Coppertown, U.S.A., south of town. (906) 337–4354. Monday to Saturday, 10–6, mid-June–mid-October. $2.

Calumet Theatre, at Sixth and Elm Sts. (906) 337–2610. Monday to Thursday, 10–4, Friday, 10–1, and weekends, 12–4, Memorial Day–mid-September. $1.50.

Hancock

Quincy Mine, north of town. (906) 482–3101. Daily, 9:30–5, mid-June–Labor Day. $3.50.

Houghton

Seaman Mineral Museum, east of town, on the campus of Michigan Technological University. (906) 487–2572. Monday to Friday, 9–4:30. Also Saturday, 12–4, July–October. Free.

Baraga

Bishop Baraga Shrine, south of town. (906) 524–7021. Daily, dawn to dusk. Donation.

Ishpeming

National Ski Hall of Fame and Museum, on U.S. 41, at Second St. (906) 485–6232. Daily, 10–5. $3.

Negaunee

Michigan Iron Industry Museum, south on Maas St. (906) 475–7857. Daily, 9:30–4:30, May–October. Free.

Marquette

Maritime Museum, downtown, on Lakeshore Dr. (906) 226–2006. Daily, 10–5, June–September. $2.

Menominee

Historical Logging Museum, on Stephenson Island (Marinette, Wisconsin). (715) 732–0831. Daily, 10–4:30, Memorial Day–September. $1.

George Rogers Clark Memorial. (Photo by Richard Frear.)

U.S. 50

Belpre, Ohio, to Vincennes, Indiana

Four of the transcontinental roads of the old federal system run across Ohio and Indiana. U.S. 20 is described earlier in this book. The routes of U.S. 30 and 40 are so taken up by freeways that it is pointless to embark on them on the sort of back road trip that we are considering here. U.S. 50 is the best of all of them.

The highway once ran from Ocean City, Maryland, to San Francisco, and it still makes it as far as Sacramento before giving up its route to an interstate. Through Ohio and Indiana, it is fairly untouched by freeways and remains a very pleasant road through historic towns and scenic hill country.

U.S. 50 enters Ohio from West Virginia at the town of Belpre (see Ohio 7). It climbs from the river valley as a four-lane road, before narrowing to two lanes and winding through hills into the valley of the Little Hocking. The original Native American name for that river was something like Hockhocking, which was how George Washington referred to it on his trip through this area in 1770. But over time the first syllable was dropped and the meaning, "above there is land," became obscured. It refers, apparently, to fertile lands lying upstream.

This was once coal country, although most of the mines shut down 60 years ago or earlier. The chief industry around here now is education, centered in Athens, the seat of Ohio University. The Northwest Ordinance directed the Ohio Territory to provide for education, and it was a charge taken quite seriously by the leaders of the Ohio Co. Marietta College grew out of an academy chartered in the town of Marietta in 1798, but Ohio University was the first school organized specifically for higher education. In 1800 the site was surveyed personally by Gen. Rufus Putnam, one of the Ohio Co. founders, and its earliest buildings were named for Manasseh Cutler, chief agent for the company. Its doors opened in 1804. It now has an enrollment of about 17,000 students. The campus is built in Georgian style, and red-brick walks angle across its center. Many of the elms there were planted by William Holmes McGuffey, author of the famous McGuffey Readers, who was president of the school from 1839 to 1843. The area adjoining the campus, around Union and Court Sts., is known as Uptown Athens. It has preserved its historic texture, with narrow streets and offbeat college shops in an authentic nineteenth-century setting.

Just outside of town is the Dairy Barn. Once part of a farm, it is now a major regional arts and crafts center. Internationally recognized exhibits are scheduled throughout the year. It is open only when shows are in progress.

The stretch of road west of Athens is called the Appalachian Highway, and as it angles through the valley of Raccoon Creek, the scenery is very similar to the vistas in those mountains. This is the sort of wild, isolated country associated more with West Virginia than with Ohio. It makes for an especially scenic drive as the road twists its way through the wooded hills. Many of the people who live here originally came from Appalachia in the nineteenth century. Attracted by local industries, they settled in for good, even after the industries died away. Part of the area is now state forest, much of it rehabilitated from overcutting in the 1930s.

McArthur was named for a governor of the state, Duncan McArthur. Past this small county seat the road enters Wayne National Forest, another scenic stretch of highway. Beyond Londonderry, the landscape gradually softens. Here you will see livestock in the fields and crops being grown. But the view from the road is of rolling terrain all the way into the old state capital of Chillicothe.

This was the most important city in Ohio when the nineteenth century began. The seat of government for the Northwest Territory was transferred here from Marietta in 1803. When statehood came in a few months later, it remained the capital, but only for seven more years. Nonetheless, those years left their mark on Chillicothe.

The place was settled by Virginians, who gave the town a look of Southern graciousness. Adena, one of the showplaces of Ohio, was built in 1807 by civic leader and future governor Thomas Worthington. The mansion was built in the Georgian style that Worthington recalled from his youth in the South. Its designer was British architect Benjamin Latrobe, who planned much of early Washington, D.C. Soon to be included there was the reconstructed U.S. Capitol, after it was burned down by Latrobe's compatriots in 1814. Adena was a place pointed out with pride to visitors, and the view of nearby Mt. Logan from its terrace is reproduced on the Ohio state seal.

Worthington, the leader of the statehood party, was bitterly opposed by territorial governor Arthur St. Clair. This was a political fight, with St. Clair, a diehard Federalist, unwilling to permit a new state with a Democratic majority to enter the Union. But when his home was besieged by indignant mobs and President Thomas Jefferson strongly sided with the statehood faction, the battle was lost. Ohio became the first state carved from the former Northwest Territory. The Ross County Historical Museum, one of the best regional facilities in the state, exhibits many items relating to those rowdy days, as well as less turbulent times in Chillicothe's past.

The *Chillicothe Gazette,* the oldest continuously published newspaper in the Northwest, dates from 1800 and is housed in a replica of Ohio's first state house. In its lobby are exhibits on the history of printing.

The road goes through more lovely hill scenery as it heads west from Chillicothe. We are now entering the heart of Hopewell country, the land of the ancient culture that built most of the mounds in southern Ohio. No one knows what they called themselves. Hopewell was the name of the family who owned the farm on which the first of their mounds was scientifically excavated in 1846. The mounds on the Hopewell property were repeatedly dug into. Although the Hopewell name has been attached to the entire culture, the mounds on the Hopewell property were never restored. (For a description of the Hopewell Culture National Historical Park, north of Chillicothe, see U.S. 35.) There is a marker on the site of the Hopewell farm, about 5 miles west of Chillicothe.

Seip Mound, however, has been returned to an approximation of its original appearance. It, too, was named for the family on whose property it rested. Seip was among the largest of the Hopewell mounds, measuring 30 feet in height, 150 feet in width, and 250 feet in length. During its excavation, between 1926 and 1928, a tremendous trove of pearls was found in the mound. Newspapers headlined the find with the words "Great Pearl Burial" and publicized the place as a royal tomb. A 28-pound ceremonial axe was also taken from the mound, and the area became nicknamed "Valley of the Kings," the name being used in the Egyptian excavations going on at the same time. When an accidental cave-in at Seip almost killed the chief archaeologist, the parallel with Egypt and the fabled curses of its tombs was complete in the public mind. But nothing especially untoward has happened at Seip Mound in the years since.

Bainbridge, a hill-enclosed town just west of the mound, is regarded as the birthplace of American dentistry. A professional school was established here in 1826 by Dr. John Harris. Its first generation of graduates are regarded as the first truly skilled dentists in the country. Until late in the nineteenth century, dentistry was still regarded, especially in the West, as a craft somewhat akin to carpentry. Licensing boards finally managed to limit entry into the field and elevated it to the status of professional practice.

Seven Caves, a group of limestone caverns formed by an underground branch of Rocky Fork Creek, are just west of Bainbridge. A walking tour of the formations and subterranean waterfalls takes about 90 minutes. The trail is mostly paved, with handrails provided for the climbs. Still, it is a moderately strenuous trip.

U.S. 50 continues its run through rolling farmland, through the Highland County seat of Hillsboro. At Fayetteville, the highway joins the Little Miami River and runs alongside it for the next several miles, through Vera Cruz and Marathon, two villages named by settlers who were keen students of battlefields. Heading straight west, it reaches the East Fork of the Little Miami on the outskirts of Cincinnati.

The city was a magnet for German immigrants in the nineteenth century. Among the first German communities in the area was a settlement along the Little Miami. Established in 1798, it was called New Germany, and the first paper mill in the state was started there. It is located west of Milford and north on Ohio 126. The Christian Waldschmidt House, built in 1804, has been maintained on the site of the town and is furnished in period style. The house also contains a small museum of a Civil War training base that was situated in the area, Camp Ross.

The suburb of Mariemont was planned in the 1920s as a model community. Named after landowner Marie Emery, the place was laid out on terraces above the Little Miami, and U.S. 50 passes through its center as a landscaped boulevard. Every so often, the bells of the Mariemont Tower, situated in a Gothic structure above the town, ring out with a selection of favorite tunes.

U.S. 50 swoops into Cincinnati as the Columbia Parkway and proceeds along a rise above the Ohio River, with several of the city's parks on the right. It passes through the downtown area as a freeway, gliding by the bridges to Kentucky and Riverfront Stadium, home of the Reds. Finally, it emerges as the Sixth Street Expressway and heads west, still paralleling the river, which is seldom out of sight.

At North Bend, one of the state's oldest towns, is the memorial to a member of the Ohio dynasty of U.S. presidents. The Harrison family is more closely associated with Indiana; Benjamin Harrison, who was elected for one term in 1888, entered political life after establishing a legal career in Indianapolis. But he was born in North Bend, and his grandfather, William Henry Harrison, is buried here.

The elder Harrison rose to fame as governor of the Indiana Territory and as the military leader who defeated the Native American confederacy at the Battle of Tippecanoe in 1811 (see U.S. 231). He is also tied to one of Indiana's old territorial capitals, Vincennes, which we will reach in a few more miles. After the War of 1812, Harrison, a native of Virginia, bought property in North Bend and retired to Ohio, though not for long. He was elected to Congress in 1816 and to the U.S. Senate 10 years later, to fill out an unexpired term.

Unwise investments and entanglements in foreign politics seemed to end his public career. He retired to North Bend, with the only job offered him being clerk in the common pleas court. But odd things happened. The Whig Party was reluctant to run a presidential candidate in 1836 against Martin Van Buren, successor to the tremendously popular Andrew Jackson. Henry Clay, the party's most forceful figure but already a two-time loser in the presidential race, decided to sit this one out, figuring Van Buren was unbeatable. So the party leadership hit on the novel plan of running four candidates, each from a different region of the country, in hopes of throwing the election into the House for a decision. To his utter astonishment, Harrison was chosen in the West. The scheme failed, but Harrison ran a surprisingly strong race. Cheered as a war hero, he even gave Van Buren a scare in New York. Although the Whigs privately mocked him as an ignoramus, they could not ignore his appeal.

The financial collapse of 1837 made Van Buren vulnerable in the next election. This time Clay wanted the nomination, but the political bosses in the East felt he could not run strongly enough in their part of the country to win. Remembering Harrison's showing, they again turned to him in 1840. Through intricate maneuvering at the national convention, the bosses got Harrison the nomination over an embittered Clay. "My friends are not worth the powder and shot it would take to kill them," Clay said on learning the news. Harrison swamped Van Buren in the election.

But the 67-year-old president-elect was overwhelmed by office seekers when he arrived in Washington for his inauguration, and the weather turned foul as well. He developed a chest cold during the ceremonies, his condition steadily worsened into pneumonia, and exactly 31 days after assuming office, Harrison passed away. It was the briefest presidential term in history and the first time that a sitting vice president was called on to assume the top office. Harrison's body was returned to North Bend for burial, behind a 75-foot-high sandstone shaft overlooking the Ohio River. Adjoining the Harrison State Memorial is the Congress Green Cemetery, where Harrison's wife and son (the father of Benjamin) are buried. Also buried here is John Cleves Symmes, who owned thousands of acres in the area and founded the towns of North Bend and Cleves.

U.S. 50 heads into Indiana and turns back again toward the Ohio River, into Lawrenceburg. This was once a bustling port, such a high-rolling place that in 1819 Jesse Hunt built a three-story brick inn and tavern on the river. The area around it was known as Gamblers' Row and was regarded as the most wide-open vice district north of New Orleans. The building was a marvel of its time, the first brick structure of that height in the Northwest. It still stands at the foot of Walnut St.

By the time Rev. Henry Ward Beecher arrived in Lawrenceburg, things had calmed down considerably. The famed cleric, brother of novelist Harriet Beecher Stowe, received his first pastorate at the Presbyterian church here in 1837. The original church was replaced by another on the same site in 1882, but the congregation remembered its most famous minister. The new church was called the Beecher Presbyterian Church, and it still stands on Short St.

The town was founded in 1801, and just eight years later the first whiskey distillery opened. That remains one of Lawrenceburg's leading industries. The Seagrams distillery, which offers tours of its plant, was actually a latecomer. It moved here in 1933, after the repeal of Prohibition, when operations rich enough to have survived bought up the idle plants of the area's former distilleries. The building now occupied by Seagrams made alcohol-based solvent in the 1920s. Now, along with the nearby Schenley distillery, it carries on the local tradition. The mansion of one of the industry pioneers is a few blocks north of the Seagrams distillery, on Ridge Ave. William P. Squibb founded his company in 1868, and 10 years later he built Acorn Hall. The Italianate landmark is in private hands but can be seen from the road. His business was taken over by Schenley in 1933.

Aurora, the next river town on the road, faces east. So it was named for the Roman goddess of the dawn by its classically educated founder, Judge Jesse Holman. The place is laid out on a hillside and is one of the more atmospheric river towns in the state. Hillforest, the mansion built for industrialist Thomas Gaff in 1852, is a steamboat Gothic masterpiece, its fantastic wood carvings giving it the look of a fairy-tale confection above the Ohio. It has been restored to its pre–Civil War appearance.

U.S. 50 leaves the river and roars off into the Indiana hinterland as a four-laner, narrowing to two lanes near the town of Elrod.

You will pass many houses of worship along this road, but none quite so striking as Versailles' Tyson Memorial Church. It was built by a local lad who went off and got rich in the chain drugstore business in Chicago. James H. Tyson returned in 1937 to leave this legacy to his hometown. The church, built as a memorial to his mother, combines various elements of traditional European architecture—from British to Byzantine—expressed with contemporary materials. It has a cast-aluminum spire and a concrete exterior. The heavenly constellations in the interior dome are supposed to represent the position of the stars at Mrs. Tyson's death.

North Vernon grew up as an adjunct to the older community of Vernon, established in 1816. But when the Baltimore and Ohio Railroad came through, along the route of U.S. 50, the newer town got the depot and most subsequent growth. It now has 15 times as many people as the older town. However, the entire town of Vernon is a national historic district, a nicely preserved slice of small-town life from the mid–nineteenth century. There are no big sights here, but it is a good place to walk around and soak up the look of another era.

H. Vance Swope left his hometown of Seymour for New York to become a much-admired artist in the early years of this century. He died at the age of 47, in 1926, but Seymour remembers him. Two years after his death, an art gallery was built here to display many of his best works, as well as those of fellow Indianan T. C. Steele (see Indiana 135).

One of the prime beauty spots in this part of the state is south of U.S. 50 at Brownstown, by way of Indiana 39. Skyline Dr., part of Jackson-Washington State Forest, looks out over miles of wooded hills in a Hoosier panorama that looks as if it comes right off a picture calendar.

Indiana limestone built some of America's greatest landmarks: the Empire State Building, Rockefeller Center, and much of the federal Triangle in Washington, D.C. Museums and skyscrapers all across the country are adorned with this material, and much of it was taken from the ground near Bedford. The limestone from the quarries here is especially prized for its uniformity of composition, fluidity, and strength. It is called oolitic limestone because its granular structure reminded geologists of tiny bird eggs. The state was aware of the vast limestone beds by 1839, but not until after the Civil War was a rail network developed enough to ship the stone to markets. Many of the quarries may be seen from area roads, especially north of town on Indiana 37. There are displays of local limestone, as well as historical exhibits, in the Lawrence County Historical Museum, in Bedford's courthouse.

Just west of Bedford is Bluespring Caverns, which visitors can explore by cruising in boats on an underground river. Filled with sightless fish and strange rock formations, this cave tour, one of the Midwest's eeriest, is worth the trip below ground.

Now the hill country becomes even more rugged, as the highway cuts across corners of Hoosier National Forest and Martin State Forest.

The town of Shoals was built at a shallow ford of the White River. West of town, fantastic rock towers, known as Jug Rock and the Pinnacle, loom over the highway. The Pinnacle offers visitors a fine view across the river valley and its high bluffs. You can also take a short side trip along Indiana 450 to the village of Dover Hill, which perches high atop one of these bluffs, about 150 feet above the river. Fabulous tales of Native American treasures buried in the caves below the bluffs abound in this area. But like the Lost Dutchman mine, none were ever found.

Loogootee's mellifluous name is a combination of last names; Lowe, after an early railroad engineer in the area, and Gootee, after the owner of the land.

Montgomery is notable chiefly because it was almost the site of Notre Dame University. The college's founder, Fr. Edward Sorin, was rector of the local church. Convinced that the state needed a great Catholic center of higher learning, he planned to build it here. Instead, the bishop of Vincennes turned over land owned by the Church on a lake near South Bend.

The route of U.S. 50 now parallels the old stage road from Vincennes to Louisville, as well as the Buffalo Trace, the road followed by the Lincoln family on their way to Illinois. These were two of the most important overland passages of Indiana's early days. The road runs through the old railroad town of Washington, which dates to 1817, crosses the West Fork of the White River, and heads straight into the Revolutionary battlefield and territorial capital of Vincennes.

A Closer Look. The streets of this old town have seen their share of drama and blood. Hundreds of miles from the eastern seaboard, it was a critical battleground of the Revolutionary War. It was an outpost of French culture on the banks of the Wabash, the home of brilliant religious leaders who brought a life of intellect to the Western wilderness. It was the incubation ground of a future president. Vincennes remembers them all.

It is a small city of about 20,000 people today, a good way removed from history's center stage. When Illinois split off from the Indiana Territory and the territorial capital moved to Corydon in 1813, Vincennes' days as a seat of government were over. But even then it was an old city by frontier standards.

There is evidence that French explorers reached this site in the 1680s. Under the direction of Robert Cavalier, sieur de La Salle, it had become colonial policy to establish a chain of forts across the Indiana frontier, to protect the fur trade from British incursions and hostile tribes. So there are reports of a fort, and even a church, in this area very early in the eighteenth century. But the date of permanent settlement is given as 1732—the year of George Washington's birth. The town was named for the first commanding officer of the stockade, Francois Morgane de Vincennes, after he was killed by the Chickasaw four years later.

The remote outpost was considered part of Louisiana and fell outside the treaty ending the French and Indian War. Nonetheless, French troops were withdrawn, and civil authority disintegrated. The lively little French community descended into lawlessness, becoming a wild fur-trading outpost. With the outbreak of the Revolutionary War, though, Britain recognized the strategic value of the place. Troops sent down from Detroit in 1777 used it as a base to harass colonial settlements in Kentucky.

The situation intrigued a young man who represented Kentucky in the Virginia legislature. George Rogers Clark had heard that Vincennes and the British fort at Kaskaskia, near St. Louis, were undermanned and vulnerable. He persuaded the state government to support an attack on them and detach the area from British control. His militia unit surprised Kaskaskia on July 4, 1778. After winning the confidence of Fr. Pierre Gibaut, leader of the French community there, they set off for Vincennes. At Gibaut's insistence, the French in the town capitulated immediately, relinquishing Vincennes to the colonies.

But Britain was not prepared to give it up that easily. Henry Hamilton, cursed on the frontier as the "hair-buyer of Detroit" for his policy of paying for American scalps, recaptured the town in December. Warned by a French-Italian trader, Francis Vigo, who made the dangerous trip to Kaskaskia in a lone canoe, Clark returned to Vincennes. Surrounded by frozen prairie and icy streams, Hamilton never expected an attack. But Clark, sloshing across the ice with his force of 170 men, surprised the town in late February 1779. Hamilton was forced to surrender—this time for keeps—and for all intents and purposes the British threat to the West was over.

So was Clark's career. His younger brother, William, would go on to glory as coleader of the Lewis and Clark Expedition through the western kingdom that the older Clark had only approached. But George Rogers Clark was a better fighter than an administrator, and under his command, the territory once again degenerated into lawless chaos. Virginia was so dismayed by the situation that it ceded the whole region to the United States, preparing the way for creation of the Northwest Territory in 1787.

Drive into Vincennes along U.S. 50 and leave your car near the George Rogers Clark Memorial. It overlooks the Wabash just south of the bridge, at the foot of Barnett St. The round building, surrounded by Doric columns, was dedicated to Clark in 1936. It contains a statue of the military leader and murals of other notable Virginians of the time, including the governor who gave Clark his commission, Patrick Henry. The visitors center explains the significance of Clark's accomplishments and also shows a short film on the taking of Vincennes.

Next to the memorial, overlooking the river, is a statue of Vigo. He was memorialized with the statue, and a nearby county was named for him. But it took until his grandchildren's time before Congress approved a monetary reward for his act of heroism.

Just to the north of the memorial are French Vincennes' proudest monuments. The Old Cathedral, built in 1826, rises on the site of the first log church in the original settlement. In its belfry is the Liberty Bell of the Northwest. According to local legend, it was rung when Fr. Gibault called the French inhabitants to swear an oath of allegiance to the United States, in 1778. Although it is no longer a cathedral—Vincennes having been merged into the Indianapolis Diocese—the St. Francis Xavier Church still serves the oldest parish in Indiana.

In the adjacent cemetery are the graves of some of the town's earliest French residents, dating back to 1741. The Cathedral Library, behind the Old Cathedral, was assembled by Vincenne's first bishop, Simon Brute de Remur. It contains thousands of rare volumes relating to the history of the Catholic Church in France and America and is the oldest library in Indiana. The library building itself was finished in 1843 by Bishop Brute's successor.

Other markers in the cathedral area locate the original building of the College of Vincennes, founded by Bishop Brute in 1837 to educate young men for the priesthood, and still operating elsewhere in town as Vincennes University, a community college. There is also the traditional site of the home of "Alice of Old Vincennes." She was the heroine of a historic novel by Maurice Thompson that was a best-seller in 1900. Thompson, a native of Vincennes, was later a friend and neighbor of Lew Wallace, author of *Ben-Hur*, in the town of Crawfordsville (see U.S. 231).

Now walk north along Second St. Just past Main St. is the Old State Bank. This Greek Revival building, the oldest bank structure in Indiana, opened in 1838 and operated here for 39 years. It is now a state memorial and an art gallery, with exhibits by local painters.

Go one block west to First St. and continue walking north, across the railroad tracks, to the Indiana Territory Capitol at Vincennes State Historic Site. From this little wooden building, an area larger than the original 13 states was governed. The Indiana Territory covered the existing states of Indiana, Illinois, Michigan, and Wisconsin, as well as part of Minnesota. Built as a residence in 1800, the capitol was converted into a legislative and administrative headquarters by Gov. William Henry Harrison. The building fell into disuse after the government moved in 1813, but many of the original furnishings, including desks and benches, were saved. When the capitol was restored in 1919 it was again filled with these priceless items.

Adjoining the capitol is the print shop of Elihu Stout, who began publishing the *Indiana Gazette* here in 1804. The printing press on display was the first in the Northwest Territory. Also on the grounds is the birthplace of writer Maurice Thompson. The house dates from 1842, and Thompson came along two years later.

South of the capitol, at Park and Scott Sts., is Grouseland, the official residence of Gov. Harrison. This was the first brick building in Indiana at its construction in 1803. It was modeled on the gracious Georgian homes Harrison recalled from his youth in Tidewater Virginia. But it was built for strength as well as for domesticity, with many defensive features more in line with a fortress than a house. The home has been restored to its appearance at the time of Harrison's residence. From here he planned the campaign against Tecumseh and the Battle of Tippecanoe in 1811 (see U.S. 231), the engagement that led Harrison to the White House 29 years later. The Treaty of Grouseland, by which hostilities against the Indiana tribes ended, was signed in his chambers here. From the grounds, you can watch traffic heading west into Illinois on the U.S. 50 Bridge.

VISITING HOURS

Athens

The Dairy Barn, north on Ohio 682. (614) 592–4981. Open during shows, Tuesday to Sunday, 11–5. $3.

Chillicothe

Adena, west on Ohio 104. (614) 772–1500. Wednesday to Saturday, 9:30–5, and Sunday, 12–5, Memorial Day–Labor Day. Weekends only, Labor Day–October. $4.

Ross County Historical Museum, at 45 W. Fifth St. (614) 772–1936. Tuesday to Sunday, 1–5, April–November. Weekends only, rest of year. $2.

Chillicothe Gazette, at 50 W. Main St. (614) 773–2111. Monday to Friday, 8–5. Free.

Seip Mound State Memorial, on U.S. 50. (614) 297–2630. Daily, dawn to dusk. Free.

Bainbridge

Seven Caves, west on U.S. 50. (513) 365–1283. Daily, 8 to dusk. $7.

Lawrenceburg

Seagrams Tours, north of U.S. 50, on Main St. (812) 537–0700. Monday to Friday, at 10:30 and 1. Reservation required. Free.

Aurora

Hillforest, at 213 Fifth St. (812) 926–0087. Tuesday to Sunday, 1–5, April–December 23. $3.50.

Bedford

Lawrence County Historical Museum, on Courthouse Square, in the basement of the courthouse. (812) 275–4493. Monday to Friday, 9–11 and 1–4. Free.

Bluespring Caverns, west on U.S. 50. (812) 279–9471. Daily, 9–6, May–September. Weekends only, April and October. $7.

Vincennes

George Rogers Clark Memorial, south of U.S. 50 Bridge. (812) 882–1776. Daily, 9–5. $2.

Old Cathedral, on Second and Church Sts. (812) 882–5638. Daily, 7–4. Donation.

Cathedral Library, behind the Old Cathedral. (812) 882–5638. Daily, 11–4, May–August. 50¢.

Old State Bank, 112 N. Second St. (812) 882–7422. Wednesday to Sunday, 1–4, mid-March–October. Donation.

Indiana Territory Capitol at Vincennes State Historic Site, at First and Harrison Sts. (812) 882–7472. Wednesday to Saturday, 9–5, and Sunday, 1–5, mid-March–December. Donation.

Grouseland, at Park and Scott Sts. (812) 882–2096. Daily, 9–5, March–December. Daily, 11–4, rest of year. $3.

U.S. 52

Burlington, Ohio, to Finly, Indiana

U.S. 52 cuts a diagonal across the eastern half of the country, running from the balmy South Carolina coast to the frigid plains of North Dakota. It follows that same northwestern course through Ohio and Indiana.

After U.S. 52 crosses the Ohio River at Huntington, West Virginia, it becomes the River Road, one of the great historic highways in the region, following the north bank of the Ohio all the way to Cincinnati. From there it again strikes off due northwest, across Indiana. En route are outstanding scenery, historic river and canal towns, and the birthplace of a president. Four-laned and freeway for a portion of the trip, U.S. 52 is still one of the best of the old roads.

The green hills of Ohio were the symbol of freedom for the slaves who gazed across the river from Virginia and Kentucky. While the number of slaves in these states wasn't nearly as high as it was in the Deep South, the system still operated in all its cruelty on the far side of the river. The town of Burlington, the first community in Ohio on this road, was founded by a clergyman from Ceredo, West Virginia (which was then Virginia), as a place for freed slaves to live. He bought the land and resettled his own former slaves on it.

The name of South Point is something of a misnomer, because Burlington actually is the southernmost community in Ohio. From South Point, though, you can see where the Big Sandy River, which forms the border between Kentucky and West Virginia, flows into the Ohio. We are at the edge of the Wayne National Forest here, and as you ride along the shoulder of its wooded hills, the Kentucky city of Ashland comes into view across the water.

These were nineteenth-century industrial cities through here. You

The *Ben Franklin III* on the Whitewater Canal. (Photo by Deb Alvey.)

can tell by the names, Coal Grove followed by Ironton. Both coal and iron were once sources of immense wealth in this area. Ironton is still a coal producer, but its iron industry shut down in the 1920s. The city was founded by an ironmaster, John Campbell, in 1848, about 20 years after ore was discovered in the surrounding hills. The Vesuvius Furnace, one of the first in Ohio, was built 10 miles north of here—you can still see the remains of its chimney near Ohio 93. Ironton shipped its iron throughout the East on the three major rail lines that converged here, one of which was that of the Detroit, Toledo, and Ironton Railroad. Many of the heavy guns used by the North in the Civil War were made from iron mined here. The ore deposits gave out shortly after the war, and Ironton now is a varied manufacturing center, with Allied Signal as its biggest employer.

The old town of Hanging Rock, built on an outcropping above the river, is barely visible from the freeway that passes by the area, replacing the narrow road that wound tortuously along the cliffside.

You can hear another echo of the iron era as you pass Franklin Furnace. It was the home of one of 40 iron furnaces concentrated in this part of Ohio during the peak of the industry's strength. Just north of town is Greenup Lock and Dam, with fine views from the observation building on the Kentucky side of the bridge.

New England money financed much of the industrial growth of this area. You may have noticed that just off the highway a few miles back was a sign for Haverhill, another old iron town funded from Massachusetts. Just ahead is New Boston, which is where the money came from to establish that industrial community. New Boston is now completely surrounded by the bustling city of Portsmouth—the largest town on the Ohio side of the river, aside from Cincinnati.

Portsmouth was built on high ground, where the Scioto flows into the Ohio, by a Virginia land speculator. Because of its river connections, it quickly developed into a thriving port, and in 1832 it also became the southern terminus of the Ohio and Erie Canal. You can still see the riches that flowed into the city in those years in the Boneyfiddle Historic District downtown, an area of well-kept nineteenth-century structures now filled with antique shops and boutiques. Portsmouth has been a leading brick-making center since 1865, and the quarrying of clay and flagstone still plays a part in the city's economy. This was also the hometown of Leonard Sly, who headed west to become a singing cowboy and changed his name to Roy Rogers. The Southern Ohio Museum and Cultural Center contains displays about Portsmouth's history, as well as art exhibits.

Once across the Scioto, U.S. 52 narrows to a two-lane road and winds along in leisurely accord with the Ohio. The Shawnee State Forest, one of the most thickly wooded areas in the state, begins near Friendship. The views across the river are splendid.

This is one of the most scenic portions of the River Road, and it was one of the most remote areas of Ohio until well into the twentieth century. A paved road wasn't cut through until 1931, and no railroad ever served these towns. They were vestiges of an earlier time, when people were totally dependent on the river for travel and communication. Just past the aptly named village of Buena Vista is a spot with a good view into Kentucky. Nathaniel Massie, the land speculator who founded Portsmouth and bought title to much of this land, was so fond of the vista that he built his own home nearby.

Massie also established the town of Manchester, in 1791. It claims to be the fourth oldest community in the state, and for many years it was an important steamboat stop. Moyer Vineyards now produces wine on the sunny slopes above the Ohio. It gives tours of its winery throughout the year.

Aberdeen grew up as a ferryboat landing at the southern terminus of Zane's Trace, the first overland route across Ohio. Opened in 1798, the road ran from Wheeling (in what was then called Virginia) to here, where it connected by ferry to Maysville, Kentucky. Parts of the trace were later incorporated into the National Road when it was extended across Ohio in 1825. But in the early years of statehood, it was Ohio's sole land connection with the East.

While Ohio's hills were a beacon to escaping slaves along this entire drive, nowhere did the light shine as brightly as in Ripley. On the heights above this old river town was the home of Rev. John Rankin, a Presbyterian clergyman who came to Ripley in 1825. A committed abolitionist, he deliberately sought out a place from which he could best provoke Southern authorities and be of greatest assistance to escaping slaves. He mounted a bright light on the bluffs, shining it into Kentucky as a guide for those trying to make their way to freedom under cover of night. For the next 35 years, he is credited with helping 2,000 slaves escape to the North, risking his own property and well-being in the effort. Under the terms of the Fugitive Slave Law, he could have lost his house for sheltering slaves, and many members of his congregation did not share his antislavery views. One of his most dramatic rescues involved a young woman who crossed the Ohio on ice floes while clutching her children in her arms. Rankin's friend, Harriet Beecher Stowe, incorporated the tale into the famed episode of Eliza on the ice in *Uncle Tom's Cabin*. The Rankin home was acquired by the state in 1938 and turned into a historic memorial. Guides in period dress show visitors through the house, which has been restored to its appearance of the 1840s.

The town of Ripley was severely damaged in the Ohio River floods of 1937. Its business section and the route of U.S. 52 had to be relocated on higher ground, away from their original sites. In recent years, Ripley has developed a lively antique and crafts business in old storefronts and in a former piano factory.

The villages in this area are all tiny places, lightly brushed by the years. Their remoteness is evidenced by the fact that there is no bridge across the Ohio River all the way to the outskirts of Cincinnati.

One of these places, Utopia, was once the site of an experiment in communal living. Started in 1844, it broke up after just two years, over the usual issues of personal freedom and individual differences. A group of Spiritualists then moved in, but apparently they were not well enough connected with the other side. They failed to get advance word of the flood of 1847, which inundated their buildings and drowned 17 of them.

All of these communities were devastated by the 1937 flood, the worst on record in the entire Ohio Valley. Many had to be relocated, and all vestiges of the old ports were swept away. In Neville, for example, two-thirds of its 61 houses were destroyed, and in Moscow the toll was half of 90 houses.

One of the buildings that did come through the flood was the birthplace of President Ulysses S. Grant. The military leader who would ignite the hillside beacons on the Ohio into the blaze that destroyed slavery was born in the town of Point Pleasant in 1822. His name at birth was Hiram Ulysses Grant, but the initials H. U. don't quite have the same ring as U. S. It was the army that made the mistake, though. The initials were written incorrectly on his original officer's commission.

The Grant family's stay in Point Pleasant wasn't long. Within a year the family had moved to the nearby community of Georgetown, where Grant attended school. His career is more closely bound to Illinois, where he was plucked from obscurity after leaving the army to enter the Civil War as a drillmaster for a local company. But his two terms as president, from 1869 to 1876, began a 55-year period in which seven men from Ohio held the highest office. His birthplace is now a state memorial.

Past Point Pleasant, U.S. 52 becomes four-lane again, in preparation for the onrush of suburban Cincinnati. It passes the old river port of New Richmond and River Downs Racetrack just before entering the city. It runs through parkland, across the Little Miami River, and becomes Eastern Ave. as it follows the Ohio toward downtown.

U.S. 52 becomes a freeway just east of downtown, then follows north-bound Interstate 75 and westbound Interstate 74. Just before the state line, it runs through the town of Harrison, named for yet another president with Ohio roots. Though William Henry Harrison was born in Virginia and rose to fame in Indiana, he retired to Ohio and then served the state as a congressman and senator. His grandson, Benjamin, was Ohio-born and became the twenty-third president. This town was named for the first presidential Harrison.

U.S. 52 breaks free of the interstate across the Indiana line and begins a northwestern course along the Whitewater River. This stream, which branches off from the Great Miami just north of its junction with the Ohio, brought the first wave of settlement into the interior of southern Indiana. Little Cedar Baptist Church, south of Brookville, one of the oldest churches in the state, was built by the new arrivals in 1812 and has changed little since that time. A churchyard, with graves antedating Indiana's statehood, adjoins the brick building.

Brookville is a town of about 2,500 people today and hardly looks the part of a political powerhouse. But Brookville men dominated state politics until 1840. Indiana's first two U.S. senators, its governors for 15 years, and every member of the state supreme court came from here. It was also the birthplace of author Lew Wallace (see U.S. 231), whose father was governor of the state in 1837–40.

Because of the political influence of the Brookville gang, one of the earliest public-works projects approved by Indiana was construction of the Whitewater Canal. It was a shortsighted venture that nearly bankrupted the state treasury. But it left some fascinating mementos in the town of Metamora.

A Closer Look. In October 1825, a small boat called the *Seneca Chief* pulled out of the turning basin at the western end of the Erie Canal. Crowds cheered. Politicians waved. Cannons went off all the way from Buffalo to New York City. No one had to tell the people who had come to witness this event that they were seeing history being made.

The Erie Canal took eight years and $7 million to complete. But it is surely no exaggeration to say that it transformed America. It connected the new Great Lakes states to the markets of the East Coast. It provided cheap and certain transportation to settlers bound for Michigan and Wisconsin. It turned New York into not only the largest city in the United States but a trade center for the world.

Other states watched and noted. If the Erie Canal could accomplish all that, surely, they reasoned, a canal would bring prosperity to them too. Nowhere did canal fever burn more avidly than in Ohio and Indiana. By the end of the decade, Ohio had opened the Ohio and Erie Canal, connecting Portsmouth to Cleveland, and was nearing completion of the Miami and Erie Canal, from Cincinnati to Toledo. Indiana started work on the Wabash and Erie Canal. Then in 1836 it passed the whopping Internal Improvements Bill, committing $13 million to transportation projects.

Most of the money went to the Wabash and Erie Canal. Work on that project would go on for 25 years and cost almost double the amount in the appropriations bill. But this was the period in which the town of Brookville was at the peak of its influence in the capital. Its heavy hitters made very sure that some of that money would come their way. By the end of 1838, work was completed on the Whitewater Canal, connecting the Ohio River, at Lawrenceburg, with Hagerstown, near the National Road. Unfortunately, eight months later the state went broke. The canal had bankrupted the treasury. Contractors' bills went unpaid, thousands of workers were thrown into unemployment, and bondholders found themselves with worthless paper. By 1840, Indiana was $13 million in debt. In the ensuing litigation, most of the canal system was turned over to private hands. But repeated flooding, caused by flawed engineering and a site-selection process that placed politics ahead of intelligence, made the Whitewater Canal untenable. The coming of the railroads completed its destruction as an economic force. By the Civil War, it was abandoned. Much of the Whitewater's towpath became a right-of-way for the Pennsylvania Railroad.

Metamora was one of the hopeful towns that sprung up along the canal's path. It was named for the leading character of a popular play based on the life of the Native American leader Metacomet, better remembered in history as King Philip. But its era of prosperity was brief, lasting only through the 1840s. The aqueduct that carried the canal across Duck Creek fell into disrepair. The railroad shut down its line. By the time Metamora reached its centennial, in 1938, only a few businesses remained open. Its population was down to 250, and the place seemed destined for oblivion.

Oddly enough, it was again some people from Brookville who turned things around. Alfred Brown and John P. Goodwin, two history-minded businessmen from that town, formed the Whitewater Canal Association, with the goal of restoring the aqueduct and canal. After World War II, Indiana agreed to commit funds for the projects and also for a gristmill at Metamora. A few businesses opened to take advantage of the historic setting. In 1964, a canal boat started making short trips through the area. Seven years later the Whitewater Valley Railroad began running sightseeing trains, originating in Connersville, along the old Pennsylvania Railroad tracks. By 1976 more than 100 businesses had opened in the little town, many of them in historic buildings that were restored on the site or moved from nearby locations.

Metamora today is a delightful place, with shops and restaurants clustered along both sides of the old canal and in the narrow alleys that lead to the waterway. The gristmill hums, there are bed and breakfasts in the heart of the village, and the scenic railroad makes its run. On peak weekends, the commercial spirit may even seem a bit intrusive. But remember that the history around you is largely authentic, and that the state of Indiana did go broke trying to build towns like this on its canals. The least you can do is stop by for a look.

U.S. 52 continues its run to the northwest and into Rushville, named for the physician who signed the Declaration of Independence, Benjamin Rush. This was the home of Gen. Pleasant Hackleman, whose log-cabin birthplace rests in the city park. The Civil War was not a good war for generals, partly because the selection process was frequently based on political or ethnic concerns rather than competence. Lincoln elevated Alexander Schimmelfennig to that rank because his name was obviously German and the president felt he could use some help with voters in that group. He died of malaria. Felix Zollicoffer was a Confederate general who was so nearsighted that he rode out ahead of his troops and began shouting orders at a mounted Union officer. The officer shot Zollicoffer dead. In all, 18 percent of Southern generals were killed in the course of the war, while 8 percent of the Northern officers of that rank died in combat. Hackleman was one of them, the only one from Indiana.

There is confusion ahead in a town called Carrollton. Or is it Finly? No one seems sure. Many of the signs in the place declare that you are in Carrollton, but the post office officially bears the name Finly. Just to muddy the situation even more, the Baltimore and Ohio Railroad decided to call its station here Reedville and that's how its timetables listed it for several years. This situation has existed for quite a while. James Whitcomb Riley wrote a poem about the place, "The Little Town o' Tailholt," which described how the confused citizenry simply referred to their place of residence as Tailholt since no one in authority seemed to be able to decide on what its name really was. Since we do not know where we are, it seems like a good place to end this ride on U.S. 52, before we really get lost.

VISITING HOURS

Portsmouth

Southern Ohio Museum and Cultural Center, at 825 Gallia St. (614) 354–5629. Tuesday to Friday, 10–5, and weekends, 1–5. $1.

Ripley

John Rankin House State Memorial, off U.S. 52, at the western edge of town. (513) 392–1627. Wednesday to Sunday, 12–5, Memorial Day–Labor Day. Weekends only, Labor Day–October. $1.

Metamora

Whitewater Canal State Memorial, just off U.S. 52. (317) 647–6512. Daily, dawn to dusk. Free, but charge for parking varies. The gristmill is open Wednesday to Saturday, 9–5, and Sunday, 1–5, mid-March–December; admission is free. Canal boat rides are given Wednesday to Friday, 12–4, and weekends, 11–4, May–October; fare is $2.

Whitewater Valley Railroad round-trips, begin in Connersville, 18 miles north of Metamora on Indiana 121. (317) 825–2054. Schedule varies through the year. Call ahead for information. $11.

Rushville

Hackleman Log Cabin, north on Park St. (317) 932–2792. Call for appointment to see interior. Free.

Buggies at barn. (Courtesy of the Ohio Division of Travel and Tourism.)

U.S. 62

Youngstown, Ohio, to Aberdeen, Ohio

The drive along U.S. 62 is one of Ohio's most pleasant rides. It takes the traveler on a trip from the edge of the state's old steel belt, past the rolling fields and rich farms of Amish country, and through the scenic hills in Ohio's southern half.

U.S. 62 overall is among the best of the country's old roads. It begins in Niagara Falls, New York, and then heads steadily southwest to El Paso, Texas. The highway may give the most diverse portrait of America of any of the old federal highways.

The road enters Ohio near the town of Sharon, Pennsylvania, then runs right through the center of Youngstown. This is a crowded, not especially scenic trip. So rather than beginning at the beginning, we'll skip ahead a few miles and pick up the road at the southbound U.S. 62 exit of Interstate 680, part of the beltway that encircles Youngstown.

This is Market St., and in a few miles the highway turns left to become Indianola St., then Canfield Rd. As it crosses Mill Creek Park, Youngstown's scenic jewel, stop off at Lanterman's Mill. The old gristmill, built in 1846 and restored to working condition, stands on the site of the Western Reserve's first mill, which gave the creek its name. Adjacent to the mill is a covered bridge. You can take the park drive north from here to spend some more time in the area. This is a lovely road, with several scenic overlooks and the Fellows Riverside Gardens near the park's north end. The gardens are noted for their rose displays. Return to U.S. 62 by taking Glenwood Ave. along Mill Creek Park's eastern border.

The road then runs through Canfield, with its oval-shaped green. One of its first settlers was Elijah Wadsworth, chief aide to General

Washington during the Revolutionary War. He came here in 1800, and his home stood for many years on the southern side of the green.

Salem was settled by Quaker pioneers from the like-named community in New Jersey. This was a popular town name wherever Quakers resided, being a contraction for *Jerusalem* and an Anglicized rendering of the Hebrew word for "peace." (The original Salem in America, however, was in Massachusetts and was named by Puritans, who were none too friendly to Quakers. But the Quakers were never ones to hold grudges.)

This Ohio town developed a militant streak early on. A center of fervent abolitionist sentiment, it became one of the state's most active anti-slavery communities, publishing Ohio's first abolitionist newspaper. One of its natives, Edwin Coppock, ran off to join John Brown and was captured with him at Harpers Ferry in 1859. After being hanged, he was returned here for a martyr's burial. There is a monument to Coppock in Hope Cemetery, on N. Lincoln Ave.

Damascus was another Quaker community, so named because its site on two rivers matched the biblical description of that city in Syria. Other members of this religious group were responsible for the settlement of Alliance. Actually, there were four separate towns around the Mahoning River as it ran through the area. In 1854 they decided to unify, and the town's name reflects that decision. The name of one of the old communities lives on, though, in Mt. Union College. The liberal arts school was established in 1846 in that town and came with the package when Alliance was formed a few years later. It now has an enrollment of about 1,200 students on its Clark Ave. campus. Crandall Art Gallery is a nice place from which to base a short walk.

West of Alliance, U.S. 62 begins an uncharacteristic stretch of four-lane road, which turns into freeway as it enters Canton. One of Ohio's leading industrial centers and the hometown of President William McKinley, Canton is best known today for activities that took place in an automobile showroom in the fall of 1920. That was when a group of sport enthusiasts anted up $100 apiece to gain a franchise in the new American Professional Football Association. Within a year, things were going so poorly that the entry fee was cut in half. The organization was then renamed the National Football League. That name worked much better, and the NFL is now the most profitable sports association in the country. Professional football won its foothold in tough manufacturing towns like Canton. The city's Bulldogs were one of the early powers in the NFL. So 43 years later, when the sport decided to return to its roots to build a Hall of Fame and museum, Canton was the top choice for the honor. The football-shaped building is reached by taking the Fulton Rd. exit from the U.S. 62 freeway (also numbered Interstate 77).

Canton's memorial to McKinley is a mile south of the football museum. The future president moved to Canton as a young Civil War veteran and opened a law practice. He was elected a congressman 10 years later and then became governor of Ohio in 1892. His political mentor, Mark Hanna, used his substantial influence in the Republican Party to get McKinley the presidential nomination in 1896. In a campaign fought so bitterly on economic issues that it would define the identities of the two national parties for the next century, McKinley campaigned for "hard money" from his front porch in Canton. Described by historian Barbara Tuchman as "a man made to be managed," McKinley was content to let Hanna call the shots. Hanna is best recalled now for remarking on Theodore Roosevelt's election as McKinley's vice president in 1900, "that damned cowboy is only one heartbeat away from the presidency." His fears were realized less than a year later, when McKinley was assassinated in Buffalo. Roosevelt's ascent ended Hanna's control over the Republican Party. The outpouring of grief over the country's third martyred president was genuine, though, and a memorial to McKinley was erected here in 1907. The statue, granite shaft, and burial vault adjoin a contemporary museum of history, science, and industry. A special hall in the museum is dedicated to events of McKinley's five years in office and contains personal items.

The road leaves Canton, still as a freeway, and then drops south, along the route of the old Ohio and Erie Canal. Navarre grew up along the canal and was a major port for farmers carrying in their crops for shipment. The town was given the French name for a province in Spain by its founder's wife, who spoke French and wanted people to know it.

U.S. 62 now turns sharply southwest and enters the territory of the Ohio Amish.

A Closer Look. Amid the carnage and social upheaval of Germany's religious and political wars in the seventeenth century, a message of hope slowly began making its way across the land. A man named William Penn from America was offering a refuge. There was land to be had in a place where there was no military conscription and no religious persecution.

To the Protestant minorities in the Rhineland and the German principalities, these were powerful words. Hardly a family had come through the wars without terrible losses. But none had suffered more than the Mennonites and Amish, small sects who practiced pacifism and lived as closely to biblical mandates as they could. The wars rolled over them, ruining their lands and decimating their families. The Mennonites were regarded as the most radical group coming out of the Reformation. They separated themselves from the world through plain dress and strict religious observance. But even this was not enough for Jacob Ammon, who thought the Mennonites too worldly and preached an even plainer way of life. The Amish, as his followers were known, broke away from the main body of Mennonites in 1609.

Penn felt a strong affinity for these groups. Their beliefs and practices seemed to closely resemble those of his own Quaker religion. They were skilled and industrious workers, the very sort he needed to populate the western lands of his colony. The first group arrived from Germany in 1683 and settled north of Philadelphia, in an area that is still called Germantown. Over the next century, they made their way west to the valleys that lie between the Schuylkill and Susquehanna Rivers. There they became known as the Pennsylvania Dutch. Stubbornly unassimilated and prosperous, they became, in the words of historian J. C. Furnas, "the only sizeable mass of peasantry that America knew . . . the first large, self-encapsulating ethnic enclave."

By the early nineteenth century, though, a certain restlessness came over many of the younger members of the group. The Pennsylvania land that once had been so ample was now costly and scarce. But stories of rich new land in Ohio, land that could be acquired as cheaply as their forebears had obtained theirs, began raising uncharacteristic excitement in the religious communities. Starting in 1815, they began moving west. Ohio's current Amish community in Holmes County is regarded as the largest in the country, and U.S. 62 runs through its heart.

Although the Ohio Amish are far less publicized than their brethren in Pennsylvania, don't get the idea that this area is a secret. On weekends, you will find plenty of traffic in the small towns, and a place to park can be hard to come by in communities like Berlin and Sugarcreek.

But the degree of commercialization, the jam-up of tour buses, is far less intrusive than what you'll find along U.S. 30 in Pennsylvania. You still have some breathing room in Ohio.

The land is a joy to the eye. U.S. 62 follows a roller-coaster track along an old Native American trail, and the neat barns and rich fields of the Amish spread to the horizon. The town of Wilmot is generally regarded as the start of Amish country. This place has developed a strong Swiss identity and a bustling cheese trade. A restaurant-shopping complex west of town, Alpine-Alpa, allows you to observe the cheese-making process, although its atmosphere is way too hokey for some tastes. Its restaurant is decorated with wall murals illustrating the cantons of Switzerland. Also there is what is billed as the world's largest cuckoo clock, and a talking Heidi carving greets visitors. Beyond Wilmot is Winesburg, another country town. It is frequently confused for the setting of Sherwood Anderson's book *Winesburg, Ohio* (see U.S. 20).

Then comes Berlin, ground zero of Amish country. Half a century ago this was a sleepy village of 232 souls. The population has multiplied by 10, and Berlin has long since awakened. It is now an Amish shopping town, its old buildings converted into craft stores, quilt shops, fresh cheese and meats stores, and stores featuring handcrafted furniture. Old barns have been turned into woodcrafting displays. Former farmhouses are now bed-and-breakfasts. Gift shops, restaurants, bakeries—everything but do-it-yourself barn-raising kits—all cluster along the town's bustling and fascinating Main St.

The onetime Miller farm, just east of town on Ohio 39, is now the Amish Farm, showing off the way the Plain People run their farms and homes. It also contains a complex of shops. Nearby, on County Road 77, is "Behalt," a cyclorama explaining the religious heritage of the Amish and Mennonites.

The most popular side trip from Berlin is Ohio 39 east, to the villages of Walnut Creek and Sugarcreek. Both are situated in a tranquil, lovely landscape and have their own assortment of shops on their respective Main Sts. Walnut Creek, especially, has the widest variety of overnight accommodations in the area. (See U.S. 250 for a description of the nearby Amish town of Kidron.)

Despite occasionally heavy traffic, this is still a drive into another era.

Looking out over these rolling valleys or sharing the road with a black horse-driven buggy, you'll find it hard to believe that you are less than an hour's drive away from some of the greatest industrial cities in America.

From Berlin, U.S. 62 continues on to Millersburg. As you might expect from the county seat of America's most Amish area, this is a neat little community, built on a series of ridges around a pleasant courthouse square. Cleveland industrialist L. H. Brightman built a Victorian mansion here in 1902 and moved in with his family of eight children. The house grew to 28 rooms, with three kinds of parquet flooring, leaded stained-glass windows, a ballroom, and gas chandeliers. It remained in private hands until 1971 and then was acquired by the Holmes County Historical Society. Victorian House is now run as a domestic museum of the era.

The road continues through wonderful hill scenery, so unlike what most peoples' image of Ohio is like. The town of Killbuck was named for a Delaware leader, known to pioneers who settled the place in 1811. Once past the turnoff to Tiverton Center, the land starts to flatten out a bit. This is still lightly populated country, though. The towns along the road are tiny places, giving no hint that you are nearing the geographic center of the sixth most populous state in the Union.

Just past Utica is the turnoff to Homer. This nondescript place on the Licking River is notable as the hometown of the Claflin sisters, two of the most notorious women of the 1870s. Both Tennessee and Victoria were striking beauties, but the entire family was made up of con artists. They seized on the craze for spiritualism in the 1850s to wander the country separating the gullible from their money. They reached their apogee of influence when Tennessee managed to wangle a meeting with the aging Cornelius Vanderbilt. The rail tycoon, one of the richest men in America, was convinced that the sisters had the power to cure his various ailments. In gratitude he set them up as the first female stockbrokers in the country. Tennessee and Victoria used this as a springboard to gain influence in the women's suffrage movement and published a weekly magazine that took a strong feminist stance. Unfortunately, they also were outspoken advocates of free love. Their notoriety got the two issues hopelessly intertangled in the public mind. Finally, they became involved in lawsuits involving Vanderbilt's will (in which they were generously remembered) and in a sex scandal that ensnared the famed minister Rev. Henry Ward Beecher. In the midst of all this, the sisters set sail for England, where they married wealthy men and spent the rest of their lives in charitable works. These remarkable women are credited with setting back the cause of women's rights in America at least a generation with their antics and are fondly recalled nowhere, least of all in Homer.

The road continues on, with farmland gradually giving way to the outlying suburbs of Columbus, the state's capital and its largest city. U.S. 62 enters the city as a freeway, then emerges on the east side of Columbus to make the run into downtown as Broad St., the main east-west thoroughfare. Many of the city's major cultural institutions lie along the route. Just where the highway joins Broad St. is Franklin Park Conservatory. The original part of this showcase of exotic plants dates from 1895 and was modeled after London's Crystal Palace. An 18,000-square-foot addition was opened in 1992 for an international floral show, held in conjunction with the 500th anniversary of Christopher Columbus's landing. It makes the conservatory one of the top facilities of its kind in the country.

Just north of Broad, at 77 Jefferson Ave., is the home of James Thurber, the Columbus-born writer whose sketches of his early years here are memorialized in *My Life and Hard Times,* one of the peaks of twentieth-century American humor. In his plays and many articles for the *New Yorker,* Thurber repeatedly turned to Columbus and Ohio State University for comic inspiration. Personal items and many of Thurber's drawings are exhibited in the Thurber House.

A few blocks west on Broad is the Columbus Museum of Art, built in 1931. It contains a wide-ranging collection of old masters and some noteworthy works by Columbus-born George Bellows. He was one of the realists, whose often brutal portraits of urban life were a powerful influence on American art in the early years of the twentieth century. Two blocks farther along is Ohio's Center of Science and Industry, an excellent museum that teaches scientific principles through a wide variety of interactive displays.

The road now dips south on Third St., running behind the Capitol building, built in 1861. It turns west once more as Town St., passing the downtown area's largest indoor mall, City Center. The road then crosses the Scioto River, before turning south on the way out of town, as the Harrisburg Pike.

It passes Beulah Park, the first thoroughbred racetrack in Ohio, opened in 1923. Nearby Grove City, named for its agricultural products, shows off historic gardens at Gantz Farm. The grounds feature plantings of herbs and flowers that were popular in the nineteenth century and a restored farmhouse also dating from that era.

The look of the land changes radically south of Columbus. The northern half of Ohio was settled predominantly by New Englanders, who laid out their townships and farms along the orderly lines of their former homes. But the southern part of the state was settled predominantly by Virginians, who were not accustomed to imposing strict lines on the natural contours of the land. So this area has an irregular appearance to it. You can see that in the stock-raising area the highways passes near Mt. Sterling, named for the Virginia estate of its founder, John J. Smith. This is rich dairy land, and the herds speckled across these fields present as reassuring a spectacle as the Amish farms, several miles back along the road.

Washington Court House is described in the chapter on U.S. 22.

Leesburg is another place whose name gives away its Virginia origins. Quakers were also among the early settlers, and the Old Quaker Meeting House here was the site of major religious gatherings throughout the nineteenth century.

Now the landscape starts to roll again as we enter Highland County and its aptly named seat, Hillsboro. From here, the road heads through ranges of hills to the Ohio River. This was one of the major escape routes on the Underground Railroad. The highway reaches the river at Ripley (see U.S. 52), from which John Rankin helped more than 2,000 slaves escape and proudly boasted that he never lost one. Rankin delighted in outthinking bounty hunters. He would send off wagons carrying farm produce along this road at night when he knew the slavers were expecting human cargo. He deliberately spread false reports that these wagons contained escapees. Then in broad daylight he would manage to move the real slaves to freedom.

U.S. 62 twists its way through increasingly hilly terrain, past several towns that are no more than crossroads, before reaching Ripley. It runs east for a few miles with U.S. 52 before crossing the river at Aberdeen into Kentucky.

VISITING HOURS

Youngstown

Lanterman's Mill, in Mill Creek Park, at 980 Canfield Rd. (216) 740–7115. Tuesday to Saturday, 10–5, and Sunday 11–6, May–October. $1.

Alliance

Crandall Art Gallery, on the campus of Mt. Union College, at 1972 Clark Ave. (216) 821–5320. Monday to Friday, 9–5, September–April. Free.

Canton

Professional Football Hall of Fame, at exit 107A of Interstate 77. (216) 426–8207. Daily, 9–5. $5.

McKinley National Memorial, at exit 106 of Interstate 77. (216) 455–7043. Monday to Saturday, 9–7, and Sunday, 12–7, Memorial Day–Labor Day. Closes at 5, rest of year. Free.

McKinley Museum of History, Science, and Industry, at exit 106 of Interstate 77. (216) 455–7043. Same hours as McKinley National Memorial. $5.

Wilmot

Alpine-Alpa, south on U.S. 62. (216) 359–5454. Cheese-making operation is open Monday to Saturday, 10–3. Free.

Berlin

Amish Farm, east on Ohio 39. (216) 893–2951. Monday to Saturday, 10–5, April–October. $5.50.

"Behalt," east on Ohio 39 and County Road 77. (216) 893–3192. Monday to Saturday, 9–5. $5.

Millersburg

Victorian House, north of downtown, on Ohio 83. (216) 674–3975. Tuesday to Sunday, 1:30–4, May–October. $2.50.

Columbus

Franklin Park Conservatory, at 1777 E. Broad. (614) 645–8733. Monday to Saturday, 10–5, and Sunday, 11–5. $3.50.

Thurber House, north of U.S. 62, at 77 Jefferson Ave. (614) 464–1032. Daily, 12–4. $2.

Columbus Museum of Art, at 480 E. Broad. (614) 221–6801. Tuesday to Friday, 11–4, and weekends, 11–5. Free.

Ohio's Center of Science and Industry, at 280 E. Broad. (614) 228–2674. Monday to Saturday, 10–5, and Sunday, 12–5:30. $5.

Grove City

Gantz Farm, at 2255 Gantz Rd. W. (614) 871–6323. Daily, dawn to midnight. Free.

U.S. 231

Crown Point, Indiana, to Rockport, Indiana

U.S. 231 is a fine old road, running the length of Indiana, down the western edge of the state. It dodges most major cities, has few miles of freeway, and is the perfect Hoosier sampler. U.S. 231 runs from the edge of the Great Lakes to the rolling hills of southern Indiana and embraces personalities as dissimilar as John Dillinger, Lew Wallace, and Abraham Lincoln.

The route of U.S. 231 through Indiana is made up of three different state roads that were combined as a federal highway after World War II. The road eventually makes its way south, through Kentucky, Tennessee, and Alabama, before reaching the Gulf of Mexico, at Panama City, Florida. It actually begins 5 miles west of Crown Point, Indiana, at the intersection with U.S. 41. But for the sake of convenience, let's start in the town.

For a few weeks in March 1934, Crown Point was the best known dateline in America. The notorious bank robber and killer John Dillinger, was awaiting trial in the Lake County Jail here. With time on his hands, he fashioned a model gun from a block of wood and turned it on a guard. Knowing Dillinger's reputation and entirely unaware that the worst injury he could get was splinters, the guard opened the cell, and the criminal fled into the night.

It was called the most audacious prison break in the annals of American crime. The Dillinger manhunt became the number one story of 1934. It ended four months later, when he was gunned down by federal agents outside the Biograph Theater in Chicago. A native Hoosier who went bad, there are elements of Dillinger lore all across Indiana. A hoard of buried treasure from his holdups is still supposedly buried somewhere in the Indianapolis suburbs. There is even a museum of his exploits in

General Lew Wallace Study and Monument. (Photo by John Penrod. Courtesy of Penrod/Hiawatha Co.)

Nashville (see Indiana 135). Crown Point, too, has capitalized on the legend. The former jail, with its original interior, is now a museum.

The courthouse, one block away, is another landmark, with its massive tower visible from miles away. The building is located atop a divide. According to local lore, Crown Point got its name from a settler who built the original courthouse on this site. Solon Robinson was nicknamed "King of the Squatters" by his neighbors, most of whom similarly had moved in without clear title to their land. Since his cabin was at the highest point in town, the community adapted Robinson's sobriquet and named the place Crown Point. He later returned east to become an editor with the *New York Tribune*.

The road angles southeast to Hebron, a biblical name especially favored by Connecticut-born settlers, then turns due south through open farmland. It crosses the Kankakee River, the great route west to the Mississippi from the Great Lakes taken by the seventeenth-century French explorers. The town of Aix, a few miles down the road, was named by French settlers of about 200 years later.

Rensselaer was founded by a member of the New York patroon family who figured prominently in the early years of the Hudson Valley. James Van Rensselaer moved here in 1837 and was the local miller. The town was the home of Civil War hero Gen. Robert H. Milroy, who held back Lee's troops for three days during the Confederate invasion of Pennsylvania in 1863.

Just south of town is St. Joseph's College, founded as a boarding school for Native Americans in 1888. It was reestablished as a Catholic men's school in 1891. Drexel Hall, the oldest building on campus, was funded by a member of a wealthy Philadelphia family, noted for its philanthropy to Catholic education in the late nineteenth century. It is registered as a national historic landmark.

The road joins U.S. 24 (featured earlier in this book) at Remington and runs with it for 7 miles to Wolcott, before turning south again. Continue on U.S. 231 for 10 miles to the junction with Indiana 18, then turn left for 8 miles to Brookston. Now turn right on Indiana 43. In about 7 miles you will see signs on the left to a county route that leads to the Tippecanoe Battlefield State Memorial.

On this field, in the autumn of 1811, the clash that broke the power of the tribal confederacy in Indiana was fought. The Battle of Tippecanoe was a prelude to the oncoming War of 1812 with Britain. It also created a political legend that would lead the American general William Henry Harrison to the White House, 29 years later.

Harrison, who governed the Indiana territory from the town of Vincennes (see U.S. 50), was alarmed by reports of the growing strength of the northern tribes under a charismatic Shawnee leader, Tecumseh. Harrison had managed to secure much of southern Indiana by treaty in 1809, paying $10,000 for three million acres of land. Most Native American leaders went along with the terms. But Tecumseh, aided by his brother, Laulawasikau, known as the Prophet, urged resistance. The Prophet preached a return to traditional ways while Tecumseh tried to put together a grand tribal alliance, gaining converts even among the Creek in distant Alabama.

Those who allied themselves with the two brothers moved to Tippecanoe Creek and formed a village, called Prophet's Town. A meeting between Harrison and Tecumseh resolved nothing. Reports of warlike preparations by the tribes reached Washington, and President James Madison urged Harrison to move north and attack. With Tecumseh away on a visit to his Creek allies, Harrison left Vincennes in October 1811 and reached the Tippecanoe on November 6. The Prophet was an inspirational leader but lacked the military skills of his brother. He allowed Harrison to take the high ground and then flung his forces against him in a frontal assault. In brutal hand-to-hand combat, Harrison lost 61 men. The tribal losses were smaller, with 38 dead. But feeling betrayed by the Prophet's false promises of immunity from bullets, the Native Americans retreated and then withdrew from the area. While Tecumseh managed to ally himself with the British, he could never again muster the numbers that had been pledged to him before this battle. Harrison, running on the famed slogan "Tippecanoe and Tyler too," would win the presidency as the Whig candidate in 1840. There is a monument and a museum on the site of the battle, as well as picnic facilities and hiking trails.

Now return to Highway 43 and take it south into Lafayette, where the road rejoins U.S. 231. This manufacturing town on the Wabash River was named for a Revolutionary hero, the Marquis de Lafayette, in a burst of appreciation during his triumphal return visit to America in 1824.

The road runs along the west side of the Wabash. In West Lafayette is the campus of Purdue University, founded as a land-grant college in 1869 and well known for its school of engineering. It was named for local businessman John Purdue, who helped raise $200,000 to establish the school here. Walking maps of the 30,000-student campus are available at the Memorial Union, at State and S. Grant Sts., a few blocks west of our route by way of Indiana 26.

U.S. 231 crosses the Wabash to head through downtown Lafayette. It then speeds straight south, paralleling the old Chicago, Indianapolis, and Louisville Railroad right-of-way, before entering Crawfordsville.

A Closer Look. Had it not been for "the book," Crawfordsville would have remained a small, charming, rarely visited Indiana town. There are some fine old nineteenth-century homes here, including one, Lane Place, that is a showplace. The campus of Wabash College is in the western end of Crawfordsville. A Victorian shopping district has been brightly restored downtown.

But it is Lew Wallace and the book he wrote more than 100 years ago that keep the visitors coming. *Ben-Hur,* published in 1880 and written mostly under a large beech tree near Wallace's home, was the best-selling American novel of its time. It was made into a stage production that toured the country for more than 20 years, and it was the basis for three movies, the last of which is regarded as the greatest spectacle ever put on the screen and is unlikely ever to be duplicated.

"Do you mean to tell me that I put all this in motion," said Wallace, on seeing the preparation for the first theatrical production of his novel in 1899. Some disbelief is understandable, because Wallace's entire life itself seems almost like a novel.

He was an apparent failure by the time he reached his fifties. His military career, which began brilliantly in the Civil War, ended in near disgrace. He was the youngest general in the Union army at the age of 34, but he misunderstood orders at Shiloh, failed to reinforce his end of the line fast enough, and was relieved of command by Ulysses S. Grant, who never fully forgave him. He served on the commissions that investigated Lincoln's assassination and Andersonville Prison, but he was also used as a dupe by Mexican rebels, obtaining aid for them and then being turned down when he asked for mining concessions.

His chosen profession was law and he hated it. The son of a onetime Indiana governor and congressman, Wallace was a man of whom great things were expected. But his legal and political career was a disappointment, because what he really wanted to do was write novels. This only added to his aura of failure. He kept scribbling away at an idea that had come to him, an intermingling of the lives of Jesus Christ and a young Jewish nobleman of the Roman period. He wrote it out in longhand under his favorite tree and finally finished the book while serving a term as governor of the New Mexico Territory.

Initial sales were disappointing. Critics did not care for it. "I protest as a friend of Christ that He has been crucified enough without having a Territorial Governor after Him," wrote one. But by 1888 it had sold

400,000 copies, and as word-of-mouth spread, *Ben-Hur* turned into a publishing phenomenon. By the turn of the century it had sold an unprecedented one million books. Novels were regarded then as vaguely disreputable. Because of its religious subject matter, however, many Baptist and Methodist homes, which otherwise would have been closed to such writings, welcomed this book. Many of its readers proudly boasted that it was the first novel they had ever read.

But that was just the start. The theatrical version, climaxed by a chariot race on treadmills, was a huge hit in New York, despite gloomy prophecies. "You're up against it, boys," said Charles Frohman, veteran producer. "They just won't go for Christ and a horse race in the same show." Seldom has an insider been so wrong.

The first movie version appeared in 1907, although it was made without obtaining copyright permission. In a historic lawsuit, the Wallace family won $25,000 in damages and established the principle that producers must pay for film rights. Its second screen version, in 1926, was a classic silent film, helping to build the reputation of the new MGM Studios. It cost an unheard of $4 million, but it earned back even more when it was rereleased, with sound added, in 1931. The final version, made in 1959, won a record 12 Academy Awards, including Best Actor for Charlton Heston in the title role. The race scenes alone cost more than $1 million to film, a figure that would be multiplied by a factor of ten in current costs.

Florid and overwritten by today's standards, *Ben-Hur,* nonetheless, was one of the most influential books ever published in America. Wallace himself returned to Crawfordsville, a wealthy and famous man, and in 1896 he built a study near his favorite tree. A square-shaped building, the architecture is best described as eclectic. The entrance gate is modeled after that of a French abbey. Many of the decorations were inspired by Wallace's tenure as minister to Turkey in the Garfield administration. "A pleasure house for my soul," is what Wallace called it in his autobiography published in 1906, and its appearance reflects the varied nature of his life.

The study is filled with memorabilia of Wallace's public career and of the book that he created. He died in 1905, before his novel went multimedia. The study is a place of pilgrimage for fans of the movie, and several of its stars have also visited. But the tree Wallace loved survived the writer by only three years and had to be cut down. A statue of Wallace, a duplicate of one that stands in Washington, D.C., marks the spot.

The General Lew Wallace Study is three blocks east of where U.S. 231 enters Crawfordsville, at Washington St. Leave the car near the corner of Washington and Market Sts. The Old Jail Museum, on Washington, just north of the intersection, preserves a unique 1882 cell block. It was circular and could be rotated by 360 degrees, reflecting the utopian penal ideas of British political theorist Jeremy Bentham. The jailer could check up on all his prisoners without ever moving.

Walk one block south to Main St. and turn left. This is the heart of the business district, and there is an assortment of specialty shops here, housed in glowingly restored nineteenth-century storefronts. Turn right at Wallace Ave. for the short walk down to the Lew Wallace Study. The area around it is called Elston Grove and was developed by Maj. Isaac Elston, an early settler and rail magnate. Wallace married his daughter Susan, and the prestige of her family was another reason his lack of success into middle age weighed so heavily on him.

The study is surrounded by a block-square, well-shaded park. Walk to the opposite gate and head south to Wabash Ave. The far southeastern corner of the property marks the site of the Wallace house, where he lived while actually writing *Ben-Hur*. Walk a block and a half west on Wabash to the entrance of Lane Place, which is also worth a visit. Henry Lane, who married another of the Elston daughters, was an officer in the Mexican War and later became an Indiana leader of the new Republican Party. He is credited with being one of Lincoln's top supporters during the Republican nominating convention of 1860, and among the memorabilia in the mansion is a lock of the president's hair. Lane Place was built in 1845 in the Greek Revival style and is regarded as one of the finest homes of its era in the state.

To round out a visit to Crawfordsville, continue west on Wabash, three blocks past Washington St. This will bring you to the entrance of Wabash College. The first nonsectarian school west of the Alleghenies, Wabash was founded in 1832. Its lovely, oval-shaped campus is surrounded by red-brick buildings in the colonial style. Among them is Forest Hall, the original college building, now the Information Center.

Lew Wallace was a graduate. So was Vice President Thomas R. Marshall, who served under Woodrow Wilson and is credited with the observation "All this country needs is a good five-cent cigar."

Beyond Crawfordsville, U.S. 231 proceeds directly south, through rich farmland, across Raccoon Creek, and then into the town of Greencastle. This is the home of DePauw University, founded five years after Wabash College, its great rival. The two schools maintain the oldest uninterrupted college football rivalry in the country. Every November thousands of their graduates attend closed-circuit telecasts of the game, which is too small to be carried on network TV yet is part of a rivalry too old to be ignored. DePauw is noted for its schools of music and journalism. It was the birthplace of Sigma Delta Chi, the national journalism society, and of the oldest Greek sorority, Kappa Alpha Theta. East College is in the *National Register of Historic Places* and houses the Indiana Journalism Hall of Fame. The campus is on S. Locust St.

The road continues south, through Cloverdale, whose name hints of the rich pastureland surrounding it. A short side trip on Indiana 42 takes you to Cataract Lake, where the state's largest natural waterfall tumbles off a hillside into the water. Located opposite the entrance to the Lieber State Recreation Area, it is a scene well worth a detour.

The country begins to roll a bit here as we approach the White River, which is reached at Spencer. The town was named for one of the officers killed at the Battle of Tippecanoe. In the Spencer-Owen Civic Center is a collection of works by local artist E. M. Viquesney, sculptor of the statue titled *American Doughboy*.

Along this stretch of the river road are old canal towns, and you can still see vestiges of that 1830s era in commercial buildings at Freedom and Worthington. With the completion of the railroads and the removal of commerce from their paths, these villages settled into a restful oblivion that goes on to the present day.

South of Bloomfield, the road is new, straight, and unencumbered by any settlement until it reaches the town of Loogootee (see U.S. 50). The highway crosses the East Fork of the White River at Haysville, a pleasant little village dominated by St. Paul's Lutheran Church. The town was so rooted in German heritage that all religious services were conducted in that language until World War I.

Jasper is another German-flavored community, although its religion is predominantly Catholic. St. Joseph Church, the largest in southern Indiana, was built between 1867 and 1880 by parishioners, who donated their material and labor. Its roof is supported by native poplar pillars, and the 206-foot bell tower is modeled after London's Big Ben. The stained-glass windows were imported from Germany. Jasper is also the home of the Kimball Organ Co., and tours of the assembly process may be set up on weekdays.

Huntingburg is another German town. Old Christian Church, built in 1852 with a potbellied stove to warm the sanctuary, is still a house of worship. It is on N. Washington St. This town had the largest surviving wagon-manufacturing firm in the country, until its demise in the 1940s.

The town of Gentryville was named for a local merchant, James Gentry. He would be long forgotten were it not for the fact that he once employed a gangling farm boy named Abraham Lincoln. While working for Gentry, in 1828, the future president was hired to take a flatboat of goods down to New Orleans. Lincoln later wrote that the trip was one of the most significant events of his life. It gave him his first look at the cruel face of slavery in the Deep South and also an exposure to the wider world, beyond the limits of his family's Indiana farm. He returned home restless and more than willing to accompany his father when he pulled up stakes and moved to Illinois in 1830.

The Lincoln farm was just east of Gentryville and is reached by Indiana 162. A national memorial and adjoining state park mark the site. The Lincoln Boyhood National Memorial reconstructs the farm on which the family lived from 1816 to 1830. Here his mother, Nancy Hanks Lincoln, died of milk sickness when Abraham was nine. She was buried in an unmarked grave. Many of the displays are devoted to her life and her abiding influence on her son. Thomas Lincoln owned 160 acres here but cultivated only a small portion, spending most of his time working for wealthier neighbors. A year after his wife's death, he returned to Kentucky to marry Sarah Bush Johnson. She was a kind woman with three children of her own and encouraged young Abe Lincoln's love of learning, bringing with her to Indiana some of the first books he ever read.

The memorial contains displays about the Lincoln farm and places it in historical context on the Indiana frontier of the time. There is also a film presentation. The Lincoln Living History Historical Farm is a re-creation of a family farm from that period, with costumed workers going about daily chores and crafts. In Lincoln State Park, the historical drama *Young Abe Lincoln* is presented every summer in a covered amphitheater.

The Lincoln family had already moved on to Illinois when William Jones built his home in Gentryville. A prominent local merchant, Jones went on to serve as a colonel in the Civil War. The house was restored to its antebellum appearance, and Gentryville itself has become an antiquing center.

U.S. 231 runs on to the Ohio River town of Rockport. The town is built on bluffs above the river and was the main point of communication with the outside world during Lincoln's youth. He spent time here as he grew older, using the law library of local attorney John Pitcher. U.S. 231 runs on for another 11 miles before crossing the Ohio River to Owensboro, Kentucky. But here in Rockport, surrounded by Lincoln lore in the river town he once knew, is a good place to end this drive down Indiana.

VISITING HOURS

Crown Point
Old Lake County Jail, at 212 S. Main St. (219) 769–4788. Daily, 10–9. Free.

Rensselaer
Drexel Hall, on the campus of St. Joseph College, south of town. (219) 866–7111. Daily during school year. Free.

Battle Ground
Tippecanoe Battlefield State Memorial, east on Indiana 43. (317) 567–2147. Daily, 10–4. $1.50.

Crawfordsville
General Lew Wallace Study, at E. Pike and Wallace Sts. (317) 362–5769. Wednesday to Saturday, 10–4:30, and Tuesday and Sunday, 1–4:30, April–October. $2.

Old Jail Museum, at 225 N. Washington St. (317) 362–5222. Wednesday to Saturday, 10–4:30, and Tuesday and Sunday, 1–4:30, June–August. Wednesday to Sunday, 1–4:30, April, May, September, and October. Free.

Lane Place, at Pike and Water Sts. (317) 362–3416. Tuesday to Sunday, 1–4, April–October. $2.

Spencer

Spencer-Owen Civic Center and Viquesney exhibit, at Franklin and Montgomery Sts. (812) 829–9096. Tuesday to Sunday, 1–5, April–mid-December. Free.

Jasper

Kimball Organ Co., at 1038 E. Fifteenth St. (812) 482–1600. Tours Tuesday–Thursday, 10. Reserve in advance. Free.

Gentryville

Lincoln Boyhood National Memorial, east on Indiana 162. (812) 937–4541. Daily, 8–5. $2 (includes visit to Lincoln Living History Historical Farm).

Young Abe Lincoln performance, Lincoln State Park. (800) 264–4223. Phone for schedule and ticket prices.

Col. William Jones House, on the Boonville-Corydon Rd. (812) 937–2802. Wednesday to Saturday, 9–5, and Sunday, 1–5, mid-March–October. Donation.

Birthplace of Thomas Edison. (Courtesy of the Ohio Division of Travel and Tourism.)

U.S. 250

Sandusky, Ohio, to Bridgeport, Ohio

U.S. 250 is one of Ohio's most varied roads, running from the Lake Erie shore on a diagonal to the rugged highlands on the West Virginia border. The traveler will find a lot of history and a generous dollop of scenery on this road. For most of its route, it also ducks the big cities and interstates. Once out of Ohio, U.S. 250 continues on a breathtaking journey across the Shenandoah and Blue Ridge Mountains, en route to its terminus in Virginia's capital, Richmond.

During the summer months, Sandusky, Ohio, wears the tanned face of a resort town. It is the jumping-off place for Cedar Point, the top amusement park on the Lake Erie shore since 1882. The park, now as then, attracts a following from across the Midwest. But by the 1950s it appeared that Cedar Point would not last long enough to see its centennial. Attendance was falling every year. The old lake steamers that brought the crowds were going out of business. The park went on the block, with a conversion planned to lakefront housing. Inspired by the success of Disneyland, however, its owners changed their minds in 1959 and went for renovation instead. Its nostalgic setting was enhanced, and some of the country's most astonishing roller coasters were added. Cedar Point was reborn and is again a major tourist destination. Record crowds flock in to squeal at its demonic coasters, dropping abruptly from great heights or getting turned upside down at high speed. On summer weekend mornings, U.S. 250, one of the main access roads to Cedar Point, is backed up for miles, between Sandusky and the Ohio Turnpike. It is best to avoid the road at those times.

But Cedar Point isn't the only thing Sandusky has going. The town sits at the center of Lake Erie's most expansive recreation area. Ferries leave the docks here for Kelleys Island and Canada's Pelee Island, while a steady stream of recreation boats heads out into the waters of Sandusky Bay. (The Native American word from which the name Sandusky was derived refers to fresh springs found in the area.)

Even before the vacationers found it, Sandusky was a busy port. After the completion of the Erie Canal, it challenged Cleveland for commercial dominance on the lake. It lost that battle when the builders of the Ohio and Erie Canal chose Cleveland as its lake outlet in the 1830s. Sandusky responded by becoming the state's first rail center. The Mad River Railroad was built to Bellevue (see U.S. 20) in 1839 and 12 years later had reached Dayton. Throughout its history, Sandusky has remained a commercial fishing center and coal port.

The best place to start this ride on U.S. 250 is Battery Park, right on Sandusky's long bayfront. This is an excellent vantage point for viewing the harbor and marina. It is located on E. Water St., just off downtown. A few blocks away is the Follett House. Oran Follett was a president of the Mad River Railroad, and his house, built in 1837, was a local showplace. It now shows off local history exhibits, including items recovered from the prison on nearby Johnson Island, in which Confederate officers were interned during the Civil War.

Our highway becomes the Milan Rd., and just past the Ohio Turnpike, it arrives at Milan.

A Closer Look. America's greatest inventor is associated with many places across the country. Thomas Edison spent his boyhood in Port Huron, Michigan, where he worked as a vendor on the Grand Trunk trains to Detroit. His laboratory in West Orange, New Jersey, from which poured the ideas and products that changed the world, is a national historic site. So is his winter home in Fort Myers, Florida. Many of Edison's personal belongings are exhibited in Dearborn, Michigan, in Greenfield Village, the historic park assembled by his acolyte, Henry Ford.

But Milan is where it began, the town in which Edison spent the first seven years of his life. This Yankee village, a little piece of New England transported to Ohio by its settlers, shows off the great man's birthplace as its primary attraction. But there is more to Milan than this. The Edison associations get people to stop in, and the rest is there for the discovering.

Milan was part of the Firelands, territory claimed by Connecticut and reserved for its citizens who had been burned out in the Revolutionary War. Most of them didn't arrive here until Ohio already was a state, because the area didn't become free of Native American or British raiders until after the War of 1812. But then the settlers, many of whom weren't even born when the losses that gave them this land were suffered by their families, began to pour in.

By 1847, the year the inventor was born, this was a booming place, one of the greatest shipping ports for grain in Ohio. Its founders had determined that proximity to Lake Erie made Milan a perfect candidate for a canal, cut through to the Huron River. The first ships came in 1839, and by the time of Edison's arrival, the town was sending out $1.25 million in goods annually.

Within a few years, though, competition from the railroads put Milan's canal out of business, and the town went into an economic decline. Among the results of that reversal of fortune was the departure of the Edison family to better prospects in Michigan. In later years, Edison admitted that his memories of Milan were hazy at best. In an article written late in his life, he recalled the grain elevators, the passing of the boats on the canal (which ran almost in back of his family's home), and the farmer's wagons filled with produce unloading in Public Square.

The square remains the center of Milan's life. The road into town from U.S. 250, Church St., is the southern boundary of Public Square. Many towns settled by Connecticut families, including Cleveland, were planned around such a central square. Milan's square remained a hitching lot for horses and teams, as Edison remembered it, until 1868, when it was planted with trees and shrubs to form the park that exists there now. The Civil War memorial at its center was erected at that time. The statue of young Edison standing at his mother's side was dedicated in 1984.

A few of the buildings on the square's perimeter date from the 1820s. The oldest of them, at the corner of Front and Main, was built by merchant Nathan Jenkins in 1821. This two-story structure with upstairs shutters was later moved farther back on the lot and replaced by a tavern. But when that enterprise burned down in 1853, the Jenkins Building was spared and returned to the front. There it has stood ever since. Two doors to the east is the Andrews Building (it now houses a tavern), which was built in 1826. On the east side of the square, the offices of the Society Bank also date from 1826. The structure was built as a store, later became a Masonic hall, and was taken over by the bank in 1912.

Repeated fires destroyed most of the other pre–Civil War buildings on the square. Local entrepreneur Henry Kelley, who made a fortune in shipbuilding and real estate, left his mark with erection of the Kelley Building (you can still see the name over the front entrance), which dominates the square's eastern side. That building was completed in 1870, then 18 years later Kelley donated the clock tower that rises above the town hall. The Milan Inn dates from a fire in 1888 that wiped out most of the southern end of the square. It still serves meals, but it takes no overnight guests. Notice, incidentally, the name of the restaurant at the square's southwestern corner—The Invention. Everybody wants to get in on Edison's action.

Now let's head over to the great man's birthplace. Walk east from the square along Front St. This is one of the most evocative blocks in the town, lined on either side with fine nineteenth-century homes. You'll find everything from Federal-style houses built in the 1820s, to the Italianate look of the 1860s, to the Queen Anne homes that were popular in the century's final two decades. The home at 21 E. Front was built by Ebenezer Merry, the town's founder, in 1823.

The street on which Edison's birthplace stands was long ago renamed Edison Dr. in his honor. The house is just a few steps north from Front St. Local historians estimate that it was built in 1842. The neat, red-brick home backs up to the bluff overlooking the canal. Restored to its appearance of the 1840s, the house shows off a typical domestic arrangement of that period. A few family belongings have been brought here, as well as models of some Edison inventions. But so many years passed between Edison's departure as a child and the conversion of the place into a museum that very little connected with the man remains.

The Milan Historical Foundation acquired several nearby buildings on Edison Dr. and turned them into a museum of local history. They are grouped on the east side of the drive, south of Front St. Just at the corner is the Sayles House, a Greek Revival home built in 1843. Next door is the Wadstrom House, which was built in the same style in the previous decade. Finally, the main building in the complex is the Galpin House, which was owned by the physician who delivered Edison.

Adjoining these homes is an exhibit building, in which a re-created country store and blacksmith's shop and fine collections of glasswork and dolls are displayed.

At the corner of Church St. is the landmark Presbyterian Church, with its high Gothic steeple. The church was rebuilt after the fire of 1888 destroyed it. Diagonally across the street is the Dr. Lyman Fay House. Although Victorian enlargements were superimposed on it, the Federal core of the house, built in 1819, can still be discerned. It is the oldest residence in Milan.

Now walk four blocks south on Edison to Judson St. and turn right. At the corner of Center St. is the Zenas King House (also referred to by the name of its present owner, J. P. Henry). King got rich building iron bridges, and the Greek Revival mansion he built here in 1848 is Milan's architectural showplace. Its front entrance, with four Ionic pillars supporting the portico, is regarded as exceptionally beautiful work. There are several other Greek Revival homes on Center St. built at about the same time as this one. You can admire them as you stroll north along Center, back to Public Square and the beginning of this walk.

From Milan, the road continues on to Norwalk, another of the old Firelands towns, and the site of the museum dedicated to that era (see U.S. 20).

This route traces the old turnpike that ran from the Ohio grain country to the canal outlet at Milan. The small towns along the road grew up in the 1830s to serve the farmers who had to drive their wagons to the shipment points. Both Olena and Fitchville were overnight stops, and their inns often put up 100 people at a time. Fitchville also boasts that one of its overnight guests was Abraham Lincoln. Almost no trace of those days remain in the tiny villages today.

The road crosses the Vermilion River and angles steadily southeast into Ashland. This was part of Johnny Appleseed's domain (see U.S. 24), and a monument to the pioneer fruit dispenser, built by subscription of schoolchildren in 1915, stands near the center of town. This is also the home of Ashland College, founded by German Baptists in 1878 for the training of ministers. It is now an independent institution with an enrollment of over 3,000 students. Although part of the Firelands grant, the town turned south for its name. Settlers changed it from Uniontown, in 1822, to honor Henry Clay, of neighboring Kentucky, whose estate was known as Ashland. One of Ashland's early industries was a pump factory. The place has been transformed into an antique mall, called, logically enough, the Pumphouse. It is located downtown on Orange St.

Rowsburg is another town that grew up because of the traffic along this road. It was a stagecoach stop on the Wheeling to Sandusky route. The West Virginia city was something of a transportation hub in the early nineteenth century, because that was where the National Road reached the Ohio River. Several overland routes through Ohio, including this one, branched off from there.

Just east of Rowsburg is a plaque marking the site of the Studebaker Farm. It was from this place in 1852 that the Studebaker brothers, Henry and Clement, decided to move to South Bend, Indiana, and get into the wagon-making business (see U.S. 20), with profound results for American industry.

An even more profound event in American popular culture occurred in Wooster in 1847, a few years before the Studebakers left the area. Another immigrant of German ancestry, August Imgard, was sorely disappointed at the blandness of the Christmas celebration he found in America. So, according to local tradition, he marched into the woods, chopped down a spruce and decorated the country's first Christmas tree. The German custom was then adopted throughout Ohio and the nation. Wooster has maintained its affection for green things. The Agricultural Research and Development Center of Ohio State University is just south of town. Established here in 1891, its rose gardens and arboretum, as well as its exhibits on research projects, make the center a worthwhile stop.

Wooster was named for the Revolutionary War general who commanded American forces entrenched at the siege of Quebec. Unfortunately, David Wooster was not up to the task. The colonials were cut to ribbons by counterattacking British troops and forced to retreat. Nevertheless, Wooster made a name for himself in Ohio. The College of Wooster, one of Ohio's fine, small private schools, was opened here in 1866. It operates its own inn on campus, at Wayne and Gasche Sts., and is noted for its science curriculum. The Wayne County Historical Society Museum is situated in a home built in 1815 by the Beall family and still contains many of their personal furnishings. It also has local history displays, and in the adjoining Kister Building are exhibits of pioneer tools used in typical carpentry and blacksmithing shops.

The countryside starts to roll beyond Wooster, with prosperous farms and sturdy barns making for a beautiful rural ride. This is the start of Ohio's Amish country (see U.S. 62), which U.S. 250 traverses on its steady southeastern course.

Past Apple Creek, take the turnoff to Kidron. This tiny Swiss Mennonite village, named for a creek mentioned in the Bible, is loaded with craft and antique stores. Look for the Lehmann Hardware Store, stocked with hard-to-find traditional tools for its Amish clientele. Kidron's livestock auction on Thursday morning (at 11 A.M.) has been held every week since 1924 and is one of the best attended in Ohio. There are flea and produce markets on the grounds during auction day.

The highway continues through the old Swiss towns of Wilmot and Strasburg. It crosses Beach City Lake, created by the Muskingum Watershed District, which was built after the devastating floods of 1913 washed through this area. The highway then hooks up briefly with southbound Interstate 77.

Dover is an old canal town, but its chief attraction is its steam locomotives. They are miniatures, carved by local craftsman Ernest Warther over the course of half a century, out of ebony and walnut wood, as well as ivory. One of his carvings has 10,000 moving parts; another reproduces the steel mill at which he worked. Many are trimmed in pearl. Frieda Warther contributed to this unique family museum by collecting more than 70,000 buttons and by planting a traditional Swiss garden on the grounds. Warther's workshop is maintained just as he left it at his death in 1973.

This was the area chosen by Moravian missionary David Zeisberger for his first community among the Delaware. The tribe, eager to learn about Christianity, had sent for the Pennsylvania clergyman and encouraged him to live with them. Schoenbrunn (the name of which means "beautiful fountain"), regarded as the oldest European settlement in Ohio, was built here in 1772. But the tribe's contact with white civilization was brief and unhappy. These lands were a battleground, bitterly fought over by Americans, British, and Shawnee. The Shawnee, encouraged by England, wanted to keep all colonial settlements out of the area; the Americans wanted all Native Americans removed, whether they had been Christianized or not. Zeisberger sadly concluded that he could not risk the lives of his converts. He moved most of them back to safety in Pennsylvania in 1776 at the outbreak of war. A few of the Delaware, however, insisted on staying on at the nearby settlement of Gnadenhutten, with tragic results (see U.S. 36). They were massacred by Pennsylvania militia in 1782.

In time the very location of Schoenbrunn was forgotten. New Philadelphia, another town settled by Moravians from Pennsylvania, grew up nearby. But Schoenbrunn's memory lived on. Almost 150 years after it was abandoned, a map showing its location was found in a Moravian church in Bethlehem, Pennsylvania. Archaeologists dug at the indicated spot and uncovered the foundations of the village in 1923. Since then, Ohio has engaged in an ongoing restoration effort, rebuilding the village to its appearance of the 1770s. The Schoenbrunn Village State Memorial is just east of New Philadelphia. The site features 17 log structures and fields planted as they would have been tilled in that period. In addition, an outstanding historical pageant, *Trumpet in the Land,* is put on here every summer to retell the story of Ohio's first white settlement and its unhappy end.

The scenery becomes increasingly rugged as we continue southeast, resembling vistas in the nearby southern highlands. Dennison, just south of the highway, was a railroad town, growing up to service the rolling stock of the Pittsburgh, Columbus, and St. Louis line. The shops left in 1922, but Dennison remained a stop for trains bound across the country's midsection. During World War II, the depot here became famous for dispensing free food and refreshment to servicemen passing through. The hometown-like canteen came to be known as Dreamsville. The depot, built in 1873, has been turned into a museum of those years, with memorabilia of the troops who passed through and the local people who served them. It presents a unique picture of the home front of the 1940s.

The road runs along the eastern shore of Tappan Lake, holding the dammed waters of Little Stillwater Creek, another part of the Muskingum flood-control project mentioned earlier. From a vantage point along the highway, travelers can look out across the water to the hills on the far shore.

Cadiz is a town well known to movie buffs as the boyhood home of screen legend Clark Gable. But numerous attempts to put together a museum of the actor's life here have never connected. One local resident who was honored with a statue is John A. Bingham. He never played Rhett Butler, but he did his best to beat him. Bingham was a member of Congress during the Civil War and was a leader in efforts to impeach President Andrew Johnson for, among other things, being too soft on the defeated Confederate states. He capped his career by serving as minister to Japan from 1873 to 1885.

The road now begins to climb and wind in earnest, through lightly populated hill country. At Ohio 150, turn north for the short side trip to Mt. Pleasant. This was a Quaker community and an early center of national abolitionist activity. The first antislavery newspaper, the *Philanthropist,* was published here in 1817, and Mt. Pleasant was a major stop on the Underground Railroad. The Quaker Meeting House State Memorial, a red-brick structure built in 1814, was once the gathering place for all Quakers settled west of the Appalachians. They were expected to journey to Mt. Pleasant to attend yearly meetings. It can seat 2,000, and the interior has been remarkably preserved after decades of disuse.

The highway continues to twist its way through the hills to the Ohio River, finally making its descent into Bridgeport. This town was founded in 1806 by Ebenezer Zane, one of the great names in Ohio's early history. He called it Canton. This was a popular name for frontier settlements, and there are two explanations why. The more plausible one for this Canton, in view of the nationality of many of Ohio's early settlers, is that it referred to the government districts of Switzerland. The other story is that many towns were named Canton because they lay at the opposite side of the earth from China. Whichever applied here, the name was soon changed to Bridgeport, because of its connection to Wheeling, across the Ohio River. A larger Ohio city to the north then appropriated the original name. After Bridgeport U.S. 250 runs across the bridge to West Virginia.

VISITING HOURS

Sandusky

Cedar Point, east of the city, by way of U.S. 6. (419) 626–0830. Daily, 10–10, mid-May–Labor Day. Weekends only, 12–8, rest of September. $28.95.

Follett House, at 404 Wayne St. (419) 627–9608. Daily, 1–4, June–Labor Day. Tuesday, Thursday, and Sunday, 1–4, April, May, and September–December. Free.

Milan

Thomas Edison Birthplace, at 9 Edison Dr. (419) 499–2135. Tuesday to Saturday, 10–5, and Sunday, 1–5, Memorial Day–Labor Day. Tuesday to Sunday, 1–5, February–May and September–November. $5.

Milan Historical Museum, at 10 Edison Dr. (419) 499–2968. Tuesday to Saturday, 10–5, and Sunday, 1–5, June–August. Tuesday to Sunday, 1–5, April, May, September, and October. Donation.

Wooster

Agricultural Research and Development Center of Ohio State University, north on Ohio 83. (216) 263–3779. Monday to Friday, 7:30–4:30, mid-June–Labor Day. Monday to Friday, 8–5, rest of year. Free.

Wayne County Historical Museum, east on Ohio 585, at 546 E. Bowman St. (216) 264–8856. Tuesday to Sunday, 2–4:30. $1.

Dover

Warther Museum, west on Ohio 83. (216) 343–7513. Daily, 9–5. $5.50.

New Philadelphia

Schoenbrunn Village State Memorial, east on Ohio 259. (216) 339–3636. Monday to Saturday, 9:30–5, and Sunday, 12–5, Memorial Day–Labor Day. Weekends only, Labor Day–October. $4.

Trumpet in the Land historical pageant, at the Schoenbrunn Village State Memorial. (216) 339–1132. Monday to Saturday, 8:30 P.M., mid-June–August. Reserved seats are $10.

Dennison

Railroad Depot Museum, at 400 Center St. (614) 922–6776. Tuesday to Saturday, 10–5, and Sunday, 11–5. $3.

Mt. Pleasant

Quaker Meeting House State Memorial, on Ohio 150. (614) 769–2893. Open by appointment. Donation.

Lanier Mansion. (Courtesy of Madison Area Convention and Visitor's Bureau.)

U.S. 421

Michigan City, Indiana, to Madison, Indiana

U.S. 421 cuts a diagonal across Indiana, running from the shores of Lake Michigan on the northwest border of the state to the Ohio River on the southeast. A portion of it retraces the route of the Michigan Road, the pioneer trail that led from the southern settlements to the frontier around Chicago. It passes through the heart of Indianapolis and also runs with Interstate 74 for about 40 miles southeast of the capital. But for most of its length, U.S. 421 is rustic and tranquil.

Like U.S. 231, this federal route was stitched together in Indiana from several state roads in the 1940s. Once out of the state, the road continues to angle steadily southeast, through the Cumberland and Blue Ridge Mountains and across North Carolina, until it reaches its terminus at the resort of Carolina Beach on the Atlantic.

Indiana's only lighthouse stands at a point that has been a crossroads of the state's history. Early explorers followed Trail Creek to the Lake Michigan dunes near here, then made their way west to the Chicago area along the lakefront. A spring named for Fr. Jacques Marquette, who came through in 1675, is not far away. One hundred and five years later, an American raiding party from Illinois was overtaken by British pursuers at Trail Creek and routed. So it was a natural progression that Indiana's first lake port, the settlement that is now Michigan City, grew up where that creek empties into Lake Michigan. The Old Lighthouse, the second built on the site, dates to 1858. It is now a museum of Michigan City's maritime history, situated within Washington Park, the town's beachfront facility.

U.S. 421 runs through Michigan City as Franklin St., the main north-south thoroughfare. Washington Park lies at its northern end.

There is a pier and marina here, with fine views over the big lake. It is also a favorite gathering place for local anglers, who take in coho and lake trout. There is a 200-foot-high observation tower, a small zoo, and a new lighthouse operated by the Coast Guard.

The road drops straight south from the lakefront. Once out of Michigan City, it settles in beside the old Chicago, Indianapolis, and Louisville Railroad right-of-way. The route is arrow-straight through rich farmland. The area's Potawatomi heritage is recalled at the town of Wanatah, named for a nineteenth-century tribal leader.

At westbound Indiana 143 is the turnoff to the Jasper-Pulaski State Fish and Wildlife Area. Within this 8,000-acre tract is a breeding ground for pheasant and a refuge for migratory birds, especially sandhill cranes. They may be observed in profusion in the early spring and late fall.

The highway continues past fields and farms. It meets U.S. 24, running east with it for 6 miles, before branching off to head south again. Just to the west here is Lake Freeman, formed by the damming of the Tippecanoe River in 1925. The bass fishing here is reputedly excellent.

The highway now starts to angle decidedly southeast, crossing the Wabash River at the town of Delphi. Growing up as a canal town, Delphi has an especially well-kept courthouse square, with a small local history museum in the courthouse building. Just south of town is Riley Dam, on Deer Creek, built by public subscription in 1930 to honor Hoosier poet James Whitcomb Riley, who often fished nearby.

Frankfort is another pleasant county seat, named by its founders for their hometown in Germany. The Washington Gallery is housed in a local landmark, an 1890s Victorian Romanesque mansion, and shows off the works of state artists.

The road now jogs sharply east and in 6 miles turns south again. It now is on the route of the Michigan Road. This trail was opened in 1826, a right-of-way through the heart of Potawatomi lands, acquired by treaty. The road led from Madison to Michigan City (although taking a different course than the way we have just come from the Lake Michigan port). Kirklin, the next town on the route, is fairly typical of the communities that sprung up along the road then. Its founder, Nathan Kirklin, anticipated that a new east-west road would pass this way (it is now Indiana 38) and bought up all the land at the Michigan

Road junction. He was a good guesser, and for a few years his village prospered. But when newer highways supplanted the Michigan Road, Kirklin settled into somnolence. It now has a population barely over 600, but its business section speaks of a vanished prosperity.

Zionsville, which lies just west of the highway on Indiana 334, grew up where the route of the Big Four Railroad crossed the Michigan Road. In reality a suburb of Indianapolis, Zionsville manages to maintain a distinct separation from the city. Its brick streets and nineteenth-century architecture are the result of concerted restoration efforts, and the town has become noted for its antique shops. The Patrick Sullivan Museum, which contains exhibits on local history, contributes to the ambience of the village.

Before the interstate era, the highway entered Indianapolis as Northwestern Ave. That is the route we will follow now. It passes through fine residential neighborhoods on its way to the city core. Just as the road crosses the White River, at Thirty-eighth St., is the Indianapolis Museum of Art. This is a first-class facility, well worth a stop. The core of the museum is organized around the former Lilly Mansion, originally owned by the Indianapolis family that made its fortune in the pharmaceutical industry. The estate was donated to the city in 1966 by the family, and the Pavilion of Decorative Arts displays the Lilly collection of tapestries, porcelains, and furniture in an exquisite setting. Other major collections in the museum complex are Turner watercolors in the Clowes Pavilion and Chinese art in the Krannert Pavilion. The museum overlooks the river from a park atop a bluff.

A few blocks south of this point is the entrance ramp to southbound Interstate 65. Unless you have an overwhelming desire to explore downtown Indianapolis, get on the freeway. Take it to eastbound Interstate 465 and then to eastbound Interstate 74, which now shares the route with U.S. 421 as it leaves Indianapolis.

We are still running along the route of the old Michigan Road here, but it has undergone a twentieth-century transformation. The interstate shoots past Shelbyville, and we exit, along with our old road, at Greensburg. This is a county seat, and thereby hangs a tale—or rather a tree. It grows on the roof of the courthouse. Greensburg has become celebrated among collectors of arcana and American oddities because of this odd spectacle of branches in the courthouse gables. The structure was built in 1858, and the tree, presumably, took root in the crumbled brick and mortar atop its tower. It is now a beloved part of the local flora.

You can tell the French origins of this area's early settlers as we continue south, by the town names of Napoleon and Versailles (see U.S. 50).

The highway runs along the eastern edge of the former Jefferson Proving Ground. Once used by the federal government to test artillery and small firearms, it was donated in 1994 to the three counties in which it is situated, and it is being converted for use as a commercial park. The road now descends through a range of hills to reach the old river port of Madison.

A Closer Look. In the years before the Civil War, Madison was the biggest, busiest city in Indiana. Its position on the Ohio River, at the start of the Michigan Road, gave it a strong geographic advantage. For a time it rivaled Cincinnati and Louisville as a port.

Eventually new roads with more direct connections to the state's growing interior were built, and Madison's influence waned. But the riches that came through the place remain in its fine homes and striking architecture. Madison has become Indiana's river-town museum, a living picture of how a port of the 1840s appeared.

Its founder, Col. John Paul, platted the place in 1809 and named it after President James Madison, who had just been inaugurated. Protected from severe winters by hills that close it off from the north, Madison grew up with the look and ambience of a town much farther south. Tobacco quickly became a staple crop, and the growing of burley retains its economic importance to the town today. Still, there was no mistaking where the community's loyalties lay. At the start of the Civil War, local banker James F. D. Lanier, a distant relative of George Washington, made Indiana an unsecured loan of $1 million to raise and equip troops. Although the southern part of the state was ambivalent toward the struggle, and though the Knights of the Golden Circle openly sided with the Confederacy, Madison and all its wealth stood firmly for the Union.

This is a beautiful place to visit in May and October, when the town's shaded streets burst into blossom or shower the pavement in a torrent of red and gold leaves. Leave your car near the courthouse, at the eastern edge of the business district, at Main St. and Jefferson (which is U.S.

421). The courthouse was built in 1855, when Madison was at the peak of its influence, at a cost of $36,000. The exterior came through a 1960 modernization almost unchanged. The Old Jail, a few doors farther east on Main St., is the oldest in Indiana, dating from 1849, and can be toured by appointment. In summer a farmer's market is held in the courthouse square on Tuesday, Thursday, and Saturday mornings.

Look back along Main St., down the row of storefronts. This is one of the best preserved nineteenth-century commercial districts in the Midwest. Most of it was built in the Federal style of the 1840s, with some Italianate and Victorian embellishments added a generation later. Madison's downtown remains economically strong, and this is a bustling stretch of pavement. Walk one block west to Mulberry and stand on the south side of the intersection to get the best view of the storefronts. Many of the buildings on Mulberry date from the 1830s, when it was the major thoroughfare leading up from the river docks. The old Central Hotel, at the corner of Second St., was used as an exterior set when the 1958 movie hit *Some Came Running* was filmed here.

Now head west on Second St. to Poplar. At 217 W. Second St. is the Schofield House, the first two-story residence in Madison. Built in 1816–17, it was used for a time as a tavern, and the first Masonic lodge in Indiana was organized there. The Masons are the current owners and have restored the house to its original appearance.

Across the street, on the next block, is the home of Jeremiah Sullivan. This is among the best preserved Federalist mansions in the Midwest, built in 1818 by a Virginia-born justice of the state supreme court. Sullivan is credited with naming Indianapolis, and two of his descendants went on to become mayors of that city. The stone and glass detail work on the front entrance door is especially fine, and the interior is furnished in period.

Sullivan's neighbor across Second St. was Richard Talbot, a local official who was killed in the Mexican War. His home is also a landmark of the Federalist era, but of equal interest is the pioneer garden on the grounds. This small tract shows off the plants favored by the area's first settlers. Many were brought here from Virginia, where several leading families of Madison originated.

Now walk back to Poplar and turn right. At the corner of First St. is the Shrewsbury House, built in 1846 by one of the wealthiest riverboat captains on the Ohio. Charles Shrewsbury's boats were a familiar sight from Pittsburgh to St. Louis, and the galas held in this home were legendary. The decorative wrought iron on the exterior was made locally and can be found on many of Madison's finest homes. The architect was Francis Costigan. Trained in Baltimore, Costigan was the best in his field in the early days of Indiana. The freestanding staircase he designed for Shrewsbury's house is greatly admired today. Drawn here by the wealthy patrons of nineteenth-century Madison, he left a lasting mark on the town.

Continue down the hill on Poplar to the river. Madison began dressing up its riverfront in the 1980s, and you can read the local pride in the red bricks on the pavement, each one bearing the name of a subscriber to the renovation. The view of the Kentucky hills across the water is gorgeous in autumn. During the summer months, the historic *Delta Queen* steamboat ties up here, and in July this is the site of the Governor's Cup Race, when the top powerboats in the country compete on the Ohio.

Now walk back up the hill along Broadway and turn left on First St. This is an absolutely lovely street, with its overarching trees and warm old homes. In the autumn, it is like a scene from a calendar, the perfect evocation of October in the Midwest. At the end of the block is Madison's proudest monument, the Lanier Mansion.

This Greek Revival home, with its sweeping river view, was designed by Costigan and built for Madison's wealthiest citizen, James F. D. Lanier. Completed in 1844, the home has the look of a great plantation house, as if it were the setting of a Southern romance novel. Its river side, with a 50-foot-high entryway supported by four pillars, is as splendid as that of any house in the region. The home is surrounded by a park and is now a state historic site. Some of the Lanier family's furnishings are inside.

At the western end of the park is Vine St. Walk north, one block past Main, to Third. At 408 W. Third is the townhouse Costigan built for himself in 1851. Although situated on just a 22-foot-wide lot, the home incorporates many of the grand features Costigan placed in his mansions. It is regarded as a masterpiece in economy of design.

A few blocks east on Third is the Dr. William D. Hutchings Office, which offers a unique look at the way medicine was practiced a century ago. Hutchings used this old house as an office and hospital for 21 years, until his death in 1903. The building and its furnishings remained sealed up and almost untouched for the next 64 years. Then, in 1967, it was reopened as a museum, with all of the doctor's instruments, books, and equipment displayed just as they were left on the day of his death. It is a fascinating look at family medicine in a bygone era.

Now continue along Third to Jefferson, where a right turn will bring you back to the courthouse and the start of this walk. From Madison, U.S. 421 crosses the Ohio River to the town of Milton, Kentucky.

VISITING HOURS

Michigan City

Old Lighthouse Museum, in Washington Park, at the foot of Franklin St. (219) 872–6133. Tuesday to Sunday, 1–4. $2. Park admission is an additional $2 per car on weekdays, $3 on weekends and holidays.

Medaryville

Jasper-Pulaski State Fish and Wildlife Area, west on Indiana 143. (219) 843–4841. Daily, daylight hours. Free.

Delphi

Carroll County Museum, in the courthouse. (317) 564–3152. Tuesday, 1–4, and Saturday, 9–12. Free.

Frankfort

Washington Gallery, at 500 E. Washington St. (317) 659–1641. Tuesday, Friday, and Sunday, 1–5, September–May. Free.

Zionsville

Patrick Sullivan Museum, at 225 W. Hawthorne St. (317) 873–4900. Tuesday to Saturday, 10–4. Donation.

Indianapolis

Indianapolis Museum of Art, at 1200 W. Thirty-eighth St. (317) 923–1331. Tuesday to Saturday, 10–5, and Sunday 12–5. Free.

Madison

Schofield House, at 217 W. Second St. (812) 265–4759. Monday to Saturday, 9:30–4:30, and Sunday, 12:30–4:30, April–November. Donation.

Sullivan Home, at W. Second and Poplar Sts. (812) 265–2967. Monday to Saturday, 10–4:30, and Sunday, 1–4:30, May–October. $2.

Shrewsbury House, at 301 W. First St. (812) 265–4481. Daily, 10–4:30, April–December. $2.

James F. D. Lanier State Historic Site, at W. First and Elm Sts. (812) 265–3526. Wednesday to Saturday, 9–5, and Tuesday and Sunday, 1–5. Free.

Dr. William D. Hutchings Office, at 120 W. Third St. (812) 265–2967. Monday to Saturday, 10–4:30, and Sunday, 1–4:30, May–October. $2.

INDIANA 135

Indianapolis, Indiana, to Corydon, Indiana

Indiana 135 is the road between the state's capitals, from the metropolis of Indianapolis to the little town it replaced as the seat of state government, Corydon. It runs through some of the finest scenery in the state in Brown County, into Indiana's Quaker country, and finally to historic Corydon. Here some of Indiana's great historic events, including its only Civil War battle, were played out.

As population began moving into the state's interior from the older Ohio River communities, it became apparent to the legislature in Corydon that the capital should be moved closer to the center of things. The commissioners charged with making the selection took their work quite literally. Indianapolis, which was then a collection of shacks known as the Fall Creek Settlement, is almost precisely in the geographic center of the state. Moreover, its planner, Alexander Ralston, laid out the new planned capital in a 1-mile-square pattern. Running right down the center of this square, in effect the main street of the state, is Meridian Ave.

This is the thoroughfare by which Indiana 135 leaves Indianapolis on its run to the former capital. The best place to begin the ride is at Union Station, at S. Meridian and Georgia St. The site of this rail terminal was a famous symbol of transportation progress in its day. Before 1853, every railroad built its own station in the big cities. This was confusing and difficult for travelers who had to change lines. Indianapolis, which had become a leading rail center, was the first urban area to promote a consolidated terminal. This first "Union" Station ended much of the difficulties associated with early rail travel. It also grew into a transportation palace, a vast showcase of the city. The station that occupies

Corydon Capitol. (Courtesy of Corydon Capitol State Historic Site, Indiana Department of Natural Resources, Division of Museums and Historic Sites.)

the site replaced the original in 1888. It still operates as a functioning Amtrak station but has also been converted into a shopping mall and entertainment center, with interior connections to a Holiday Inn.

Head out on Meridian, through the city's warehouse and industrial belt. The highway soon settles in beside the old Illinois Central Railroad right-of-way. This is tomato-growing country, and rich farmland stretches off in either direction. After the junction with Indiana 44, the countryside begins to roll perceptibly. Then the road jogs to the west, through a landscape that becomes increasingly hilly and wild.

The road enters Brown County and approaches the town of Bean Blossom. This town's name is thought to originate in the name of a local Native American. In recent years, Bean Blossom has become familiar to fans of country music as the home of the late bluegrass icon Bill Monroe. He was credited with founding the bluegrass musical style, with its emphasis on the traditional sound of the southern highlands and the strong presence of fiddles on lead melody.

Brown County has become a famous symbol of Indiana. Its landscapes are a staple of wall calendars and living-room art. The representation of these rugged hills, especially in autumn, evokes a sense of what people usually visualize when they hear the word *Hoosier*.

The origin of that name, by the way, is still a subject of debate in Indiana. According to one theory, it was derived from an Anglo-Saxon word, *hoo,* meaning "hick" or "rube." Other historians have traced it to a canal contractor in 1825 named George Hoosier, who preferred hiring laborers from Indiana. His employees came to be known as Hoosiers, and the tag was applied over the years to the entire population. By the time artists first came to Brown County, it was so accepted as an appellation for Indiana that they called themselves the Hoosier Group. Led by a coterie of Indianapolis artists, most prominently Theodore C. Steele, they started to arrive in the 1890s. Brown County was then regarded as the most remote place in the state. No railroads penetrated the hills. People got here on a bone-jarring wagon journey through narrow mountain roads.

The artists came to depict the "real" Indiana, the way the state looked before it had been swallowed up by progress. It was a painter's version of the poems of James Whitcomb Riley, whose homespun evocations of rural Indiana made the state a symbol of American rural life. Indianapolis journalist Kin Hubbard also created a fictitious Brown County character, Abe Martin. Because of Hubbard's syndicated features and the book *Abe Martin, Brown County, Indiana* that he published in 1906, the area's reputation grew as a storehouse of rustic wisdom.

Much of the area's finest scenery is preserved in Brown County State Park, which lies just to the south and west of this road. Back roads into its campgrounds, scenic drives, and hiking trails branch off Indiana 135 as it makes its trip through the area.

Nashville, the county seat, still holds the same population it had 75 years ago, about 700. Two major artists' cooperatives, the Brown County Art Gallery Association and the Brown County Art Guild, maintain exhibit space in town, with changing shows by local painters. The Abe Martin tradition is kept up at the Brown County Historical Museum, with its displays of county life inside and its "Liars' Bench" on the front lawn. The bench became famous in a 1923 photograph showing elderly residents exchanging worldviews.

John Dillinger may not quite seem to fit into this bucolic setting. One of the more vicious criminals of the 1930s, the Indiana-born bank robber was implicated in the deaths of 16 people, many of them innocent bystanders. One writer described him as being "only five-foot-seven, but every inch was mean." Nonetheless, Dillinger's legend has only grown stronger since his death by FBI gunfire in 1934. After his burial in Indiana, local collectors managed to acquire some of his personal belongings, including articles of clothing and photographs. Many of them are on display in Nashville in the John Dillinger Historical Museum.

After that, it may be a refreshing change to take a brief 8-mile side trip west on Indiana 46 to Belmont and the T. C. Steele State Historic Site. The home and studio of the artist who founded the Hoosier Group can be seen here. About 150 of his Brown County landscapes are displayed. Steele described the scenes he would make famous as "a fairyland with its narrow, winding roads . . . picturesque cabins that belonged to the landscape, as did the people who lived in them." You see the scenes here through his eyes.

Back in Nashville, head east from town on Indiana 135. The road climbs Weedpatch Hill, at the northern edge of Brown County State Park. The observation tower atop its 1,167-foot summit offers an excellent view of the area. The road then turns south, through more hill country, and enters the Hoosier National Forest, the only such facility in the state.

Vallonia, located outside the national forest, grew up around a frontier stockade built in 1811 to protect settlers against tribes who resented their presence. Four companies of militia occupied the place during times of heightened tension. The stockade has been rebuilt and includes a museum of life at this outpost.

Indiana 135 crosses the Muscatatuck River (the name means "clear river") and runs through rich farmland into the old Quaker community of Salem. This place was settled in 1814 by predominantly German members of the Society of Friends and was named after the established Quaker community in North Carolina. The area around Salem was the setting for the film *Friendly Persuasion,* adapted from a novel by Jessamyn West. The story revolves around what happens when the pacifist convictions of a Quaker family encounter the Confederate troops of Gen. John Hunt Morgan, during his wild raid of July 1863. (We'll see the site of the Civil War battle between Morgan's raiders and local forces a few miles down this road.) The Southerners pillaged this community during a five-hour occupation, and it was here that Morgan had to abandon his plan to drive toward Indianapolis. With the home guard alerted to his coming and with units of the regular army on his trail from Kentucky, he had to wheel to the east. He began an incredible run through Ohio before being captured 18 days after first entering Northern territory.

Salem was also the birthplace of John M. Hay, who began his career as an assistant to President Lincoln's private secretary. He was only 25 years old when named to the post. It was the start of a brilliant public career, which reached its apogee during his service as secretary of state in the McKinley and Theodore Roosevelt administrations. Hay was one of the architects of American foreign policy toward China in this period, opening up the country to U.S. influence. He was also one of the leading negotiators for the Western powers during the Boxer Rebellion of 1900. Hay was credited with the remark that "in a two-hour dinner with President Roosevelt, the guests are only responsible for four and a half minutes of conversation. The president supplies the rest." An elegant writer and biographer of Lincoln, Hay hated in his later years to acknowledge his Hoosier roots. He referred to his birthplace as "the barbarous West." Nonetheless, Salem forgave him. The house in which he was born in 1838 is now a museum of his life and is furnished as it would have appeared when he lived there.

Indiana 135 runs along the highway that Morgan's raiders followed on their way north. The landscape and villages through which it passes seem little changed from when his men galloped through on that long-ago July. This is southern Indiana at its best, typified by the historic streets of the old capital city of Corydon.

A Closer Look. For 12 years, at the birth of Indiana's statehood, the little town of Corydon was at the heart of major events. This is where the state constitution was drawn up, where legislators decided on the course the new state would take, and where the decision was made to move the capital to Indianapolis. That switch, which took place in 1825, left Corydon as a pleasant little county seat with big memories. Not much has changed since then.

There didn't seem to be many hard feelings about losing the state government. It was a bit of a fluke that Corydon ended up with it in the first place. Vincennes (see U.S. 50) had been made the capital of the Indiana Territory in 1800. But when Illinois and Indiana were split off as separate candidates for statehood, the feeling in Indiana was that Vincennes was too far from the rest of the population. So the capital came to Corydon, a town named by the popular Gov. William Henry Harrison, on whose land it was built. Harrison, a bit of a classical scholar, had named it after a shepherd in Virgil's poetry. The character also turned up in a popular ballad of the time, "Pastoral Elegy," one of Harrison's favorites. The town lay near the road from Vincennes to the federal offices in Jeffersonville, and Harrison was a frequent visitor. So the decision to move the new capital here was strongly supported by the territory's most prominent citizen. Even then it could be seen that the population was rapidly fanning out from the Ohio Valley and into the interior. It was just a matter of time before the capital would follow, but Corydon made the most of its years at the center.

Indiana 135 comes into Corydon from the north as Capitol Ave. Leave the car near High St. for a short walk. At the northwestern corner of this intersection stood the original territorial courthouse. Corydon wasn't quite ready for the arrival of the government, so a log structure on this hilltop was used to house both territorial and county officials. In the summer of 1816, delegates from across the new state met here to frame a constitution. In the heat of June, they decided to move out of the courthouse and meet, instead, under the branches of a giant elm, just down High St. That's where most of their work was done. The Constitution Elm fell victim to beetle infestation in 1925. But its trunk was preserved within a memorial and still stands here. The old log courthouse was torn down shortly after the constitution was signed. Its salvage value of $301 was used to defray part of the cost of putting up the new capitol.

Walk south on Capitol past the Branham Tavern, built by Harrison in 1800 and operating during the capital era as a place of refreshment for thirsty legislators. Turn left on Walnut St. and walk along Courthouse Square, just past Elm St. On the north side of the street is Gov. Hendricks' Headquarters, the official residence of Indiana's second governor, William Hendricks. He lived there from 1822 to 1825, and the house is now a museum of Indiana domestic life in the nineteenth century. Just down the block and set well back from the sidewalk is the State Office Building. Erected as a private home in 1817, it was used for a variety of functions. Most prominently, it was where Indiana kept its funds. They were stored in the form of silver in strongboxes in the cellar. The house is once again a private dwelling, and one can imagine that its owner occasionally does some digging in his basement.

Walk south along Elm St., past the businesses lining the block, to the walkway that leads to the entrance of the Corydon Capitol. This two-story limestone structure is where Indiana's House and Senate met from 1816 to 1825. It reverted to the function for which it was first built, as a county courthouse, when the capital left town. It served in that capacity for the next 104 years, until a new courthouse opened next door. This building was then acquired by the state and restored to its original appearance. The legislative and supreme court chambers appear as they would have looked in its capitol days, and documents pertaining to that era are exhibited on the walls.

From the capitol entrance, cross the road and walk one block down Cherry St. At the end of the street is the Posey House. It was owned by Thomas Posey, son of the last territorial governor and a prominent early citizen. Although a bachelor, Posey raised 14 orphaned children in the home, which was built in 1817. The Posey House is maintained as a museum of the Federal era in Indiana.

Now walk back to Capitol Ave. and return to your car. Leave town on southbound Indiana 135, across Little Indian Creek, and watch for the signs that lead to the Battle of Corydon Memorial Park. This is where local forces made their stand, on July 9, 1863, against Morgan's raiders, in the only Civil War battle fought on Indiana soil.

Morgan had harassed the Union rear throughout the western campaign. He and most of his men were Kentuckians and found ample support for their raids in their home state. In the spring of 1862 he had captured Union supply depots in central Kentucky and even threatened Louisville. He repeated the exploits in December. Early in the summer of 1863, he was ordered by Gen. Braxton Bragg, Confederate commander in the West, to disrupt supplies and try to siphon off Union forces with yet another raid.

This was a desperate time for the South. Morgan left the Confederate lines in Tennessee on June 11. By the time he reached the Ohio River, four weeks later, there had been Southern disasters at Gettysburg and Vicksburg. Bragg had never given authorization for Morgan to cross into Indiana with his 2,500-man force. Why he decided to carry his raid into Northern territory is still a matter of debate. But on July 8, he commandeered two steamboats and transported his troops to the town of Mauckport, Indiana.

When word of the crossing reached Corydon, the home guard was called out to resist. At this point, no one in Indiana knew Morgan's intent. The governor mobilized all available troops in the southern half of the state. Moreover, Union cavalry had been sent from Kentucky in pursuit. A force of 450 militiamen was gathered and sent out from Corydon to make a stand behind hastily erected barricades on a hill south of town.

The home guard was no match for the veteran campaigners of Morgan. His riders managed to flank both their wings, and in a hard-fought engagement of about an hour the militia was routed. Four were killed and most of the rest were taken prisoner, to be released at the end of the day. Morgan, however, lost 11 dead and 40 wounded in the skirmish, an unacceptably high toll for such a raid.

Morgan occupied Corydon for several hours, looting stores and demanding money from shopowners under threat of burning them out. That afternoon the raiders left town for Salem (which we passed through earlier on this road). Morgan eventually turned west across the southern part of the state, menaced the suburbs of Cincinnati, then rode across the entire width of Ohio before finally surrendering at the town of West Point, almost at the Pennsylvania border. Morgan lost all but about 300 of his men before surrendering on July 26. While interned as a prisoner of war, Morgan told interrogators that he had hoped Southern sympathizers in Indiana and Ohio would rise to his support. But the raid was eventually seen as a blunder. It solidified feelings in the border areas against the Confederacy and its political allies in the North. After his escape from a prison camp, Morgan was killed in battle in 1864.

The raid has acquired a patina of gallantry over the years and has become the subject of fond local lore. A few of the Southerners in later years even recalled brief romances with the local ladies. But on one summer day, a terrible war came home to Corydon, and this hilltop memorial marks its passing.

The road continues south to the old town of Mauckport, where Morgan made his fateful crossing, and ends at the Ohio River bridge to Brandenburg, Kentucky.

VISITING HOURS

Indianapolis

Union Station, at S. Meridian and Georgia Sts. (317) 267–0701. Stores open daily at 10. Free.

Nashville

Brown County Art Gallery Association, at Main St. and Artist Dr. (812) 988–4609. Monday to Saturday, 10–5, and Sunday, 12–5. Donation.

Brown County Art Guild, south of Indiana 135, on Main St. (812) 988–6185. Monday to Saturday, 10–5, and Sunday 11–5, March–December. Weekends only, rest of year. Donation.

Brown County Historical Society, on Courthouse Square. (812) 597–4900. Tuesday to Sunday, 10–6, May–October. $2.

John Dillinger Historical Museum, at Franklin and Van Buren Sts. (812) 988–7172. Daily, 10–6, March–November. Daily, 1–5, rest of year. $3.50.

Belmont

T. C. Steele State Historic Site, south of Indiana 46. (812) 988–2785. Tuesday to Saturday, 9–5, and Sunday, 1–5, mid-March–December. Donation.

Vallonia

Fort Vallonia Museum, south of town. (812) 358–3137. Weekends, 2–4, May–October. Free.

Salem

John Hay Center, at 307 E. Market St. (812) 883–6495. Tuesday to Sunday, 9–5. $2.

Corydon

Corydon Capitol State Historic Site and Gov. Hendricks' Headquarters, on Courthouse Square. (812) 738–4890. Tuesday to Saturday, 9–5, and Sunday, 1–5. Free.

Posey House, at 225 Oak St. (812) 738–2553. Tuesday to Sunday, 12–5, May–September. Closed weekends, rest of year. Donation.

OHIO 7

Martins Ferry, Ohio, to Chesapeake, Ohio

Not only is Ohio 7 one of the top scenic drives in the Midwest; it ranks very high among the most historic too. This is the Ohio River Road. It retraces the path of settlement on which colonists first broke through the Alleghenies in the late eighteenth century into the rich lands of Ohio. The inability of British officials to hold back this tide was one of the precipitating factors of the American Revolution.

Ohio 7 actually begins at the Lake Erie shore, in Ashtabula. But for much of its northern portion it has surrendered to freeway. It doesn't spring clear until it gets past Steubenville. We will pick it up near the western end of the Interstate 70 bridge to Wheeling, West Virginia.

One mile north of the interstate bridge is the town of Martins Ferry, which is the proper starting point for this ride, since it was one of the starting points of Ohio. A few tentative incursions into Ohio had been made by westward-moving Americans as far back as the 1760s. The Moravian mission among the Delaware at Schoenbrunn (see U.S. 250) is regarded as the first white settlement in the state. But as hostilities broke out on the frontier in the 1770s, the mission was abandoned, and Ohio became a war zone, with Native American allies of the British attacking scattered settlers wherever they could be found. Not until 1785 was a town made permanent, and the site was Martins Ferry.

This place was laid out by Absalom Martin, who was granted the land in return for surveying services. He called it Jefferson. His son, Ebenezer, was responsible for its present name. Ebenezer had renamed the place Martinsville, but the Ohio River ferry that he operated here was a major landmark. So people simply called it Martins Ferry, and the name stuck.

The *Valley Gem* steamwheeler, in Marietta. (Courtesy of the Ohio Division of Travel and Tourism.)

The ferry actually had been initiated by the Zane family. Ebenezer Zane was one of those hearty individuals who had penetrated the wilderness alone. He knew Ohio better than any other European, and after the war he laid out Zane's Trace, the first overland route through the state. His wife, Betty, was just as daring and resourceful as he was. During the Battle of Fort Henry, which occurred across the river in 1782, in what was then Virginia, Betty Zane ran from the besieged stockade to fetch gunpowder for the troops. More than a century later, one of her descendants used the incident in a novel, which he called *Betty Zane.* The book launched the professional writing career of Zane Grey. The Zane family settled here after the war. Betty remains very much a local heroine. A celebration recalling her courageous run is held here each August, and a memorial to her and Ebenezer stands in the town's Walnut Grove Cemetery. A sculpture of her is also situated at the cemetery gates.

Now we can head south on Ohio 7. Bridgeport was another community established by the Zanes, who recognized its importance on the path of the western extension of the National Road. It was also the starting point of the original Zane's Trace. But a bigger city grew on the eastern side of the river, at Wheeling, when construction of the road was held up by a political wrangle for more than a decade. So while Bridgeport became known as "the Gateway to Ohio," the key to that door is in West Virginia.

The road is still four-lane here, and the scenery consists of Wheeling's industrial suburbs. In view of that, Bellaire's name seems a bit of an anomaly. But the town was named for its founder's estate in Maryland, where the air, presumably, was a bit more salubrious.

Finally, at Dilles Bottom, named for five brothers who occupied the land here in 1793, the roadway narrows to two lanes and the river scenery improves. Between its origin at the Golden Triangle at Pittsburgh and the rail center of Wheeling, the Ohio is a densely industrialized stream. Much of that muscle fell slack after the collapse of the American steel industry in the 1970s. But from this point on this is a river of dreams, a lovely passage through old towns and misty hills. You can understand the inspiration for Ohio's state waltz, "Beautiful Ohio."

Powhatan Point, a former coal town, occupies an outcropping over the river, looking across to the rugged hills on the opposite shore. The town's name is based on one of the earliest errors made by English-speaking settlers in dealing with Native Americans. John Smith, head of the Jamestown colony, wrote with assurance about everything, even when he was wrong. Smith declared that the name of the most powerful tribal leader was Powhatan, which is not even close. His name was Wahunsonacock. Powhatan, or something like that, was the name given to the tribal confederacy he headed. Pocahontas was, in fact, his daughter. But the story of how she pleaded for Smith's life was, most historians feel, simply another of the colonial leader's tall tales. Eleven states besides Ohio have towns named for Powhatan, a man who never existed.

Between here and Marietta, the road seems to wander into another century. Sleepy old river towns—none with more than a couple hundred inhabitants—line the shore. A few larger communities are on the West

Virginia side, but only two bridges make the crossing. Past Sardis, the road enters Wayne National Forest. This is the easternmost unit of the 200,000-acre facility that covers much of Ohio's southeastern corner. Here it preserves the scenery much as the first arrivals saw it as they floated downriver on flatboats in the 1790s. Except for a few places between here and Cincinnati, the river's north shore hasn't changed that much.

Fly was so named simply because its residents wanted a short, easily remembered tag. They got it. Across the river is Sistersville, recalled by fanciers of Gothic thrillers as the setting of the classic *Night of the Hunter,* later a Robert Mitchum film.

New Matamoras got its name from the town on the Texas border captured during the Mexican War. The origin of Grandview's name will need no explanation as you cruise past. The river then makes a great bend north, and at the farthest sweep is historic Marietta.

A Closer Look. In the summer of 1787, while the Constitutional Convention met in Philadelphia to create a new nation, the Congress it would soon put out of business was passing the most significant law of its brief existence. The Articles of Confederation, under which the former colonies were governed, had many weaknesses. The greatest of them was the absence of a strong central authority. But when facing the most profound question put before it, what to do with the western territories, the Confederation Congress responded brilliantly.

Seven states had claims on these lands, some of them overlapping. They had to be sorted out and ceded. The vast territory, reaching from the western borders of the original 13 states to the Mississippi River, had to be organized. Then there was the question of statehood. What form would it take? Would western states be admitted to the new Union with the same rights as existing states? "Would not such equality prove a dangerous policy," wrote historian Catherine Drinker Bowen, "a swamping of older, experienced government councils by a horde of wild men in fringed leggings, uncouth, untutored, uncivil altogether?"

By July, most of those questions had been answered. The Congress, meeting in New York, enacted the Northwest Ordinance, one of the seminal documents in the history of American freedom. It provided that the region north of the Ohio River would be ruled by a governor and eventually divided into three to five separate territories. Whenever one of these territories reached a population of 60,000, it could be admitted to the Union on terms of full equality with the older states. Slavery was prohibited. A bill of rights, securing freedom of worship and trial by jury, was included. Schools were provided for. The ordinance had laid out a road map for the future of the new country that was being created in Philadelphia.

The work was especially impressive because Congress was operating under the greatest kind of pressure. In 1787, three flatboats a day, filled with new settlers, were making their way down the Ohio River into the new lands. Facts on the ground were quickly outrunning the capacity of government to deal with them. Manasseh Cutler was the foremost lobbyist for the territories. He had organized the Ohio Co., which sought to purchase 1.5 million acres near the junction of the Ohio and Muskingum Rivers. Many of the most prominent men in America, including George Washington, were strong backers of the scheme. It was rumored that Cutler also had given several members of Congress special purchase rights in order to speed passage of the legislation. By whatever means it was accomplished, the Northwest Ordinance brought order and stability to this new frontier.

Within five months, Cutler and his chief partner, Gen. Rufus Putnam, a close associate of Washington's, were on their way to Ohio. It took almost four more months to transport the first colonists to the selected site. On April 7, 1788, they came ashore at what was to become Marietta, the first capital of the Northwest Territory. The landing place is on the eastern bank of the Muskingum, where it meets the Ohio, at the foot of Ohio St. This is now the levee. In a plaza built as part of the two-hundredth anniversary observance of the event, the approximate spot of the landing is marked with a memorial.

The town was called Muskingum, but the name was changed to honor Marie Antoinette, who still had one more year left to her as queen of France. There were other changes as well when territorial governor Arthur St. Clair arrived in summer. The first site for the settlement had been chosen because it lay right across the river from Fort Harmar, built here in 1785. The town would depend on the fort for military protection. But St. Clair preferred a place farther up the Muskingum, and it was there that Campus Martius, the stockaded town center, was constructed. We can walk there by heading north along Front St.

A footbridge crosses the Muskingum just a few yards north of the original landing place. Built in 1873, it operated as a railroad link to the settlement of Harmar, which grew up around the site of the old fort across the river. It has carried pedestrians only since 1962. There are some fine views from the span, and the outline of the old fort is marked out on the far side. In the former rail depot in Harmar, there is now a museum of antique toys and dolls.

Back on the Marietta side of the bridge, Muskingum Park occupies the land between Front St. and the river as we walk north. The park is studded with monuments, the most significant being the *Memorial to the Start Westward*. Dedicated in 1938, this sculpture of three pioneers was done by Mt. Rushmore artist Gutzon Borglum. It stands at the place where St. Clair was inaugurated as governor. Across Front St. are several historic buildings, including the town's original post office, built in 1806. It is on the southeastern corner of Front at Putnam.

Continue walking along the park, through a residential area, to Washington St. On the river here is the *Valley Gem,* a stern-wheeler that cruises the Muskingum and Ohio on sight-seeing trips. Just beyond the bridge is the Ohio River Museum. This facility depicts the history of the great river road to the West and the development of transportation and commerce along its shores. A major attraction is the *W. P. Snyder, Jr.,* built in 1918 as the last steam-powered stern-wheeled towboat in America.

Now walk one block up Washington to Second. Here is the entrance to Marietta's top attraction, the Campus Martius Museum of the Northwest Territory. Built on the site of the first territorial capitol, it is filled with exhibits and items relating to the history of the Northwest. The log cabin of Rufus Putnam, built in 1788 as part of the original settlement, is preserved here and furnished with belongings of the pioneer families. Also in the museum is the Ohio Co. Land Office, where the vast tracts acquired by the firm were mapped and sold.

Now turn left on Second and walk one more block north to the broad boulevard known as the Sacra Via (a Latin name meaning "sacred way"). Before Europeans came to Marietta, the site was occupied by one of the ancient cultures of Mound Builders. The pioneers discerned that this wide pathway had been laid out from the river to lead to several of the mounds. Putnam, who was trained as a surveyor, understood its religious significance immediately. So in Marietta, unlike in many other Ohio cities, the mounds were not leveled but instead were incorporated in the town plan. The Sacra Via was maintained as a dignified thoroughfare, and some of the finest homes in town were built along this boulevard. You can still see the elevated square, called Quadranaou, to which the Via once led. It is between Third and Fourth Sts.

Now turn right on Fourth. This is another fine street, lined with nineteenth-century homes. The Castle, at 418 Fourth, is the most imposing and is the town's best example of Gothic Revival architecture. Continue on to Scammel St. and turn left. At the end of the block is Mound Cemetery. The burial ground was built around a 30-foot-high mound, called Conus by the settlers. They left the mound untouched and buried their own dead around its base. Among the people buried there are 24 Revolutionary War officers, including Putnam; it is believed to be the largest concentration of such graves in existence.

Continue left on Fifth. On the far side of Putnam St. is the campus of Marietta College. Chartered in 1835, the school traces its roots to the Muskingum Academy, which was founded in 1797 as the first college in the Northwest Territory. As you stroll across campus, look for the clock tower on Erwin Hall, a local landmark built in 1850. From the southern entrance, walk down Butler St. back to Front and the start of this walk.

Ohio 7 leaves Marietta as a four-laner, passing through the town named Belpre, which is French for "beautiful meadow." This town was founded by a group of Revolutionary War veterans who moved here from Marietta in 1789. Israel Putnam, a son of Marietta's founder, Rufus Putnam, was among those who settled Belpre. He is credited with establishing its library, the first in the Northwest.

Just past town, look for the turnoff to the Rockland Cemetery and the vantage point for Blennerhassett Island. This 3-mile-long island in the Ohio belongs to West Virginia and is reached by boat from that side of the river. But its story also figures in Ohio's history. The island was the focus of a secret plot (whose details are still not fully known) to establish an empire in the Southwest by obtaining concessions from

Spain. One of the chief conspirators was U.S. Vice President Aaron Burr. A dark figure in American history, Burr was a fugitive when he came here in 1805. He had killed Alexander Hamilton in their famous duel the previous year. Indicted for murder in New York and New Jersey, Burr fled to Washington, D.C., for the protection his federal office gave him. Though President Thomas Jefferson was appalled by Burr's actions, he nonetheless found it politically expedient to appoint some of Burr's relatives and cronies to positions in Louisiana. This fit right in with Burr's ambitions. When his term expired he became a fugitive from justice, but he consulted first with both British and Spanish ministers about his scheme to create a new country out of American holdings within the Louisiana Purchase.

The visit from Burr was fatal for Harman Blennerhassett. An Irish aristocrat, the eccentric Blennerhassett built a mansion on this remote island and spent his time studying political philosophy and composing tunes for the cello. After his connection with Burr became known and supply boats suddenly appeared at the island, an alarmed Jefferson sent militia to investigate. Blennerhassett had already fled, but he and Burr were captured and were later put on trial in the state capital (which was then Richmond, the island still being part of Virginia) for a variety of offenses. The evidence was insufficient for conviction, and both men were acquitted. Blennerhassett, however, was ruined. The militia had sacked his home when it landed on the island, and Blennerhassett was never able to recover damages. He eventually moved back to Britain. In contrast, Burr returned to New York and conducted a successful legal career until his death in 1836. After seeing the fine view of this island of mystery from the side road, turn around and rejoin Ohio 7.

The Little Hocking River tumbles out of the hills to join the Ohio at the town of Little Hocking. George Washington came this far down the river on a scouting trip in 1770 and mentioned camping at this place in his log. As I mentioned earlier, Washington was an enthusiastic supporter of the Ohio Co., and he purchased 40,000 acres himself in this vicinity.

Ohio 7 now cuts away from the river to head straight across the Ohio bootheel to the town of Pomeroy. That's not what we want to do, though. Instead, turn south on Ohio 124, for one of the great river drives in America. The landscape here, with the river passing between towering hills on either side, made homesick German immigrants think of the Rhine. The towns here don't compare with those in the Rhineland, but the scenery is quite similar. Just past Hockingport is a tremendous view of the river as it winds off into the distance. The last colonial governor of Virginia, Lord Dunmore, camped near this place with his army during the campaign against the Shawnee and their allies in 1774. This nasty clash, known as Lord Dunmore's War, drove the tribes out of Virginia and was a prelude to the larger war that was about to come to this frontier.

Forked Run State Park, with swimming and picnicking facilities, is just north of Long Bottom. This area, shielded from northern winds by the hills, is a fruit-growing region, and in the spring the budding trees growing down to the river make a splendid spectacle.

Just past the town of Portland is the memorial to the Battle of Buffington Island, the only Civil War engagement fought in Ohio. This was the climax of Gen. John Hunt Morgan's raid through southern Indiana and Ohio in the summer of 1863 (see Indiana 135). Morgan managed to evade his pursuers by heading across the Ohio backcountry, looking for a way to get back across the river to comparative safety. He thought the crossing could be made here, but a small group of Union soldiers kept him away from the river until pursuing forces and some gunboats could catch up. In the battle on July 19, nearly one-third of Morgan's force was either killed or captured. A few days later the remnant of his raiders had to surrender. About 300 of his men, out of a force of 1,900, managed to escape into West Virginia.

Ohio 124 branches west past here. Instead of taking that route, stay on Ohio 338, which follows the river, past more outstanding scenery. The road runs through forgotten little villages with names like Apple Grove and Antiquity, the latter of which got its name from inscriptions found on some boulders. At Racine the road becomes Ohio 124 again, and it rejoins Ohio 7 at Pomeroy.

This old coal town reached its peak in the 1880s, when it was among the top bituminous-producing areas in the country. Its salt industry also went into decline at about the same time, snuffed out by cheaper competition from Michigan. The place has been in a slow economic slide ever since, offering a rather picturesque sight as you pass through. It sits at the top of the river's Pomeroy Bend, and from here on Ohio drops to its most southern geographic point.

Beyond Pomeroy, the valley widens a bit, and the highway runs fairly straight. Near Kanauga (named after the Kanawha River, which joins the Ohio across the way, in West Virginia) is a memorial to one of the worst highway disasters of the twentieth century. On December 15, 1967, the Silver Bridge across the Ohio collapsed and threw 45 people to their death. This was the country's first bridge built with steel eye-bars, which were used instead of suspension cables at the bridge's construction in 1928. An undetected crack in one of the bars destroyed the bridge. It was reopened in 1969 and carries traffic to Point Pleasant, West Virginia.

Ohio 7 continues into Gallipolis. The name means "city of Gauls," and its origin comes from one of the more notorious land swindles in Ohio's history. An organization called the Scioto Co. sent sales agents to Paris in 1788 to offer land in an earthly paradise in America. The pitch was greatly overstated, but many members of the city's middle class— artisans and small businessmen—were nervous. Revolution was in the air, and they were looking for any strand of hope that would give them a reason to leave France. The Scioto Co. provided that. When the French investors arrived in America, however, they discovered a major hitch to the plan. The company did not own the land, and their titles to it were worthless. They were headed for a near wilderness with their investment capital gone. They petitioned Congress for relief, and Rufus Putnam managed to send some Ohio Co. workers from Marietta to clear land for them. But they had to pay for it again after arriving there in 1790.

Gallipolis survived, even though all the original French settlers and their descendants left the place within 50 years. City Park, which was called La Place by the settlers, was the site of the original stockade. A law passed in 1885 ensured that the view of the riverfront from this point could never be obstructed. The park is on First Ave., at State St., and is surrounded by homes and commercial structures dating from the early nineteenth century. The whole area is a national historic district.

One block east is Our House, a tavern and inn built in 1819. Among its guests were the Marquis de Lafayette and Louis Philippe, the latter of whom would become king of France in 1830. He visited this settlement of Royalist supporters during his American tour of the 1820s. The inn's name originated in owner Henry Cushing's telling travelers to "come up to our house." The tavern has been restored to the appearance of its early years and furnished in keeping with that era. It also contains a small museum of the French settlers.

One more block east is Riverby, a Federal mansion overlooking the Ohio. It is now the French Art Colony Gallery, a local cultural center honoring the memories of the artisans who founded the town.

The best view in Gallipolis is from Fortification Hill, reached by following Ohio 141 out of town to Mound Hill Cemetery. Cannons were mounted here during the Civil War, and you will understand why when you see the sweeping view of the river that this vantage point commands.

Ohio 7 continues due south, past the huge Robert C. Byrd Dam, the first in the country built with steel rollers to control water flow. It was built by the Army Corps of Engineers in 1938, one year after the worst Ohio River flood in history.

Where the river bends to the west is the marker for Hannan's Trace, one of the earliest roads into the West from Virginia. It was laid out in 1798 by Thomas Hannan and ran from this point on the river to Chillicothe, the first Ohio state capital.

As the river plain widens, we enter another fruit-growing region. The farm town of Athalia was named for the founder's daughter, although his first and last names are unknown.

Now the suburbs of Huntington, West Virginia, come into view on the far bank. The town of Chesapeake, named for the rail line that connected Ohio with the Mid-Atlantic seaboard, is also a satellite of the larger city. This is where Ohio 7 ends, at the intersection with U.S. 52. The river drive can be continued on that old road.

VISITING HOURS

Marietta

Valley Gem steamboat rides, at Front and Washington Sts. (614) 373–7862. Tuesday to Sunday, hourly 1–5, June–August. Weekends, hourly 1–4, May and September. $4.50. There are also dinner cruises and fall foliage trips. Check for rates and times. Reservations required.

Ohio River Museum, at Front and Washington Sts. (614) 373–3750. Monday to Saturday, 9:30–5, and Sunday, 12–5. May–September. Closed Monday and Tuesday in March, April, October, and November. $4.

Campus Martius Museum of the Northwest Territory, at Second and Washington Sts. (614) 373–3750. Same hours as the Ohio River Museum. $4.

Portland

Buffington Island State Memorial, south on Ohio 124. (614) 297–2630. Daily, dawn to dusk.

Gallipolis

Our House Museum, at 434 First Ave. (614) 446–0586. Tuesday to Saturday, 10–5, and Sunday, 1–5, Memorial Day–Labor Day. By appointment at other times. $3.

French Art Colony Gallery, at 530 First Ave. (614) 446–3834. Tuesday to Friday, 10–3, and weekends, 1–5. Free.

Index